3/5/14
$38.00

Building Prosperity

Building Prosperity

Why Ronald Reagan and the Founding Fathers Were Right on the Economy

Gene W. Heck

ROWMAN & LITTLEFIELD PUBLISHERS, INC.
Lanham • Boulder • New York • Toronto • Plymouth, UK

ROWMAN & LITTLEFIELD PUBLISHERS, INC.

Published in the United States of America
by Rowman & Littlefield Publishers, Inc.
A wholly owned subsidiary of The Rowman & Littlefield Publishing Group, Inc.
4501 Forbes Boulevard, Suite 200, Lanham, Maryland 20706
www.rowmanlittlefield.com

Estover Road
Plymouth PL6 7PY
United Kingdom

British Library Cataloguing in Publication Information Available

Library of Congress Cataloging-in-Publication Data

Heck, Gene W.
  Building prosperity : why Ronald Reagan and the founding fathers were right on the
economy / Gene W. Heck.
      p. cm.
  Includes bibliographical references and index.
  ISBN-13: 978-0-7425-5190-9 (cloth : alk. paper)
  ISBN-10: 0-7425-5190-3 (cloth : alk. paper)
  1. Fiscal policy—United States. 2. United States—Economic policy—1981–1993. 3.
Wealth—United States. I. Title.
  HJ257.2.H43 2006
  330.12'20973—dc22   2006019777

Printed in the United States of America

∞™ The paper used in this publication meets the minimum requirements of American
National Standard for Information Sciences—Permanence of Paper for Printed Library
Materials, ANSI/NISO Z39.48-1992.

To the memory of the late Ronald Reagan

In framing a government which is to be administered by men over men, the great difficulty lies in this: you must first enable the government to control the governed; and in the next place, oblige it to control itself.

—James Madison, fourth president of the United States, in *Federalist Paper No. 51*

Contents

Acknowledgments

The author acknowledges his debt and gratitude to many for making publication of this book possible. Foremost among them is the publisher, Rowman and Littlefield, and their superb editors, Chris Anzalone, Karen Ackermann, and Meghann French for making its publication not only possible but enjoyable; to Doug Baldwin and Tiffani Adams, as always, for their ongoing counsel, wit, and wisdom; and finally, but certainly not least, to my wife Adrienne whose counsel and support have been a source of strength for many years. Thank you all.

Introduction

Building Twenty-First Century Governance for the Twenty-First Century "New Economy"

> The ideas of economists and political philosophers, both when they are right and when they are wrong, are more powerful than is commonly understood. Practical men, who believe themselves quite exempt from intellectual influences, are usually the slaves of some defunct economist. Madmen in authority, hearing voices in the air, are distilling their frenzy from some academic scribbler of a few years back.
>
> —John Maynard Keynes

"All that we ever learn from history," lamented nineteenth-century German philosopher Georg Hegel, "is that we learn nothing from history!" As subsequent findings of this inquiry reveal, it may well be an apt corollary that "those in authority" still learn far too little from economic history's cogent lessons.

Those lessons make indelibly clear, in fact, that "profit motive," the acquisitive spirit of economic man, is profoundly impacted by the actions of government—bureaucratic transaction costs: excessive taxation and regulation. As a consequence, America remains today an economy at peril. At the federal level, the challenge is twofold:

1. an overtly expensive government whose costs depress entrepreneurial spirit; and
2. an obsolescent, obsessive one more appropriate for administering a bygone age.

Indeed, as analysis reveals, bureaucratic transaction costs levied upon U.S. citizens have today reached onerous levels. The Tax Foundation estimates that the average individual now annually pays more than $6,500 in federal income taxes, whereas the U.S. Small Business Administration estimates that the average American household spends an additional $8,000 per year in hidden regulatory compliance costs—which, at the bottom line, are no less than a cleverly disguised form of indirect taxation.[1]

Recent studies have likewise found that the United States presently relies significantly more heavily upon onerous levies on corporate income and profits—both as a share of total taxation and of gross domestic product (GDP)—than practically any of the other twenty-six major Organization for Economic Cooperation and Development (OECD) countries, with only economically moribund Japan worse. Indeed, combining all levels of government, income and corporate profits taxes account for about 48 percent of all U.S. revenues, contrasted with a thirty country OECD-wide average of just 36 percent.[2]

A year-end 2005 study completed by the Tax Foundation similarly found that at its 39.3 percent top marginal rate—with most corporations averaging 35 percent federal and 5.3 percent state taxes—U.S. corporate income tax rates are the highest among the OECD countries. While all countries levy corporate income taxes at the federal level, most do not follow with a second layer of levies at the state, provincial, or local level. Accordingly, when state corporate income taxes are factored in, American taxes become the most burdensome among the world's major industrialized countries.

These findings build upon a 2004 study commissioned by the National Association of Manufacturers (NAM) that concluded:

> The current tax system is the single largest obstacle to increased economic growth . . . while manufacturers face many challenges in the current global environment, it is the finding of this report that domestically imposed costs—by omission or commission of federal, state, and local governments—are today damaging manufacturing more than any foreign trade competitor and are adding at least 22.4 percent to the cost of doing business in the United States.[3]

But the bureaucratically imposed financial burdens are not limited to direct taxes, as NAM's international trade competitiveness study similarly found that "the total tax and regulatory compliance burden on U.S. manufacturers is the equivalent of a 12 percent excise tax" and that "[o]n a trade-weighted basis, the full burden of pollution abatement expenditures alone reduces U.S. cost competitiveness by at least 3.5 percentage points."[4]

Regrettably, the cumulative effects of such tax and regulatory disparities is that U.S. firms almost invariably confront considerably higher capital operating costs than do their principal international commercial trade rivals.

Small wonder that the national trade deficit has ballooned from 0.5 percent to 5.5 percent of GDP within the past decade, that the foreign import penetration of the U.S. market has advanced from 23 percent to more than 67 percent since 1980, or that U.S. export penetration has declined from well over

12 percent of global merchandising trade to 10.7 percent within the past five years alone.

This bureaucratic transaction cost–induced erosion of international trade competitiveness may likewise, in significant part, explain why, despite producing a growing share of the world's gross domestic product—now exceeding 30 percent, up from 22 percent in 1980—the United States is losing relative global market share, as revealed in table I.1.

Table I.1.   U.S. Population, Gross Domestic Product, and Exports as a Percentage of the Global Total

	1960	1996	2003
Population	6.0	4.7	4.6
GDP	39.9	26.2	30.4
Exports	15.3	11.7	9.8

Source: Calculations performed on IMF, "World Economic Outlook," April 2004; World Bank, "World Development Indicators," 2004; and IMF, "International Financial Statistics Database."

Such trends indicate, therefore, that while the American industrial engine remains highly capable of generating premier value-added output, other countries are finding cheaper downstream ways of producing it. Labor cost disparities play a clear role in this process, of course, but onerous bureaucratic transaction costs are equally significant in their competitiveness impact.

Small wonder also, then, that America's economy has become increasingly susceptible to escalating political charges that it is dangerously threatened by "industrial outsourcing"—with the nation enduring an ongoing hemorrhaging of manufacturing jobs that, if not soon stanched, threatens to ultimately reduce it to the ranks of second-rate economic powers.

The lessons emanating from the data aggregates thus are clear. Indeed, as economic performance data developed in chapter 5 reveal, within the past half century, only following the Kennedy tax cut of 1964 and the Reagan tax cut of 1981 has the long-term erosion of the nation's manufacturing workforce been arrested in absolute terms.

Beyond such positive employment gains, moreover, the revenue receipts were even more buoyant. After President Ronald Reagan's 1981 tax cuts, total tax revenues climbed by 99.4 percent during the 1980s, and income tax revenues also grew by 28 percent, after adjusting for inflation, by 1989. Indeed, more tax revenues were collected *every year* of the two Reagan terms than had ever been collected in any year before.

Yet this was by no means a unique outcome. The same result has happened throughout history. When Calvin Coolidge cut taxes, he produced the Roaring Twenties. When John F. Kennedy cut taxes, he produced the Prosperous

Sixties. When Ronald Reagan cut taxes, he produced the Enterprising Eight-
ies. The lessons learned—from Calvin Coolidge to John Kennedy to Ronald
Reagan: tax cuts do matter.

Tax cuts matter. The reason is both clear and simple: the prime purpose of
tax cuts is to generate economic activity, and more activity generates more
revenues—with the affluent paying larger shares—even at the lower rates, as
tables I.2 and I.3 reveal. As Kennedy himself said in 1962:

> An economy hampered by restrictive tax rates will never produce enough rev-
> enues to balance the budget, just as its trade will never produce enough jobs or
> profits. . . .
>
> It is a paradoxic truth that tax rates are too high and tax revenues are too low,
> and that the soundest way to raise revenues in the long run is to cut tax rates now.

Table I.2.   Comparison of Magnitude of Coolidge, Kennedy, and Reagan Tax Cuts

Tax Cuts	Marginal Cut	Revenue Increase	Increase
1920s Coolidge tax cuts	70 percent to 25 percent	$719 million in 1921 to $1.164 million in 1927	61 percent
1960s Kennedy tax cuts	90 percent to 70 percent	$94 billion in 1961 to $153 billion in 1968	62 percent (inflation adjusted, 33 percent)
1980s Reagan tax cuts	70 percent to 28 percent	$517 billion in 1980 to $990 billion in 1990	99.4 percent (inflation adjusted, 28 percent)

Table I.3.   Comparison of Incidence of Impact of Coolidge, Kennedy, and Reagan Tax Cuts

Tax Cuts	Proportion Borne by the Affluent
1920s Coolidge tax cuts	Income over $50,000: from 44.2 percent in 1921 to 78.4 percent in 1928
1960s Kennedy tax cuts	Income over $50,000: from 11.6 percent in 1963 to 15.1 percent in 1928
1980s Reagan tax cuts	Top 10 percent of earners: from 48.0 percent in 1981 to 57.2 percent in 1988

The message from the economic data, then, is: Want to stop outsourcing?
Quit pricing Americans out of the job market through excessive bureaucratic
levies!

And it is here that the lessons of economic history afford clear answers. For it is the challenge of economists and historians—and overarchingly of would-be public policy makers—to ponder why twenty-two separate civilizations have risen and fallen in man's brief sojourn on the planet. What caused them to ascend? What precipitated their demise? What are the policy implications of the messages resonating from these profound societal evolutions and de-volutions in forging public governance?

From the standpoint of enduring economic governance, this inquiry seeks answers to these questions—producing findings demonstrating that in the as-cendancies of most free societies, a spiraling series of crucial economic in-teractions eventually coalesce. To wit: as man's modus operandi ascends from merely acquiring the necessities of sheer survival to a more sedentary lifestyle, the ambitions of *economic man* concomitantly rise.

For economic man is acquisitive man—as his society matures, so do his ambitions. In his quest for material gain, he is increasingly driven to convert current earnings into savings in order to accumulate and invest his surplus capital in future cherished goods and services. And it is these individual and collective savings, committed on the promise of a fair return, that generate the investment capital that underwrites those productivity-enhancing technologi-cal breakthroughs that empower societies to progress.

It is free society's ability and willingness to divert those savings into noneconomic intellectual and aesthetic activities, in turn, that produces those scientific, literary, and artistic achievements that are the hallmarks of civi-lization. It is the accumulation of such wealth that empowers its owners both to finance the development of intellectual property and to fund the activities of educational institutions.

It is the cumulative volume of a society's savings, made up of the contri-butions of its institutions and individual members, moreover, that ultimately determines its living standard—that liberates economic man from the need to focus exclusively upon basic necessities and, in the end, distinguishes be-tween his eking out a living and attaining the highest levels of culture.

Though the desire to accumulate such social overhead capital is resilient, however, it would obviously be greatly diminished should some predatory external force—private mob extortion or public unjust government, for example—arbitrarily intervene to expropriate the savings of individuals to fund its own objectives. For just as productivity within the hive is disrupted when the energies of worker bees are diverted to subsidize the indolence of drones, so inordinate bureaucratic costs to fund nonproductive causes viti-ate the dynamism of profit-driven, job-producing private enterprises.

This, in fact, is precisely why communism died. It fell because it could not resolve the internal ideological contradictions between its steadfast commit-ment to radical equality and its belief that there was no need for individual incentives to optimize the full potential of productive economic individuals—thereby rendering it largely incompatible with the motivational realities of human beings in a modern industrial age.

Communistic socialism thereby denies the workings of free market process and indeed is its antithesis. It is contemptuous of individualism and personal achievement. Thus, socialism and freedom can never be effectively combined. Indeed, should an aspiring entrepreneurial nation ever cease to enjoy a "decade of greed," its ruling system of democratic capitalism—historically demonstrably capable of providing citizens with greater bounty than any other—will, at that moment, have commenced upon its inexorable decline.

Yet modern nations are not the first to embark upon such an imprudent policy course. As analysis will reveal, the annals of economic history are strewn with the triage of ruinous tax and fiscal policies and replete with the political obituaries of those who would try to "fool the market" by masking private capital confiscation in the guise of serving the public good.

The reason for this reality is basic. Profit motive remains at the core of man's aspirations and accomplishments. Unfettered, it can be a powerful economic force. At the same time, it is perishable. It can be destroyed by inordinate taxation; it can be ruined by rampant regulation—which is no less than indirect taxation in a more insidious form—and unequivocal examples of the excesses of each presented in subsequent discourse illustrate the inevitable results.

It follows, then, that those who would seek to preserve or restore a nation's historic economic strengths must commence by taking it back to its economic roots—striving to reignite within it the competitive spirit of enterprising individuals while concurrently promoting both their desire to succeed and the rewards for those who do—cognizant that contrary to liberal contention, competition is not mean-spirited, acquisitive spirit is not selfish, and profit is not greed. They are, in fact, the very ingredients that create inventiveness.

That economic surplus is quintessential to the advance of civilizations is central to the thesis of this inquiry. Its corollary, however, is that when any government taxes away that surplus, it sows the seeds of its own demise. Those individuals, empires, and eras most successful throughout history have invariably been those characterized by indomitable entrepreneurial spirit. The deaths of such empires and eras, in turn, have usually occurred when onerous public policies have suffocated the competitive spirit that is nurtured at the roots of its private enterprise foundations.

Yet in the political arena, sage economic advice, based upon lessons of history and time-tested experience, too often goes unheeded. And thus it is that today, despite its spectacular and nearly unbroken string of success, traditional Anglo-Saxon capitalism—economic determinism shaped by human motivation, called by some the "triumph of individuality," or, indeed, "the ultimate triumph of motive over method"—remains precariously under siege.

Its prime threat no longer comes from repressive socialism, perhaps, nor just from those who, for self-serving political purposes, would bureaucratically cap its productive capacity—but equally from the export of its own successes. For elsewhere around the world today, the free market system that America has done much to create and promote is setting ever-deeper roots.

Real-time examples are legion. The fall of the Berlin Wall has, in itself, liberated a vast European marketplace of more than 300 million consumers, rivaling America in size. China is likewise mobilizing its billion citizens to employ its emerging economic freedoms to achieve a surge economic prosperity unthinkable a mere two decades ago.

With its 700 million citizens, India is rapidly following suit, doubling its economic growth rate and achieving a dramatic 8 percent annual GDP growth rate. How? Through cutting taxes, deregulating industry, and practicing precisely that unique brand of entrepreneurial capitalism that made the twentieth century the American Century.

Paradoxically, then, while the United States is now economically recoiling from the twin threats of outsourcing and global competition bred of the exorbitant costs of its government—with some even seeking remedy by calling for a return to trade protectionism and still higher taxation in the name of an ethereal "social justice"—the nation's global competitors have stumbled upon its erstwhile cherished secret of trade competitiveness: a free marketplace, as more than three billion new capitalists have recently been reborn.

The need for closer public policy attention to the messages that economic history's cogent lessons teach thus remains an imperative unrequited. For just because there are today plausible excuses, such as 9/11, and the attendant costly war on terror that it has occasioned, shaping the parameters of America's emerging and escalating fiscal crisis, that reality doesn't mean that there are no economically fixable problems that need fixing—and fixable with the very system that has historically generated for it the planet's greatest prosperity—unfettered laissez-faire capitalism.

Indeed, the economic synergies that it has produced have proven to be both powerful and durable. For while as late as just two decades ago Western capitalism was perceived to be under grave challenge from the communistic economic model, today both that challenge and that perception have collapsed, as its dreams of a socialistic nirvana lie in shambles practically everywhere on the globe except perhaps in select isolated outposts of left-leaning academia where "intellectuals"—notoriously defined by Bishop Fulton J. Sheen as "those educated beyond the limits of their intellects"—still cling to a failed notion that top-down governance is smarter than the rationale of the free market.

Yet statist intervention has never outsmarted the laissez-faire market in the past—and the chances for it doing so within the foreseeable future remain problematic at best. For no socialist state has ever, even once, produced enduring economic prosperity. The crucial question thus becomes: Will America's free market, as currently constituted, continue to prosper?

While countless examples of the perils of authoritarian intervention into the private marketplace exist, three of the more classic presented in analysis—those of ancient Rome and of its successor, the Holy Roman Empire, as well as that of the Islamic imperium—highlight the dangers that feckless autocratic tax and fiscal policy poses to even the most powerful of world-class economic superpowers, including the United States.

Top-down political economic engineering notwithstanding, then, this is no cause for great rejoicing. For history leaves no doubt that both Roman empires and that of Islam fell precisely at that point when their citizens came to view predations of their own governments as worse than those of their would-be invaders. Will this be America's fate as well? Will increasing public-sector excess levied from within do more harm to the nation's future well-being than the threats posed by predatory competitors and terrorists from without?

The answer may perhaps be found in exploring the reasons for the nation's incipient success. Those of the nation's primary international trade competitors that are prevailing in today's global marketplace are doing so because they have correctly learned that the master key to economic success is the active promotion and mobilization of private surplus capital—with the outcome of the intense market confrontation that they have, in the process, precipitated destined to be the ultimate determinant of whether the twenty-first century will again be the American Century, or will instead witness the nation slipping abysmally but inexorably, albeit initially slowly perhaps, into the ranks of second-rate economic powers.

This inquiry is focused on that answer—and in its quest, the lessons that economic history offers are both striking and sobering—directly framing the decisive issues at stake in the ongoing quest for optimal economic governance both within the context of the historic "conservative-liberal"/"capitalistic-socialistic" confrontations and the framework of contemporary global marketplace realities.

Its findings are critical. For because inordinate governmental intervention—in the form of excessive fiscal or regulatory taxation—directly impacts upon the private sector, its effective constraint becomes a vital policy imperative—as the market costs of noncompetitiveness are themselves foremost causes of economic retreat.

The quest for remedy, then, must be no theoretical abstraction. For as findings that follow vividly reveal, every major civilization that has retrenched within the first two millennia of the Christian era has, without exception, done so from economic cause precipitated by government fiscal, tax, and regulatory compliance cost extravagance.

The reason is basic: While the market can, at times, be foiled—and often is through public sector intervention—it ultimately cannot be fooled. Taxes and affiliated bureaucratic transaction costs *do* matter. They remain the foremost determinants of economic growth within any jurisdiction. How, then, is remedy best approached?

The answers lie in the economics. Classic development theory holds that the main objective of any successful development initiative is to create wealth—and that net wealth is derived primarily through the production of exportable goods and services. Such production, in turn, results from a process of free market innovation—finding new ways to employ resources more effectively to create the things customers need and want.

Only private business enterprise is equal to this challenge, as government doesn't create wealth, it merely consumes it. Its proper role in public policy, therefore, must be to facilitate, or at least not hinder, the private sector in its vital task of combining financial, human, and natural resources to produce those marketable cherished goods and services that contribute to new wealth creation.

Nations build net wealth, then, not by implementing new public programs per se, but rather by stimulating new private-sector business investment. Generally, this goal is best approached by reducing, not increasing, the public-sector role in the private-sector marketplace. Indeed, in those success scenarios where public intervention has made a significant growth impact, positive results have been produced primarily because policy makers have actively sought to create an operating environment propitious for private entrepreneurship to evolve.

More relaxed tax and regulatory milieus have almost invariably been the foci of such enlightened policy efforts. For leading-edge economic development remains a free market process, not a legislated act. To the extent that it can be impacted by public policy, such policy must be aimed at the goals of both changing public attitudes toward private profit and removing public barriers to private-sector growth.

This time-proven economic reality remains the greatest challenge to any sound, balanced national development agenda operating within a free market system—and wherein such development enjoys a certain self-generating reciprocity. It is dynamic economic growth that fuels technological innovation and scientific progress; it is such economic growth that raises living standards for the rich and poor alike and ultimately defeats poverty.

Yet while government cannot create economic growth, and indeed can often be its enemy, it can nonetheless aspire to establish settings favorable for it to take place—environments that encourage businesses to take those economic risks in quest of equitable returns that enable civilization to progress.

This must become America's foremost forthcoming public policy objective. For today it remains governed by antiquated and restrictive late-nineteenth-century federal public institutions and policies created to solve early twentieth-century socioeconomic problems. Indeed, "modern government," as most in the United States know it, is a relic of the 1880s civil service reform movement.

The net result is that the nation finds itself frenetically attempting to provide twenty-first-century economic government while functioning at a nineteenth-century administrative pace—conjuring up vivid images of Cray computers operated by a run-amok bureaucracy framed within a backdrop of ink bottles, quill pens, gaslights, green shades, and ornate roll-top desks.

The examples of obsolescent bureaucratic dinosaurs still roaming the inner environs of the Washington Beltway are legion. The U.S. Department of Commerce is advanced as the nation's frontline federal development agency. Yet it is regulatory focused and wholly ill structured to promote twenty-first-century economic growth. Its obsolescent research and regulatory functions likewise were formulated in an age when mass assembly production operations were coming to the fore a century ago. Certainly, they are inadequately equipped to provide the levels of forward-looking collaborative technological research policy vision needed to succeed in this dynamic new information age.

Indeed, if the motto on the portal in the lobby of the CIA Headquarters Building in Langley, Virginia—"You shall know the truth, and the truth shall make you free"—accurately signals that agency's vital mission, then an analogous one prominently posted on the portals of the Herbert Hoover Commerce Building might appropriately warn business people: "Abandon all hope all ye who enter here"!

The U.S. Department of Agriculture has similarly grown big—its workforce size soon to rival the number of farmers in America—without concurrently growing strong in its ability to support modern farming. At the same time, the Treasury Department often appears more determined to, and more appropriate for, penalizing U.S. business interests than promoting them—and the Justice Department has likewise gotten into forging "industrial policy" by challenging the monolithic operational efficiencies of the nation's most successful corporations.

At a historic juncture in the nation's economic history when developing state-of-the-art workforce skills is paramount in global competition, moreover, federally funded job-training programs remain largely unstructured and inefficient mosaics of well-intended, but ineffective, "bureaucratic cures."

Clearly if America is to prevail in the modern global market, massive institutional reorganization is required.

Much of this systemic governmental inefficiency stems, of course, from the traditionally reflexive knee-jerk nature of the public policy formulation process itself. For public problems invariably emerge in the form of urgent "crises"—and the remedies proposed address symptoms rather than their underlying causes. Superficial manifestations are treated, therefore, without their systemic determinants ever being effectively explored.

Yet when the actual causes are ultimately, and quite predictably, not abated by the short-term patchwork solutions, are the palliatives ever repealed? To the contrary, they are too often merely amended into infinite complexity until even the original purpose of the precipitating initiative is lost. Thus it is that bureaucratic inefficiency and obsolescence accrete within the federal system to the degree that it is now near axiomatic that a dinosaur is a "governmentally owned lizard"—and a "pelican," a bureaucratic compromise between a peacock and a swan.

America today faces critical policy choices—tectonic opportunities to fundamentally alter the way that government now operates—with the course of action chosen not simply about economics but instead about national character and what future society itself will become.

In this quest, there can be no equivocation—for action or inaction, in themselves, are choices. America can bureaucratically streamline to restore, but failing that, it will retreat. The nation stands at a special place in history. At no time has the need to more precisely chart its economic course been more compelling or complex.

"Where there is no vision, the people perish," the prophet Isaiah admonishes, and nations perish for that same reason. Thus, if America wishes to provide optimal economic stewardship for its citizens wrapped in the mantra of a special ethos of "democratic capitalism," the economic blueprint that is its defining gospel must be decisively declared, mindful of the counsel of biblical Corinthians that "[i]f the trumpet gives forth an uncertain sound, who shall prepare for battle?"

Humankind learns from what reality teaches. There comes a time when rhetoric and reality must intersect. If America is to prevail in the highly competitive global commercial marketplace, a new brand of "policy entrepreneurship" is invoked that creates politics that learn from the cogent lessons of economic history and replaces politics as usual.

To these ends, this inquiry explores the lessons of three millennia of history seeking to discern the impacts of bureaucratic excess—direct taxation and regulation—upon the rise and fall of nation-states. Its endgame is to develop an analytic matrix that empowers political decision makers to confront long-term economic challenges, face their underlying facts, and then act decisively upon them.

Seeking creative solutions that ensure that humankind's productive future is more than a mere continuation of its recent past, therefore, and based on the economic beliefs of Ronald Reagan and the Founding Fathers as articulated in the formula:

A Free Market Formula for Building Prosperity

			EDUCATION		PRODUCTIVITY,
	TAXATION		& TRAINING		COMPETITIVENESS,
PRODUCTION –	&	+	&	=	&
	REGULATION		RESEARCH &		GLOBAL MARKET
			DEVELOPMENT		PROSPERITY

---

recommendations for a profoundly new and comprehensive national "competitiveness agenda" are advanced.

NOTES

1. S. Dudley (2004), p. 10; Tax Foundation (April 17, 2005), p. 12.
2. P. Merrill (July 22, 2004), p. 2.
3. J. Leonard (2003), "Abstract," pp. 1, 3, 22 (quoted).
4. J. Leonard (2003), pp. 19–20.

Part I

IN QUEST OF "ECONOMIC MAN"

We have staked the whole of all our political institutions upon the capacities of mankind for self-government, upon the capacities of each and all of us to govern ourselves and control ourselves, to sustain ourselves according to the Ten Commandments of God.

—President James Madison

Agriculture, manufactures, commerce, and navigation, the four pillars of our prosperity, are the most thriving when left most free to individual enterprise.

—President Thomas Jefferson's First Annual Message to Congress

Give me control of a country's money, and I care not who makes its laws.

—Mayer Rothschild, 1790

How can one deny the absolute fascinating creativity of capitalism which in a few centuries has now passed from mechanical looms powered by running water or steam to industrial robots capable of carrying out series of complex operations; from printing to telecommunications; from the discovery of America to the exploration of space? And how can one not be haunted by the destructive capacity of this dynamic at work?

—Michel Beaud in *A History of Capitalism*

Chapter One

Reflections on the Opportunity Costs of Failing to "Seize the Moment"

The country is ruined beyond redemption. It is ruined in the spirit and character of its people. There is an abjection of spirit that appalls me.

—Senator John Randolph on aristocrat John Adams's presidential defeat at the hands of populist Democrat Andrew Jackson in 1828

"For the White House, the new year began in gloom. The President's wife had spent a sleepless and painful night, and Mr. Adams, waking at daybreak, found the dawn overcast, the skies heavy and sullen. He prayed briefly, then fumbled for his Bible and turned to the Book of Psalms, reading slowly by the light of his shaded oil lamp:

Blessed is the man who walketh not in the counsel of the ungodly, nor standeth in the way of sinners, nor sitteth in the seat of the scornful.

"On, he read, to the ultimate assurance:

For the Lord knoweth the way of the righteous, but the way of the ungodly shall perish.

"The familiar words assuaged the disappointments of four years. To an Adams, the first Psalm seemed almost like a personal pledge. "It affirms that the righteous man is, and promises that he always shall be, blessed," he noted with precise gratification in his journal, and went to his desk for his usual early morning labors. As his pen began to scratch across the paper, his lamp, its oil low, flared for a moment, then flickered out. Mr. Adams sat in the gray light.

"It was no time for righteous men; everywhere they sat in darkness. Two months before, General Andrew Jackson had been elected President of the United States. The ungodly were now in the ascendancy, and those who walked not in their counsels had little but the Scriptures for a solace.

3

"There is more effrontery," Samuel Clessen Allen, retiring Congressman from Massachusetts had exclaimed . . . in putting forth a man of his bad character—a man covered with his crimes . . . than was ever before attempted upon an intelligent people." The Reverend Robert Little, pastor of the Unitarian Society of Washington, sadly chose as his text: "When Christ drew near the city, he wept over it."[1]

Fast-forward now to Inauguration Day 1993. George Herbert Walker Bush—Yankee-born Episcopalian, scion of the "Eastern Brahmin Establishment"—sits alone in an equally somber White House bemused by a similarly ignominious fate. The leader who had promised a "kinder, gentler America" forced from power, a member of the nation's gentry swept out in a populist tide. An "age of righteousness" is now over, the piety of the patricians swept out by the masses at the gate.

It had begun so promisingly a dozen years before. A decade of prosperity had issued from a comprehensive federal tax reduction enacted in 1981 by a Congress stunned into submission by the Reagan landslide. "Morning in America" was held forth as a hallmark of national pride, as the Reagan years ushered in new hope for a country that, its forlorn outgoing president lamented, was afflicted by a "chronic malaise"—and seemingly, he was right.

"Stagflation," a product of the 1970s, had reached intolerable levels in the Carter administration's four-year term. Inordinate unemployment levels were accompanied by double-digit inflation and short-term interest rates above 15 percent.

"Reaganomics" came as a breath of fresh air to an economically shell-shocked nation. The largest tax cut in American history slashed individual marginal rates by more than 25 percent over a three-year period and dramatically accelerated tax write-offs for expanding businesses. And the nation's economy dynamically responded—producing over ninety-six successive months of growth and creating more than 19 million productive new jobs, accompanied by surging exports and declining interest rates.

As a consequence, for the next two decades in America, more net national wealth was created than at any other time in human history, and large-scale governmental intervention in the economy—in areas such as commercial taxation and industrial regulation—was reduced to a level as low as at any time within the preceding century.

The results were spectacular. Unemployment, which had exceeded 10 percent at the nadir of the 1979–1982 recession, was now slowly but steadily halved, gradually trending downward toward the level of 5 percent. Productivity averaged 3.1 percent, outstripping both Germany and Japan. America thereby regained its position as the world's foremost cost-effective exporter, *and manufacturing's share of GDP actually grew by 15 percent.*

Inflation was simultaneously reduced from double-digit levels to less than 3 percent. Real disposable incomes, the lifeblood of national economic vigor, were rising once again—and the stock market responded with a succession of all time record-breaking performances. In all, in the Reagan era, the U.S. economy grew a massive 34 percent—the equivalent of a West Germany— and in cresting patriotic recrudescence, investors and consumers alike came to believe in the U.S. economic system once again.

Morning in America! The president spoke eloquently of the 1630s Puritan Massachusetts governor John Winthrop and his vision to make America a "shining city on a hill"—and now, throughout the nation's cities and homes, lights once again shone brightly in groundswells of new hope.

Yet all was well, but for a time. For the recovery did not anticipate the consequences when fecklessness combines with fate—as a new governing philosophy, under the stewardship of a quite different administration at the close of the 1980s, soon melted down into an unprincipled unwillingness to compromise a decade of sound tax and fiscal policy.

The reckoning was visited upon the "shadow president," Ronald Reagan's vice president and successor, George H. W. Bush. A political agnostic lacking his predecessor's political savvy and economic zeal, Bush so epitomized the doctrine that "the nation governed best is the one governed least" that he devoted little cerebral energy to the noisome tasks of governance.

For four long years, then, no coherent economic themes issued from Washington, as the nation permuted into a state of industrial drift, and incessantly tormented by what Bush called the "vision thing"—indeed, so out of touch with American lifestyles that he failed to recognize a pricing bar code in a grocery store during the 1992 campaign—he surrounded himself with a palace guard of sycophants possessing no more notion of the American economic realpolitik than did their well-meaning, but ultimately haplessly ineffective, patrician boss.

Yet throughout history's course, whenever men of reason have abandoned their responsibilities, the resultant leadership void has invariably paved the path beckoning the barbarians to the gate. It did so in fifth-century Rome; it did so in thirteenth-century Islam; it did so in the 1828 Adams versus Jackson presidential contest; and it did so in the 1992 U.S. election.

Why? The answer lies in the lessons of political economic history. For analysts seeking to trace the course of America's politics, as well as the incipient factors that impact upon her relative economic well-being, may productively begin by analyzing the results of her elections. As in democracies, the fates of nations and those of their economies are inexorably intertwined. Such was clearly the case in 1992—wherein the argument that Bill Clinton, with 43 percent of total, won the presidential election is not at all compelling.

In the immediate aftermath of Operation Desert Storm, Bush's popularity stood at an astronomic 91 percent—leading to that prized Jay Leno line: "If George Bush really wants to humiliate Iraq's Saddam Hussein, he should work to ensure his selection as the Democratic Party's presidential nominee." But economically, the way Bush ran his campaign, Saddam likely could have won. Coming from way back in the pack, the long shot from Arkansas, Bill Clinton, did!

The results were as unnecessary as they were unpredictable. For the race was clearly Bush's to lose, and with studied determination, he did. He lost because he and those he led lost sight of the underlying progrowth strategies that had threatened, for a time, to make the Republicans the nation's majority party.

More particularly, after running up federal spending by 16 percent in his first two years in office, faced with a slowing economy and a rising deficit, he lost it on that fateful day of June 26, 1990, when he inexplicably lost his ability to "read his own lips," renouncing the "no new taxes" pledge that was the centerpiece of his nomination acceptance speech in the summer of 1988.

This was a disastrous revenue deal cut with a Democratic Congress that, in effect, repealed the growth-oriented economic policies of the Reagan era in favor of higher levels of taxation and domestic spending. It was "Saint George, the tax killer" in a sellout to the tax-and-spend dragons of Congress—a victory for *bipartisanship* perhaps, but tragically at the expense of the American taxpayer—as Reagan's vision for a more entrepreneurial America became no more than a distant memory.

And it was Bush's greatest political mistake, for the resulting economic and political repercussions were as predictable as they were immediate. By turning to a "liberal remedy," Bush paved the way for a "liberal recrudescence"—with the 1990–1992 recession—and his own subsequent defeat the inexorable result.

As capitalizing upon the lingering economic downturn amid the prevalent and all-encompassing void of both rational economic polity and thought, a relentless opposition now moved in for the kill, as America's airwaves bristled with the vibrant casuistry of class warfare waged in the vacuous name of "economic justice."

"Tax the rich" became the rallying cry for self-serving out-of-power politicians who now claimed that America's economic well-being could be resurrected only by restoring their own. For months, candidate Clinton pilloried a hapless Bush with a crude, but effective, campaign placard on which liberal economist Paul Krugman observed:

> Bill Clinton's advisors knew what issue would win them the election, and to remind campaign workers, they put up a celebrated sign in his Little Rock head-

quarters: "It's the economy, Stupid!" Four years earlier, Bush was swept into office on a wave of economic contentment; in 1992, he was swept out by a pervasive sense that something was very wrong with the American economy.[2]

With each iteration of this simplistic theme parroted by the national media, then, the mythical economic crisis soon grew to mass proportions within the public psyche—and in the end, a president who was elected to campaign in the same diffident manner that he governed was brought down by a coterie of unabashed partisan opportunists. The results, though decisive, were therefore predictable.

As in the absence of a positive economic record, Bush's strategists were reduced to adopting the simplistic mantra of "Don't worry. Be happy!" and elevate irresolution to an art form, substituting rhetoric for real results. In the end, absent tangible economic accomplishment, Bush elected to run against the system itself, in effect becoming an opposition leader to the very government that he had headed for four years.

When called upon to defend his weak economic performance in the 1992 presidential debates, he responded meekly: "It's not as bad as you think," and in acknowledging his performance shortfalls, declared, "I am prepared to do whatever it takes to get reelected!" Even his own running mate, Dan Quayle, was known to complain that Bush "never had a message" because "that takes a strategy."[3]

Like the emperor Nero of classic antiquity who "fiddled while Rome burned," then, Bush's administration economically accomplished little. Indeed, Reagan himself said of his successor: "He doesn't seem to stand for anything." Predicated upon this Lilliputian "master blueprint"—the problem that Bush himself scorned as the "vision thing"—antipathy to all governmental activism became the order of the day. But as Prince von Metternich before him observed: "Stability is not immobility!"[4]

As a strategy that produced so much in the Reagan 1980s had permuted into abject economic drift in the Bush 1990s "Morning in America," in the view of many, had devolved into a gloomy winter twilight. And on Election Day of 1992, America's media, which played a major role in its results, jubilantly proclaimed "the end of Reaganism!"[5]

Contrast that economic performance with that of Bush's son and presidential successor once removed, George W. Bush. For despite the stifling fiscal impacts of the 9/11 devastation and the removal from the economy of hundreds of billions of dollars to fight the ensuing war on terror, with the record-setting, across-the-board income tax cuts enacted in 2001–2003, as the 2004 election approached its close, America's economy was again in remarkably good shape.

Indeed, following the initial incidence impacts of the first Bush II tax cuts commencing in 2003, aggregate GDP growth, compared to the previous three

years, averaged 4 percent—0.4 percent higher than the corresponding performance of the vaunted "prosperous" Clinton years—combined with an increase of more than 5.5 million jobs created between August 2003 and August
2006, and steadily rising personal incomes. Concurrently, GDP growth has averaged 4.0 percent since the start of 2003, exceeding the post–World War II
average of 3.4 percent. The data thus confirm that this is one of the most dynamic economies in U.S. history—paralleling those generated by the analogous Coolidge, Kennedy, and Reagan tax cuts documented in the introduction.

Indeed, in October 2004, the month immediately preceding the election,
the national unemployment rate likewise stood at 5.4 percent—less than that
of any other major industrial country and well below the 5.8 percent Clinton,
6.1 percent Bush I, and 7.4 percent Reagan term-long average levels—and
has continued on a downward path to 4.7 percent and below ever since—
lower than the average of the 1960s, 1970s, 1980s, or the 1990s. And media
histrionics notwithstanding, the federal budget deficit as a percentage of GDP
has now been halved from 4.5 percent in 2004 to 2.3 percent in 2006, and aggregate U.S. federal debt held by the public today stands at 65.7 percent of
GDP, compared with 67.2 percent a decade ago.

In sum, the cogent lessons learned through history's course are that the outcomes of economic foresight and sound fiscal governance *do* matter. They
matter because a nation's political destiny can be forged by prudent economic
and fiscal stewardship interacting within the crucible of economic history's
vital lessons—but they can be equally undermined by ignoring them.

OPPOSING IDEOLOGICAL WILLS

The economic lessons posited by the Bush tax experience are not new. Indeed, common to all civilizations throughout history, they are embedded in an
ongoing epic—almost cosmic—"conservative versus liberal" confrontation.
It is a clash of diametrically opposing ideological wills, a substantive debate
on how proactive governance should deploy, a dialogue of choices.

Operating within the vast chasm of this ideological divide, while liberals
believe surplus capital is no more than unrequited governmental revenues
that, through some unfortunate flaw or oversight in the public taxing system,
still remains within the private sector at their sufferance, conservatives know
that it is the seed corn from which future economic growth will issue.

Conservatives, on the other hand, identify *onerous fiscal overburden* as the
prime cause of that economic stagnation that is causing financial stress for
America's wage earners and their households. They believe that liberals
have—through class warfare and the politics of dependency and fear—for too

long farmed out the nation's poor and minorities to the plantations of welfare addictions. They view liberalism as a launch pad for sustained attacks on the nation's core values, precipitating its accelerating moral decline. They see "statist values" as not only symbolic of, but a catalyst for, the deepening decay. They envision an America that is slowly toppling from its lofty role as a free market beacon into the abyss of a subsuming welfare state. They believe in a return to limited government by and for the people—and that the liberal notion that all rights and powers directly descend from Washington is not only patently absurd but singularly unconstitutional.

In this ongoing global clash of coalescing visions, then, while liberal government is "big government," conservative government is "rationalized governance." While liberals offer "statist bureaucracy," conservatives counter with "private economic opportunity." While liberals argue a public-sector *solution* for every social problem, conservatives find for every one an underlying public-sector *cause*.

While liberals propose to dramatically expand the role of government, conservatives would significantly downsize it through tax cuts and budget-balancing amendments. While liberals seek to *grow the government*, conservatives seek to *expand the private sector* to keep the macroeconomy strong. Thus, while for liberals, raising taxes is invariably a *first recourse*, for conservatives, it is relegated as a *last resort*.[6]

The political clash thus is Promethean in both its scope and its ideological underpinnings. While liberals extol the expansion of public rights, conservatives cite the importance of private responsibilities. Under the pretext of compassion, liberals sell repackaged socialism in their quest for empowerment through dependency, as theirs becomes a quasi-religious social disorder that demands that all of life be controllable.

They demonstrate their compassion by randomly throwing money—other people's money—at perceived social problems, denominating their degree of compassion in the number of people they have taken to the public trough. Thus, while conservatives call for judicial restraint in seeking recourse to government to solve problems for which it is ill-suited, liberals cry out for publicly imposed social justice to remedy all societal ills.

Their vision is not one of "a shining city on a hill" at all, then, but instead one of a pulsating socialist democracy served by a public-sector conveyor belt delivering copious portions of subsidized food, housing, welfare, medical, and pension benefits for all—paid for by a cornucopia of tax wealth confiscated from the so-called rich.

Accordingly, under the guise of "fairness," they confiscate the hard-won earnings of achievers and redistribute them to nonachieving pet constituencies—to those who have been rendered nonachievers by their deadly cocktail of taxation, regulation, and other disincentives to produce. Their battle cry—"the rich get richer while the poor get poorer"—thus culminates in their too often successful efforts to ensure that no one ever gets much richer than anyone else.

Finally, when all else has failed, to prevent "starvation in Paradise," in true *deus ex machina* fashion, they proceed to entice their "beneficiary victims" with public-sector entitlements, which further reduces them to perpetual "ward of the state" status. As a consequence, it is no accident that today more than 40 percent of the nation's income is spent not by the workers who earned it, but by America's political class who have taxed it away from them.[7]

Pragmatic conservatives counter, in response, that such a welfare state is not only unequivocally addictive, but also imposes dual drags upon national economic efficiencies—first in misallocating resources by allowing individuals the option of not having to provide for themselves; and second, by permitting politicians to overburden the private economy through pandering to the whims of the indolent at the expense of the conscientiously productive to build electoral majorities.

Yet by thus weakening the private sector, the nation as well as its individuals are concurrently weakened as the public welfare system institutionalizes dependency and perpetuates it from one generation to the next. The end result is an expanding ethical shortfall within the political system, which produces a corresponding moral shortfall in societal values, which ultimately results in devastating monetary shortfalls in the federal budget.[8]

Such compensatory social safety nets, moreover, usually merely serve to complicate the addiction problem by setting "welfare traps"—offering public-sector handouts at benefit levels that price alternate employment out of the market—thereby often making dependency an economically more rational business decision than seeking low-paying jobs.[9]

In short, America's profound "dependency crisis"—its gradual devolution from an entrepreneurial ethic to an entitlements ethic—is a product of a profound loss of both its social and its economic bearings. While able-bodied people who truly want to make a productive contribution to society still can, liberal political leadership has effectively countered with a hybrid system of disincentives for productive effort blended with rewards for indolent inactivity—a deadly combination that produces a poverty of human values by giving economic value to the state of poverty.

Thus it is that under liberalism, the progenitive sources of socioeconomic problems are inverted and recast as their cures—as the prime purpose of liberal politics is not to solve problems but to find problems to justify the empowerment of government. For liberalism itself is empowered only through the relative deprivation of others, much of which it has already been responsible for creating through the impact of the taxes required to sustain it.[10]

The consummate irony, however, is that it is firmly founded upon an unadulterated, convoluted economic logic in sheer terms of who ultimately winds up paying for the government's sublime largesse. As whenever any strategy focuses on "making the poor less poor" by "making the rich less rich," the tab invariably winds up being paid by those in between—the politically defenseless and struggling middle class.

The fiscal bottom line, then, is that most governmental redistributions of wealth do not come from high- and middle-income people to lower-income people but rather from middle-income people to sectors of society at large as a function proportionate to how well those sectors are politically organized.

For far too often liberals unapologetically do succeed in subduing political debate through treading upon the *terre sanctae* of Orwellian big government political doublespeak—rechristening their traditional big government programs with conservative-sounding names—patently misleading terms such as "deficit reduction," "reinventing government," "welfare reform," and the like.

Old-fashioned tax hikes thus become "revenue enhancements." Classic pork barrel patronage is promoted as an "economic stimulus package," budget deficits as "underfunded revenue investments," disposable personal incomes as "unavoidable 'tax expenditures,'" socialized medicine as "managed competition," employer mandates as "shared responsibility," welfare as "non-work-required human investments," ad infinitum.

Indeed, at times, quite remarkably, they succeed at the ballot box as well. Yet when the French political philosopher Jean-Jacques Rousseau advanced his general theory of democracy focused upon governance in accordance with the general will of the people in the eighteenth century, that concept was predicated upon the premise that the electorate would somehow ultimately get some semblance of what it thought it voted for. Its premise held that should a politician be elected by promising to cut taxes, then some effort probably should be devoted to seeking a postelection tax cut.

Logic again follows, therefore, that were a candidate to be elected upon the pretense of being a champion of the long-suffering middle class, then some postelection focus might be lent to formulating policy that, at the least, does no grave harm to middle-class economic interests.

Today, such is often not the case. For unlike the free market, wherein consumers vote their income dollars to purchase precisely what they want, in the contemporary political marketplace the voter generally gets something quite different from what he or she voted for—often modified in the name of changing economic circumstance.

That's precisely how, for instance, incessant Clinton charges of recession-inducing Republican economic mismanagement in the campaign of 1992 somehow became transubstantiated into the notion of an unavoidable "global recession" when he personally became responsible for the nation's economic governance in 1993. That's also how his 1992 firm campaign promise of a middle-class tax cut became in 1993 a massive *tax increase* instead.

Yet while such slick "sleight of mouth" might most charitably be called "a technical question of probity" in public-sector parlance, its probative value, at the very least, hues to an all too common political line that "a little inaccuracy can save a lot of explanation." And while compromise is inevitable in, and intrinsic to, the democratic process, malleable and duplicitous responses to good faith public commitments are not abiding strengths of character. For in implementing the opposite of what was promised and what the electorate voted for is not a characteristic of the workings of democratic practice—it is what dictators do. How can the practice be explained? Reflecting upon Mark Twain's sage observation that "a lie makes twenty trips around the world before truth takes its first step," perhaps only in the poignant words of another accomplished Democratic orator, Adlai Stevenson, when he said, "A lie is an abomination onto the Lord, but a very present help in time of trouble!"[11]

The liberal-conservative dichotomy is further defined and compounded in America by the ongoing, never-ending clash of partisan politics—explaining why the parties today remain hovered over a seemingly unbridgeable ideological chasm—yet concurrently making most political outcomes of the past half century not surprising, as Democrats have traditionally been better defenders of their liberal heritage than have Republicans of their conservative roots.

Indeed, for years, liberal Democrats have prevailed politically by dominating ideologically, seizing virtual free reign in the political marketplace of ideas—ruling the media, educational establishments, universities, foundations, mainline churches, and the halls of big government. Because of the *intellectual depth* of their activist ideological infrastructure, therefore, when the Democrats do prevail, they generally bring to the table some strategic vision tied to some specific goal.

In its quest, they appoint as policy advisers the "best and brightest" of their political persuasion, most often from their "East Coast Liberal Establishment"— namely, the Roosevelt "Columbia Brain Trust" and the Kennedy "Harvard Clique." Even the Arkansas-born Clinton's inner circle was dominated by the Rubins and the Reichs—brilliant East Coast intellects, but ones who define societal problems in terms of their particular frames of socioeconomic reference, which invariably issue from ideologies that encapsulate some form of "statist salvation."

Preferring the bureaucrat that they know to the consumer that they cannot control, their cerebral contributions have come to constitute a corpus that is the manifesto for their "politics of dependency." Thus it is that Democrats have historically focused upon public-sector cures. If traditional normative structures can't provide security and comfort, they maintain, then government should step in with the necessary economic and social infrastructures and the requisite tax increases to pay for them. Consequently, for them, the term "fiscal discipline" has become no more than a mere subliminal code name for "tax increases."

Yet decades of policy experience make clear that the *public* programs that result from such monolithic thinking serve only to undermine *private* support infrastructures—not only supplanting the nuclear family but often depriving it of the resources it needs to survive and function as an integral economic unit.

By contrast, for decades, Republican conservatives have deemed it an article of faith that, save for tax cuts, there is no constructive role for public policy in the workings of the free market. Laissez-faire purists in the abstract, their cherished and recurring refrain has become "Government has neither right nor reason to pick winners in the marketplace." Their approach to the market has thus become "If we have no stake in it, we need not address it!"—appointing as economic advisers those who brought in the most bucks and blew up the most balloons in the last election—and therein lies the problem.

Literal devotees of Adam Smith, they lend credence to the lame Keynesian joke: "How many Republicans does it take to change a light bulb?" Answer: "None . . . they just sit around and wait for the 'invisible hand' to do it!" In stark difference to the Democrats' impressive intellectual infrastructure and their incessant quest for socioeconomic change, then there is no real resolve, no countervailing force to "free" the free market—only to preserve the status quo. Only Ronald Reagan, and now George W. Bush, have reversed the stasis of the "politics of same."

For oblivious to the reality that when distraught American heads of households stay up late into the night, they are generally not worrying about whether school prayer should be voluntary or mandatory, but rather how to pay their bills, balance their household checkbooks, and fund their offspring's educations, Republicans remain strangely disengaged from those arenas where people live their lives, refusing to aggressively engage the economic intellectual debate.

Because to them, writing books suggesting where the economy should be heading smacks of verboten economic planning, they thus produce no tangible economic legacy—no substantive ideological ammunition—to sustain their political agenda. Only Newt Gingrich and his Contract with America, together with Reagan's simple but effective homilies for governance—"No nation has ever taxed itself into prosperity" and "No nation has ever been attacked because it was too strong"—are the sole recent exceptions to this trend.

Yet this phenomenon is no accident, either. It is explicitly by design, bred of the flawed aforesaid notion that "if we're not in the market, we need not worry about it." As a result, Republicans have ceased to be an economically proactive party. Instead, their sole raison d'être is one of mere reaction. Were the word "no" to be removed from their vocabularies, in fact, they would have virtually nothing to say.

The net result is that whether or not the Democrats ultimately come up with better economic solutions, in general they will have given them more focused economic thought—and while their solutions may habitually punish economic accomplishment with taxation, the Republicans have done little to create an alternative environment wherein productive achievement is rewarded—instead waiting for "invisible hands" and "mystic forces" to wend their magic work.

Consequently, the ultimate effect of the abjectly idea-free environment the Republicans have allowed to evolve is that the Democrats' parochial definitions of economic problems—carefully retrofitted to their particular policy biases—become the accepted "problem statements" within contemporary political debate.

With this built-in rhetorical advantage, then, Democratic advocates and their media surrogates are generally able to effectively agitate public opinion on why a particular public policy may or may not be geared to skewed perceptions of pressing domestic problems that they have so cleverly crafted.

Then, moving into the resulting intellectual vacuum caused by the dearth of effective opposing response, Democrats are invariably able to make political hay on such evocative but economically dicey issues as the federalization of health care, the homogenization and downsizing of the U.S. military, the creation of still more bureaucracy aimed at reinventing government, and the promotion of public infrastructure investment financing through taxing the starch out of the private industrial economy—while Republicans are reduced to sitting on the sidelines fighting economic rearguard actions and lamenting the loss of the flag and the "evil empire" as prime political concerns.

The high unemployment rate of 1992 was a product of this convoluted problem-defining approach. Despite accrued inefficiencies caused by rapid 1980s industrial expansion, combined with the recessionary effects of the 1990 Bush tax hike and the 1990–1991 Gulf War, America's economy remained in surprisingly good shape as the 1992 presidential campaign commenced. Inflation, at a mere 3 percent, remained well under control, contrasted with the high double-digit rates of the Carter years. The nation's private economy abounded with liquidity, and the stock market was setting all-time records practically on a monthly basis.

True, the national rate of unemployment had been somewhat on the rise due to the economically dampening effects of the 1990 tax increase. But still, by Labor Day 1992, the traditional kickoff date for the presidential campaign, the national unemployment rate had averaged 6.13 percent in the first three years and eight months of the Bush administration—contrasted with 6.43 percent throughout Carter's four-year term and 7.39 percent in Reagan's eight-year tour in office.

In short, there was no true economic crisis in 1992, so the opposition contrived to manufacture one. Yet the novice Bush political caretakers charged with economic formulation could not convey—or seemingly even grasp—the notion that their 6.13 percent "unemployment recession" was somehow better than Reagan's 7.39 percent "decade of prosperity."

Despite the fact that (a) the unemployment rates in the economies of major global trading partners were running as much as 3 to 5 percent higher, a reality conceded even by Clinton on the eve of his first G7 summit conference in 1993; and (b) the economy was already coming out of recession as the 1992 campaign moved into its post–Labor Day stretch run—there was no coherent Republican counterattack.

Had there been, Bush would have won reelection comfortably. Instead, the image of a depression-inducing "George Herbert Hoover Bush" was deeply ingrained into the popular conscience by cynical out-of-power politicians and an allied media that sensed a major political coup in the "journalistic deposition" of yet another modern president.

THE SYSTEMICS OF THE POLITICAL PROCESS

Thus it is today that modern public policy formulation remains precariously balanced between the "politics of crisis" and the "politics of confusion"—while crying out for effective leadership for an economy equally torn between the conflicting ideologies of atavistic statism and laissez-faire indifference. Though this ever-deepening crisis of conviction is not an entirely new phenomenon, it is one that must be effectively confronted and addressed. For both economic manipulation and economic inattentiveness are today endemic to the political process.

Many of the policy problems evident on both sides of the political divide are, in fact, intrinsic to the workings of democracy itself—as the system frequently fosters and regenerates its own socioeconomic problems—reflecting the stark reality that sound economic development remains a process, not an act. It cannot be solved with a single bill or in a single congressional session.

Yet legislators, presidents, and governors alike must be reelected every two, four, or six years. In America's crisis-driven political process, they cannot afford protracted policy results. They lack both the time and the incentive to wait as patient investment capital wends its way to a successful return. Such on-the-ground political realities thus mandate for them an endless, frenetic quest for short-term solutions to long-term problems and simple solutions to complex problems.

Regrettably, in this process, placebos are too often passed off as panaceas—often producing full-blown policy circuses that stand in steadfast affirmation of the time-proven political axiom that there are two things that one should never see being made—one is sausage; the other, law. The problem is compounded by the TV-era PR strategic operative rule known as the "Dan Rather syndrome": Don't attempt to accomplish anything that Dan Rather cannot explain in thirty seconds.

In essence, if a solution can't be reduced to a thirty-second sound bite, it probably isn't politically worth pursuing. Yet if sound governance is to prevail—and effective economic policy is to issue from it—a defining difference between philosophy and platitudes, policy and politics, true accomplishment and mere bumper sticker slogans must be reestablished.

The end result of such superficial thinking is that complex structural economic problems often remain beyond the grasp of political process. Hence they are almost invariably ignored—as lawmakers lavish still more tax dollars not upon building the economy, but upon the inevitable effects of what happens when the economy breaks down: welfare, crime, and unemployment.

For the economic bottom line, the ongoing breakdown of family and community, the rise of crime and violence, and middle-class citizens' growing anxiety about the future—all are, in fact, direct results of adverse economic change. Indeed, when people complain about welfare profligacy or affirmative action, what they are actually talking about, albeit frequently ever so subliminally, is economics—job threat and income stagnation—and not the abstract need for better social policies.

Nonetheless, prescribing legislative placebos for traumatic economic wounds will still always generate a certain modicum of street traction. For there, the illusion, at least, of short-term policy results can be achieved—making commitment of finite public capital resources to such causes a much smarter *political* investment than actual long-term solutions.

Yet tragically, the greater governmental demands in private resources, the slower is the private investment that sustains productivity growth, and the production output growth needed to ensure a prosperous economy decelerates as a result. For one enduring fiscal axiom remains: Whenever government spends citizen-funded tax dollars, the private-sector economy drinks its own lifeblood and is weakened accordingly.

How the liberal-conservative dichotomy interacts to formulate future economic and fiscal policy thus constitutes a critical ideological confrontation whose outcome will ultimately determine whether the twenty-first century will again be the American Century or whether the nation will continue upon a precarious downward-sloping path toward becoming a second-rate economic power.

The facts of life remain largely economic—and the lessons of economic history are crystal clear. Every bureaucratic fix does have its "morning after"—yet one whose antidote cannot come at the expense of private producers who constitute the sole source of abiding national prosperity.

Subsequent analysis will demonstrate vividly, in fact, that levels of bureaucratic revenue costs—be they in taxation or regulation—levied upon private job and income earners are the single most important determinant of economic growth within any jurisdiction. This financial axiom dictates, in turn, that if any national economy is to survive and prosper, solutions that preserve the free market generators of its profound economic strengths must readily be found.

As the dynamic new economies of East Asia—the vast resource potentials of China, the industriousness of South Korea, the creativity of Singapore—increasingly become prime engines of global economic growth, signs of U.S. industrial eclipse are concurrently in evidence. The trend is not a transitory one. America's accelerating state of economic drift cries out for a defining vision—a master policy for renewal that transcends partisan politics as usual.

Before the crest of civilization crescendos on its inexorable westward path to the Orient—a path that set out in ancient China's Ming dynasty, moving in the Middle Ages to the Islamic Middle East, to western Europe in the Renaissance, to making the past one hundred years the American Century, and now seemingly cascading onward back to the Pacific Rim—the nation must wake up to the reality that its continued prosperity is not a given. Instead, it is an aspiration—and potential opportunity.

While time remains, therefore, it is not infinite—making incumbent upon America's leaders the need to take decisive action. For the challenge of effective governance today presents not so much an *economic* crisis as a precursory *public policy* crisis. If this policy crisis is not addressed with effective tax and regulatory curtailment, technology development, and education upgrade measures now, true economic crisis will surely follow in its wake.

America today is not yet a materially impoverished nation. Instead, it remains a resource-rich society, indeed richer than any other in history, including its former self. Its economy remains the most powerful on the planet. It still leads the world in science and technology, which will determine the pace of progress throughout this new century.

In short, America possesses the resources to continue to lead if it retains the will. Once its policies become properly defined and prioritized, the nation possesses tremendous capabilities to deal with them. The key is to establish

those priorities while opportunity and time remain—and this quest will require no small measure of economic vision.

To these ends, to explore the full panorama of policy options in the depth
that they deserve, this inquiry seeks definitive answers within the tax and
fiscal lessons of economic history—evaluating the role of sound governance, or the lack thereof, in securing the industrial well-being of nation-
states. Analysis commences with an in-depth evaluation of the critical role
of private investment in underwriting both industrial and cultural advance.
It proceeds cognizant that such investment is selective. It takes place only
in those environments propitious for profit taking—milieus that by promising fair returns, compel investors to save from their current earnings in order to invest their capital surpluses in the production of goods and services
that will secure for them better futures. Such surpluses, then, are indispensable to both production and procurement of those capital goods that drive
a nation's economic system.

They are, moreover, the lifeblood of those downstream investments in education, the arts, and other noncultural advances that are the hallmark of civilization. It is this social overhead capital that frees talented individuals from
a need to work exclusively for subsistence and enables them to refocus upon
those aesthetic luxuries that ensure that humankind's future is better than its
past. Indeed, such private economic well-being is an incontestable precondition for any society to advance.

Government cannot create such surplus capital; it can only reallocate the
capital of others. Thus, when government expropriates capital from its private
sector—either through exorbitant taxation or regulation to aggrandize its public sector—it is killing the geese that lay prosperity's golden eggs—as prosperity can issue only from increased private investment.

This inquiry is attuned to the consummate dangers of "statist" economic
planning—attempting to "pick winners and losers" in the otherwise free
marketplace. History is, in fact, replete with examples of governmental mismanagement of enterprises and functions that rightfully belong in the private
sector. Among them, U.S. government regulation of the wellhead price of
natural gas for decades caused well-publicized and severe supply/demand
imbalances. Farm prices fabricated in federal offices are yet another egregious example of gratuitous public service that has turned into a disincentive
to stable economic growth. Had USAID been involved in its planning, the
land where Hong Kong stands would likely now be covered with rice pad-
dies rather than skyscrapers.

From a public policy standpoint, there is a clear distinction to be made between microeconomic meddling and macroeconomic policy formulation. For

the folly of inadequate discrete and prudent business climate preparation is equally egregious and an ongoing cause of policy myopia.

As pursuant to it, so long as revenues remain rosy, to even address a problem or propose a solution is implicit recognition that a problem exists. The bottom line is that it is only when a genuine economic collapse occurs that government rushes frenetically and ambidextrously about pasting legislative Band-Aids over a critically wounded economic base.

In sum, affluence is neither the archenemy nor the cause of economic decline. To the contrary, it is a foremost fount of economic strength—for the rich don't get that way through salaries alone. Most of their income derives from prudent savings and investments, the ultimate keys to a stronger economy. If more is taken out in taxes, therefore, there will be less for investment-producing savings—with fewer well-paying jobs, lower personal incomes, and a stagnant economy the inexorable result.

Indeed, when public-sector overburden breaks the backs of productive men and women through onerous taxation or excessive regulation—or both—the need for still more government is inexorably invoked. But as British commentator John Grigg has aptly put it, "It is not the duty of the State to facilitate the heavenly redemption of the rich by impoverishing them on earth."[12]

Conversely, however, because of the rising economic tide the investments of the most productive create, their commitments become a nation's most promising prosperity path for its less affluent. The key to future prosperity, then, is to ensure that sufficient surplus capital is generated so that such investments continue to take place.

Today, the United States, as a nation, is served with ample warning. The need for more entrepreneurial government and greater fiscal responsibility are not novel concepts. Indeed, as early as 63 BC, anticipating the economic causes that, in the end, would destroy his own nation, the Roman senator Cicero declared: "The budget must be balanced, the treasury restored; the public debt must be reduced; the arrogance of public officials tempered and controlled; and aid to foreign lands must be curtailed lest Rome become bankrupt."[13]

History affords clear answers. By carefully studying the economic lessons of the past—in both good times and bad—time remains for America today to confront the daunting task of preparing for its industrial future. This course is in no way a discretionary option but is instead a strategic necessity if the nation is to transcend the economic status quo and preserve its industrial vitality.

"Organizing to win" is a worthy goal as a sustaining economic vision—formulating policy in the light of studied reason rather than in the rhetoric of the campaign trail. Indeed, if prudent planning promoted by responsible leadership cannot alone excise the demons of "atavistic statism," it can, at the very least, provide new weapons to fight back, and with them, renewed hope where today the nation treads with trepidation.

This inquiry is dedicated to exploring the lessons of economic history in democracy's quest to best answer the question: Can what past capitalistic experience teaches preserve the American Dream? To this end, analysis commences with an evaluation of the role of profit motive—and its encouragement or frustration at the hands of government—in the course of civilization building within the span of the last three millennia of human experience.

NOTES

1. The opening lines to historian Arthur Schlesinger Jr.'s *The Age of Jackson*, on the changing of the political guard with the succession of populist Andrew Jackson over aristocratic John Adams in 1829.

2. P. Krugman (1994a), p. 1; C. Edwards (2004), pp. 1–2.

3. S. Skowronek (1993), pp. 239, 430, 432, 435, 441–42; M. Duffy and D. Goodgame (1992), p. 22.

4. M. Zuckerman (July 13, 1992), p. 72.

5. L. Peter (1977), p. 133.

6. Here, no value judgments are intended. These are convictions espoused on each side of the intellectual divide.

7. J. Muller (1993), p. 3.

8. R. Kuttner (1984), pp. 179, 232; R. Nixon (1992), p. 295.

9. A.Wildavsky and C. Webber (1986), p. 370; R. Kuttner (1984), p. 37.

10. On this, see P. Drucker (1949), p. 19.

11. A saying likewise attributed to C. E. Ayers in L. Peter (1977), p. 192.

12. J. Green (1982), p. 83.

13. Cicero's *Orations,* cited in "Thoughts on the Business of Life," *Forbes* (July 18, 1994), p. 340.

Chapter Two

"Economic Man" and the Quest for Capital Gain

I have always believed that there was a Divine Plan that caused people to totally uproot their lives to come to this continent to pursue their dreams in America.

—Ronald Reagan

The dramatic demise of global communism within the past two decades— leaving mercantile capitalism as the world's most enduring economic system— has been hailed as a defining moment in the ideological evolution of the West. From sundry sectors—business, politics, academia, and the fourth estate— have come paeans of praise for the remarkable triumph of the free market, defined by its proponents as a wondrous Western invention. Few have denied the merits of the claim.

Yet self-indulgence notwithstanding, the primary origins of capitalism itself remain remarkably ill defined. Did the Western free market system really arise Phoenix-like from the ashes of medieval Europe's Dark Ages, as much conventional Western business history contends? Was it a quite natural complement to the Protestant Reformation, as other various sources would suggest?

Where did this so-called Western capitalism first set roots? Did it not stem from earlier cultures and religions—such as those concentrated around the Mediterranean Basin in particular? Focused inquiry into such issues of provenance holds significant implications not only for economic historiography, but overarchingly for forging a new twenty-first-century economic governance that empowers diligent people committed to productive enterprise to succeed.

In this quest, the key questions thus become: What are those factors that motivate individuals to financial gain and, in the process, foster intellectual and social progress? Are there worthy prototypes of governance that afford insight into optimal policy approaches—precedents that illuminate those motives that incentivize the acts of economic man? In short, can man profit from the successes and mistakes of his political past? Can he learn from economic history?

WHAT WE LEARN FROM ECONOMIC HISTORY

While this inquiry will explore many facets of man's socioeconomic legacy, a rapid review of the panorama of civilizations that have preceded it renders one reality readily evident—that any macrosociety, as a whole, is invariably better served when investable capital remains productively at work within its private sector than when it is administratively appropriated for bureaucratic oversight.

If enduring economic and social progress are to advance, therefore, government as a financial catalyst must be relegated to backbench status as a last resort and not to that of a frontline economic player. For sustained social progress, almost without exception, is won through effective employment of the creative resources of private individuals and not those of the state.

But why is this axiom the case? What motivates individuals and compels them in their incessant striving to succeed? These are valid questions for any nation seeking to preserve a sound economic future founded upon individual responsibility by aspiring to learn from the accumulated wisdom of the past.

Without question, within most modern Western cultures, the term that best captures the indomitable human quest to succeed is "profit motive"—the pursuit of which was called by Adam Smith "enlightened self-interest." Indeed, the insatiable search for profit drives a person's every economic activity—his or her willingness to work, penchant to invest, and eagerness to save.

Profit motivation is encouraged not only by a desire to succeed but equally from a favorable operating milieu and an opportunity to equitably compete. Conversely, though highly durable, its perishability remains a function of economic circumstance. It can be ruined by unfavorable market conditions, undone by inordinate taxation, subjugated by excessive regulation, decimated by unfair competition, and overwhelmed by the coalescing of all these factors into a repressive business climate.

Hence the pursuit of profit remains quintessential for any civilization to progress. It is the driving force that produces economic surplus, the capital needed for investments in those noneconomic aesthetic and intellectual developments—in art, architecture, literature, music, philosophy, and science—that lend ambience to human life.

Indeed, private economic surplus keys all of those essential economic interactions at the essence of sustained human progress. It is private surplus funds that create the social overhead capital that finances technological innovation and cultural development. Those great societies that have reached civilization's socioeconomic apogee at any time in history, in fact, have all been distinguished by this one outstanding attribute—private economic surplus.

A precondition for any civilization to advance, in fact, is that it must possess such capital surplus—in the form of cash, industrial goods, and/or agricultural products—in excess of that needed for immediate survival. Such surplus can then be channeled into more creative enterprises of a non-economically essential intellectual or aesthetic nature. Exactly for this reason, then, the cultural apogee of any civilization coalesces precisely at that point where its economic decline commences to set in.[1]

Yet any economic surplus presupposes private healthy business activity—and the operation of an economic milieu wherein healthy profit taking can take place. Sound public-sector fiscal policies thus must concurrently create confidence in investors that capital commitments to entrepreneurial activity will lead to profitable downstream undertakings.

Such business confidence, in turn, must be sufficient to foster deferred consumption—savings from both corporate profits and personal salaries—so that worthy investments in other economic enterprises can continue to take place. This surplus must not be limited to affluent capitalists, moreover, for laborers too must be rewarded with adequate wage compensation to induce them both to be productive and to be high demand consumers.

Capitalistic operation thus is a holistic process—a means of organizing resources, both natural and human, to produce economic surplus. Its productive activities are propelled by the vaunted workings of the competitive free market—of Smith's "invisible hand" coordinating market exchange among individuals and firms—which is at once the secret of its success and the source of its remarkable resilience and self-regulating adaptability.

This need for private economic surplus is a reality that has existed from the dawn of written history. Despite controlling a landmass no larger than New York State, for instance, the Greeks of classic antiquity were able to amass sufficient private resources to underwrite a civilization that became the envy of the Mediterranean basin. Mobilizing investment capital to finance the development of manufacturing in a period coinciding with the era between the sixth and third centuries BC, the Greeks ushered in the Iron Age and became the "workshop of the ancient world."[2]

The evolution of the Greek industrial base, and the proliferation of marketable goods that it produced, soon set into motion a remarkable chain reaction of related commercial and financial developments. Shortly after 600 BC, for example, some of man's very first currency issues began to appear in regional marketplaces to facilitate trade.

The appearance of negotiable coins was accompanied by the bill of exchange, business letter of credit, bank lending, and individual bank accounts. The birth of a monetary economy, in turn, gave way to a price system that operated within an economy that can best be described as laissez-faire, as such state intervention in the economy as did occur was generally of a character to facilitate commerce, not disrupt it.[3]

In this highly favorable investment milieu, then, additional industry rapidly evolved to diversify the Greek economy. Water was harnessed as a means of power, trireme shipbuilding was invented, new and better weapons were developed, iron tools were perfected, the construction industry flourished, and sophisticated new techniques of transmitting power by mechanical means were mastered. The prime impetus driving them: man's relentless pursuit of private profit operating within the framework of a free market economy.[4]

The attendant accumulation of excess financial resources and the commercial system that it facilitated were soon followed by the highest levels of civilized development that the ancient world had known. The geometries of Pythagoras and Euclid, the biologies of Anaximander and Anaxagoras, the medical research of Hippocrates and Herophilus, the philosophies of Plato and Aristotle—all were by-products of the abundant social overhead capital that Greece employed at the zenith of its golden age that transpired between the sixth and third centuries BC. Their objectives were straightforward in that their quest for gain was ageless, for as Aristotle argued, the raison d'être of economic institutions, like political ones, is to ensure the "good life."[5]

Yet by the end of the Hellenistic period, the sublime grandeur that was ancient Greece gradually but inexorably came to be eclipsed by a dazzling new rising star on the Mediterranean firmament—the vaunted Pax Romana—the majesty that was imperial Rome. On the strength of her intrinsic economic dynamism, Rome likewise soon became empowered to generate the abundant economic surplus needed to reach its economic and cultural apogees in the half millennium between 300 BC and AD 200.

As with Greece, imperial Rome's ambition for personal material improvement propelled this great groundswell of socioeconomic progress. This economic dynamism was attended by a tremendous growth in trade: "From Sicily and North Africa came grains; from Gaul and Spain copper, silver, lead, tin, wood and hides; from the Orient spices, perfumes, and carpets; from the Black Sea fish; from Asia Minor cloths and dyestuffs; from Greece arts and other luxury goods."[6]

As also with ancient Greece, classical Rome's prime institutions for facilitating capital formation were generated by the ongoing requirements of commerce. A unified coinage, standard weights and measures, bank lending at a profit legally fixed at 12 percent maximum interest, pooled capital to underwrite sea voyages, bills of exchange, deposit banking, fund transfers, and stock trading in the shares of private companies all evolved in direct response to the pursuit of profit motive stimulated by lucrative economic opportunity and buoyant market demand in the centuries immediately preceding the Christian era.[7]

This age of abundant surplus capital likewise was distinguished by the appearance of numerous great masterpieces of science, literature, and art. Such works included the scientific inquiries of Pliny the Elder into the natural sciences, Ptolemy into trigonometry and astronomy, and Galen into anatomy and physiology; the histories of Polybius, Livy, Varro, and Tacitus; the geographies of Strabo; Cicero's orations and Virgil's epic poem *The Aeneid*; and the tragedies of Seneca, the comedies of Juvenal, and Julius Caesar's *Gallic Wars*.[8]

These monumental scientific and literary achievements, in turn, were matched by equally great contributions in architecture, sculpture, and other physical arts, the relics of many of which have survived unto this day—all monuments to the march of civilization made possible by the rich capital liquidity that was the empire's legacy.

When Rome eventually died from mounting taxes, a decline of central authority, the demise of internal security, and the rise of external threats commencing in the Christian centuries—in Paul Kennedy's apt phrase, "imperial overstretch"—and Europe was cast into its half-millennium-long experiment in Dark Age economics, precipitated in no small part by the church's steadfast determination to extirpate all cash returns on invested capital, which it condemned as "usury," the Islamic Empire of southwest Asia next mightily rose to become the economic superpower of the Mediterranean basin, and indeed of the entire known medieval world.[9]

Now a vast new trade zone—a dynamic and expansive Pax Arabica that became the most expansive of its kind until then in all of history—spread from Spain in the west all the way to China in the east. Again, it was the dynamism of profit motive that triggered this remarkable ascendancy, as private surplus capital became the solvent that lubricated economic progress. As commercial profit motive was woven directly into the socioeconomic fabric of this new religion, as God's revelations encouraged Muslims to practice trade and other professional pursuits, and pursue them avariciously, they did.

To support their vast and burgeoning commerce, as subsequent analysis will reveal, the medieval Muslims likewise developed highly sophisticated ancillary capitalistic tools that resembled those of modern banking. Such fiducial tools included letters of credit, bonds, credit transfers, promissory notes, bank deposits, checks, a system of uniform weights and measures, and a trimetallic gold/silver/copper coinage of unparalleled quality that would soon become the "dollar of the Middle Ages."

Thus, both doctrinally and in application, the medieval Muslims became exceedingly accomplished in their quest for capital gain—with their early attempts at creative free market exegesis later culminating in the monumental treatises of the renowned fourteenth/fifteenth-century economic historian Ibn Khaldun, whose cogent descriptions of the manifestations of medieval Arab profit motive are defined in concepts that can in precept only be described as laissez-faire.

Yet these early Muslim scholars, some writing a half millennium and more before Scottish economic philosopher Adam Smith, did not enjoy Smith's benefit of ready recourse to free market theoretical antecedents. They were, instead, working directly from empirical observation based solely upon the operational dynamics of their own contemporary economic milieus.

Contrast such forward economic thinking—addressed to the role of profit motive and surplus capital impelling commerce—with the didactic of the contemporary Christian Church which castigated as a cardinal sin "innate human greed," the vulgar quest for common capital bred of an insatiable desire for material gain.

For in the church's eyes, even virtue itself was not an end but rather merely a means to the ultimate end of attaining heaven. Thus moving into a resultant capital void that was entirely of its own making, the papacy itself now became the principal financial institution of the Middle Ages. But from a commercial standpoint, the fiscal system that it formulated and sponsored made matters not better, only worse.

As a consequence, while the church was laboriously teaching that "it is easier for a camel to pass through the eye of a needle than for a rich man to enter heaven" and "you cannot serve God and mammon," Arab caravans were carrying merchandise to the far corners of Asia—and ships bearing their commodities ranged from Japan in the east to the furthermost reaches of West Africa.

Indeed, while the church was preaching solace in Saint Paul's exhortation that "no man overreach or circumvent his brother in business," Muslim jurists were adroitly formulating new accommodations to their religion's ban on interest. Small wonder that the Islamic Empire became the world's supreme economic power—presiding over a vast new "common market" stretching from Japan and China in the east to Morocco and the Atlantic in the west— while Christian Europe sank into the morass of a deepening Dark Age.[10]

The intellectual contributions of the medieval Muslims—fostered by the economic surplus that this accumulated wealth comprised—though generally less well known than those of the Greeks and Romans, were nonetheless equally as profound and impressive as those of their imperial predecessors. Indeed, theirs was a monumental and unique scholarly achievement. For unlike those imperial predecessors, their greatest accomplishments did not initially flow from a long-standing tradition of academic genius—as the early Arabs in pre-Islamic times were a transitory Bedouin people with no documented heritage of deeply rooted intellectual pursuits. It was only because of social overhead capital, amassed through the avid pursuit of private profit, then, that their sedentary population gradually evolved—which, in turn, made systematic scientific inquiry possible—and from it, "Arab genius" issued.

It was, in reality, the wealth produced by private-sector productivity that provided the financing that underwrote the economic base that empowered the medieval Muslims to become pioneers of science and the contemporary masters of technological innovation. It was the leisure time made possible by such wealth that propelled Islamic civilization to its cultural apogee in the early Middle Ages.

Almost from the beginning, the medieval Muslims developed an interest in the arts and sciences. The Qur'an openly encouraged them to seek out learning wherever it could be found. This discrete religious mandate—directly woven into the highly international character of Islamic society that emerged— soon became a principal stimulus impelling their empire to acquire a profound knowledge of bygone civilizations and to employ that knowledge to develop contemporary civilization.

Indeed, it was Muslim scholars who preserved much of Greco-Roman science and philosophy during medieval Europe's prolonged intellectual darkness—a base era wherein, in the words of modern Near East historian Phillip Hitti, scholars at the royal courts of Arab rulers were delving into Roman, Greek, and Persian sciences, "whilst Charlemagne and his lords were still dabbling in the art of writing their own names."[11]

This was indeed a remarkable transformation—a watershed in the application of ideological methodology unprecedented in human history, and still today largely unknown to the world of scholarship at large. Suffice it here to say that medieval Islam now became imperial Rome's worthy successor and the primary catalyst for the rebirth of Christian western Europe—a civilization that then regenerated rapidly in economic and cultural advance.

For with the sparks of renaissance first flickering in the city-states of Italy—Venice, Genoa, Pisa, and Amalfi, those most directly engaged in commerce with the Arab world—the flames of productive enterprise soon spread throughout the southern basin, then upward into western Europe in the course of the eleventh to fifteenth centuries.

Trade now expanded along increasingly well-developed commercial roots. Towns grew at key intersections—and within them, factories sprang up to meet the incipient needs of distant markets. Craftsmen simultaneously flocked in droves to the newly established urban centers to capitalize upon the new economic opportunities that they afforded. A distinct diversification of industry also now evolved; as like Greece and Rome before it, Western Europe became the "workshop of the late medieval world."[12]

This industrial resurgence, in turn, generated burgeoning private economic surplus—and with it ever-increasing revenue-producing productive investment and the ability to sustain increasingly greater numbers of scientists, scholars, and artists focused upon the acquisition of knowledge as well as aesthetic activities. The attendant revival of learning, and a renewed penchant for the arts—after nearly half a millennium of mire in the morass of Dark Age indolence—thus precipitated Christian Europe's intellectual renaissance commencing in the twelfth century.

This regeneration of profound thought in intellectually reborn Europe took on many forms, while manifesting itself across a broad spectrum of scholarly spheres—in the philosophies of Thomas Aquinas, Desiderius Erasmus, Niccolò Machiavelli, René Descartes, and John Locke; in the pioneering scientific methods of Roger Bacon and Leonardo da Vinci; in the astronomy of Galileo and the physics of Isaac Newton; in the poetry of Petrarch and Geoffrey Chaucer, the literature of Giovanni Boccaccio and William Shakespeare; and in the art of Michelangelo, Raphael, and Donatello.[13]

But such spectacular attainment would have been impossible save for the restoration of capital surplus produced by profit motive engendered by the self-serving quest for personal gain—all imports from the Arab East—as the direct linkage between humankind's economic well-being and production of science, art, and literary masterpieces was again reestablished in late medieval western Europe.

Indeed, by the end of the fifteenth century, Christian Europe's renaissance was in full flower—stimulated in no small part by its ongoing contact with Islamic civilization. In 1492, in fact, the very year that Granada, the last Muslim principality of Spain, fell to the armies of Ferdinand and Isabella, a young explorer named Christopher Columbus, commissioned by those monarchs, discovered the Western Hemisphere.

Thus the shape of an entirely new civilization gradually coalesced—a profit-driven society whose materialist leitmotif holding that all things, including the quest for divine salvation, have their price—was proclaimed as a truism by none other than Columbus himself: "Gold constitutes treasure, and he who possesses it has all that he personally needs within this world, including the full means of rescuing souls from Purgatory and restoring them to Paradise."[14]

Yet this dramatic ideological evolution, like most processes of structural social change, had experienced an extremely long gestation. Commencing in the eleventh and twelfth centuries, the Italian city-states, whose profit motivations were already richly leavened by their exposures to the economically superior Near East, gradually introduced its business methods into Europe to facilitate widespread commercial and industrial development. Concurrently, the prevalent use of money, deposit banking, bills of exchange, and credit instruments, long so prevalent in the medieval Islamic East, began to reappear throughout the Christian West as well.

The Crusades, in turn, lent impetus to this active process of cross-cultural commercial fertilization—as tapping into Islamic economic wealth and technological knowledge through tiny apertures in the Levant, great socioeconomic contributions came to flow with ever-mounting velocity into the West through ever-widening sluices in the civilizational divide.

Many of Europe's new business techniques of trade were now, in fact, directly borrowed from the Muslims. For contrary to Orientalist contentions that the rise of a "hostile Islamic power" on the Mediterranean had overwhelmingly disrupted commerce and, in that process, thrown southern Europe into its Dark Age abyss, the reality was that the Muslims thrived on trade—and that it was only Christian antagonism to the rise of a rival religion so proximate to the domains of the Holy See that caused such slackening of trade as did occur.

By exchanging its goods with those of the Arab Levant, in fact, Western Europe came to realize a level of economic prosperity never before achieved. With the rebirth of profit inspiration and the gradual emancipation of her reemerging merchant class from the commercial strictures of the church, moreover, her economy now took off—and in this process, the basic crucible of modern Western capitalism was forged in spectacular fashion—with an indomitable commercial spirit reigning triumphant over the feudalistic ethos that had characterized its medieval civilization, as a mercantile European society was reborn.

The results were spectacular, as a dynamic age of exploration now began, both externally and internally. Thanks to significant innovations in shipping, *mercantile* capitalism could expand dramatically overseas—and thanks to innovations in the workplace, *industrial* capitalism could equally productively expand.

Indeed, henceforth, the pace of technological progress would proceed hand-in-hand with economic growth and political evolution. The emergence of "scientific method" in the age of Copernicus, Galileo, Descartes, and Newton further accelerated the pace of progress—and the science that it empowered in turn facilitated technological progress further still, particularly in navigation and transportation. In the words of economic historian Raymond Crotty:

> The accumulation of wealth, political adaptation, and scientific and technological progress, all proceeding over a 250 year period of mercantile capitalism, created the preconditions for a new phase of human existence. In a manner

reminiscent of the near miraculous combination of circumstances that had made possible the original emergence of capitalistic production, there was, around the mid-eighteenth century, a confluence of conditions that made it possible for Europe to progress to a new, higher plane of productivity, which may be referred to as *factory capitalism.*[15]

As a consequence, by 1764 a single nation, Great Britain, had, in the appraisal of the Marquess of Caracciolo, become "a democratic republic in which trade is God." Indeed, less than a century later, by the 1840s, it had become the new "workshop to the world"—and by 1860 it controlled some 45 percent of the world's industry, 40 percent of its trade in manufactures, and one-third of its merchant ships. In the poignant assessment of the French baron Montesquieu, the English had then "progressed the furthest of all peoples in three most important things: commerce, piety, and freedom."[16]

This was a monumental transformation. For of all of the achievements of Western civilization, none have been quite so remarkable as those it has realized in its private economic sphere, with no other society in human history having so many so soon come to enjoy so ambient a lifestyle. As combining technology, resources, enterprise, and profit motive, the captains of Western commerce and industry between the seventeenth and twenty-first centuries have created greater material wealth than ever before in the history of the planet.

Several factors have coalesced to produce this dramatic economic evolution. The clear necessity to earn a living in a laissez-faire economy has generally compelled individuals to work. The modern profits system—investors' insatiable quest for material gain—has instilled greater functional efficiency in producing goods and services. Indeed, today's proliferation of dynamic new enterprises—establishments run by private entrepreneurs employing financial capital to produce and sell high-quality, competitively priced goods and thereby gain revenue and profit—stands as prima facie evidence of the productivity of that process.

An admixture of work ethic and the elevation of the desirability of productive output as a national proclivity have characterized the rise of capitalism in the West, and most particularly in the United States. For in America, the Industrial Revolution—combining capitalistic spirit, abundant natural resources, and a focused approach to "work"—has created the twenty-first-century version of "high-tech factory to the world"—and the economic growth that has issued in its wake has brought with it buoyant financial dimensions that are both infectious and self-generating.

For more than two centuries now, the free market system has served America and its Western capitalistic allies well. As a result of the bountiful economic surplus that it has produced, its citizens have earned a level of per capita economic well-being never before achieved. This material affluence has concurrently been accompanied by equally impressive accomplishments in the natural sciences and, to a lesser extent, the arts.

Within the past two centuries, humankind has thus achieved far greater technological advance than that recorded in all of previous history. Indeed, the past two decades have produced greater scientific accomplishment than that realized in the past two centuries. Applying disciplined scientific method to an ever-expanding universe of knowledge and abundant resources, increasingly advanced technologies have been forged—causing the domain of economic progress to expand exponentially.

The principal factor underlying these developments, of course, has been the insatiable human desire for material acquisition—the economic engine of profit motive generating the capital surplus that empowers civilizations to progress. For given ample surplus capital, the desire for further capital gain has, in the West, unfailingly welded labor, raw materials, technical knowledge, and market demand into tools of technological advance, just as it did in the great civilizations that preceded it.

It is the prospect of such capital gain, as shown, that has driven Westerners to divert earnings into savings in order to accumulate and invest their surplus funds in desired goods and services. The famed German philosopher/scholar Werner Sombart in his *Der Moderne Kapitalmus* has, in fact, labeled "material acquisition" and "satisfaction of human needs" as the two greatest principles to evolve within Western economic history.[17]

But were they genuinely Western in provenance? Socioeconomic scholars seeking to quantify these twin synergistic economic phenomena have, at times, lumped them together under a single rubric: the "Protestant ethic." Yet they are "Protestant" only to the extent that their doctrinal evolutions first issued from the pens of Reformers seeking relief from those pervasive and stifling economic effects that the medieval church had long imposed in the name of "social justice" upon the erstwhile entrepreneurial life of contemporary Christian Europe.

Today, the commonly used term "Protestant ethic" is an unfortunate misnomer that is at once both stereotypic and divisive, as countless Catholics, Jews, Muslims, Buddhists, and other religious minorities have likewise contributed to building the economic greatness of Western capitalism, and that obtaining in America and Great Britain in particular. Indeed the spectacular business achievements of those enterprising Catholic and Buddhist Vietnamese immigrants who have flocked to American shores within the past four decades, successfully overcoming tough cultural, linguistic, and financial barriers, effectively dispel certain trendy theories about why minorities succeed or fail within the free market system.[18]

Hence, the ideological provenance of those founding economic doctrinal precepts that propelled the Protestant Reformation—and whose tenets, in turn, inspired the progenitors of modern capitalistic spirit—are worthy of further contemplation.

REVERBERATIONS OF THE REFORMATION

A century has now passed since noted German sociologist and socioeconomist Max Weber produced his renowned, albeit controversial, work *The Protestant Ethic and the Spirit of Capitalism*. His analysis searches for answers as to why "business leaders and the owners of capital, as well as the highest grades of skilled labor, and even more so, the highly technically and commercially trained personnel of modern enterprises, are overwhelmingly Protestant" is, in fact, the case.[19]

He purports to find them in Calvinistic doctrine, which—unlike medieval Catholicism's banning as "avarice" the quest for capital fructification—turned profit-seeking capitalism into a distinct religious virtue—equally as a sign of redemption and a devout act of faith—the technique of "seeing God manifest" in the capitalistic successes of rational economic man.

Making the marketplace its chapel by reconciling the Christian goal of salvation with the capitalistic goal of consumption, he asserts, Calvinism slammed the doors of staid monasteries forever shut behind them. Accordingly, the earning of profit now became for the devout not an effort to earn one's "daily bread," but rather a capitalistic obligation that later would find vivid expression in the admonition of Benjamin Franklin: "Remember that time is money. . . . He who idly loses five shillings worth of time loses five shillings and might just as prudently throw five shillings into the sea."[20]

Diligent labor thus became a religious ritual as well as an essential element of early Western capitalism—as John Calvin, in establishing a unique theological laissez-faire, now elevated to lofty status the role of economic virtue as a prime precondition for salvation. For under it, man ascertains his calling as one of "God's elect" in his ordinary struggles with daily business life. Accordingly, by allowing individualism to replace collective consciousness, thereby igniting personal economic energies, it gave fuller free play to the workings of Adam Smith's vaunted "invisible hand."[21]

But unlike the more classic religions whose adherents earn their salvation through a vast accumulation of good works, the Calvinist proves his redemption through a series of self-serving acts that take place within an overarching microeconomic system wherein industry, utility, diligence, thrift, frugality, and sobriety are among faith's foremost pillars.

Thus enterprise and mercantile endeavor become at once both Christian virtues and societal contributions to the goal of establishing an economic order worthy of the Kingdom of Christ. For in diligently striving to earn profit within the marketplace of free will—again a precept predominant and common to both Islamic and Calvinist Christian doctrine—man demonstrates the unequivocal signs of his election to salvation, and, in so doing, promotes the greater glory of God.[22]

Within this reformed process, then, there is no longer room for the human cycle of sin, repentance, atonement, and release over which the medieval church had long presided—as in this new doctrine, redemption through temporal punishment cannot restore a state of grace. Man is on his own recognizance; he must earn his own election. Or, more succinctly put: "God helps those who help themselves."

By sanctioning—and indeed glorifying—self-serving ends, Calvinism thus overcame the mentality that man would work only because, and as long as, he was poor. In giving new life to the virtues of heretofore suspect successful business endeavors, it was a religion formed of, and for, bourgeois entrepreneurs who actively functioned within the real-time "marketplace of life"—an eminently practical doctrine that would lend inspiration to the capitalistic spirit manifest in the strong determination of that rugged Dutch sea captain who asserted that he "would go through Hell for capital gain, though it would likely scorch his sails."[22] Hence, after Calvin, in the words of British economic historian R. H. Tawney, "The good Christian was no longer at all greatly dissimilar from 'economic man.'"[23]

Though Calvin offered an eminently pragmatic economic doctrine that was unique to the Christian West, however, he was no pioneer. For elements of the so-called Protestant ethic can be found in the varied doctrines and dogmas of other, equally zealous, "theocratic elites" as well. Among them, Islam, as shown, similarly exhorts its followers to the utmost of productive labor; and certainly the tenets of Judaism have played no small role in the industriousness that has traditionally characterized its devout.

Over time, profit-seeking Jews, in fact, became the "merchants of money" around the Mediterranean while their Islamic and Christian counterparts labored grievously under their religions' separate bans on capital fructification—and would remain so until the collapse of the Christian ban on interest-bearing transactions late in the fourteenth century. Indeed, because of the Jews' vast capital liquidity and widespread geographic dispersion, they gained great advantage in most contemporary international trade and finance and soon became a powerful force behind the expansiveness of the global economy.

Their economic accomplishments also enjoyed a strong religious doctrinal basis—as defined for them in *dispensa* authored by such renowned

medieval Jewish scholars as Moses Maimonides. Thus, the three great
"heavenly" religions—Judaism, Christianity, and Islam—have all directly
linked "industry" with "salvation" in God's economic plan for mortal man.

It is no accident, therefore, that the last two major civilizations to dominate
the planet—the Muslim East and the Christian West—both have been driven
by the identical relentless impetus—profit motive—as the "Protestant Ethic"
and the "Islamic Ethic" appeal to, and indeed are mirror images of each other
in capturing the acquisitive instincts of modern man.

Examples are abundant. Smith, the great definer and patron of modern Western capitalism, reminds us: "It is not from the benevolence of the baker or the
grocer that one gets his bread but from everyone pursuing his self interest"—
whereas his fifteenth-century Islamic counterpart, the historian-philosopher
Ibn Khaldun, appeals to the same self-serving sentiment in his exhortation,
"Buy cheap and sell high. That is commerce for you!"[24]

The motivation, in each case, is identical.

AMERICA'S ECONOMIC HERITAGE

Free market capitalism—be it Islamic, Judaic, or Calvinistic—thus is immensely practical. Indeed, the pragmatic values of rugged individualism that
it inspires are the wellhead fount of historic economic strengths. For its secular essence, as defined by Smith and Ibn Khaldun alike, is that society is best
served when its members dedicate themselves to the quest for personal gain.

It is therefore illuminating to explore how that doctrine is today applied in
America, the self-proclaimed epitome of pragmatic free market values. For in
their single-minded pursuit of enlightened self interest, American capitalists—
be they industrial tycoons or middle-class shopkeepers—have come to be
characterized by three basic business traits: (1) industry; (2) prosperity; and
(3) utility.[25]

As for the typical U.S. entrepreneur imbued with the Protestant ethic,
work is a consummate action of conscience. Hence, idle hands, like idle
minds, are the devil's instruments. To avoid serving demonic purposes, then,
they must be productively employed. Accordingly, the resulting need for
"busy-ness" that this mandate implies converts itself, definitionally, in fact,
into "business"—a transformation that sustains Weber's proposition that
Protestantism, particularly in its Calvinistic forms, is the today prime engine
of work in the Western world.[26]

America was founded predominantly by Protestants—refugees from western Europe seeking escape from the church's practice of the "economics of
asceticism" and its attendant persecution of dissent. They have thrived in their

new free markets and have inspired their neighbors to greater industrial productivity as well.

Indeed, though the long-standing economic gap identified by Weber between Anglo-Saxon Protestants and their Catholic counterparts has diminished in recent decades, this reality does not imply that the church's doctrine has suddenly become more hospitable to profit motive—only that U.S. immigrant Catholics have become Americanized into a more capitalistic mode.[27]

Many modern scholars, on the other hand, in addressing Weber's treatment of Calvin, contend that "Protestant industriousness" is actually no more than a nervous reflex—a counter-reaction against the complex doctrine of predestination, another conviction shared by Islam, offloaded onto them by Calvinism.

"For God not only foresaw the fall of man," Calvin wrote, "He arranged it through the determination of his own will." Indeed, Weber made this argument in contending that the spirit of capitalism was a secularized by-product of Calvinistic teaching on predestination as synthesized with religious calling.[28]

Yet man is simultaneously granted free will, Weber continued, in order to prove his election to salvation through service—thereby glorifying God's majesty by contributing to the Kingdom of Christ on earth. Thus seeking to rationalize the divine determinist doctrine of free will preordained by God—this argument holds—"Calvinists reassured themselves by inventing capitalism."[29]

Whatever its redemptive elements, however, Calvinistic doctrine does carry with it a clear bottom line: "Whatever man does, he must be busy at it!" Hence, it is ironic that the Protestant "religious reflex" that began four centuries ago with a precipitous rejection of the church's doctrine of salvation through good works now ends paradoxically with a glorification of prosperity, the end product of work.

For the foreordained reward of industry, of course, is "prosperity"—which capitalists also greatly admire—as in Calvinistic terms, in serving as the imprimatur for meeting the capitalist's nervous need for reassurance, business prosperity is the outward sign of grace. "By your works, ye shall be known," the Bible says, and the true capitalist believes this admonition fervently.[30]

The notion that success follows industry is likewise an American, as well as a Calvinistic, tradition. Indeed, it is the very formula that has produced the dynamic, uniquely American economic system. As such, the incessant quest for success that capitalism imbues has today become an indivisible part of the "American ethic."

In an early harbinger of this integral capitalistic dimension to the American modus operandi, James Madison, in the *Federalist Papers*, directly placed ambition as the centerpiece of the U.S. business psyche—the focal point upon which future prosperity hinged—and clearly he was right. For the great industry that capitalism has imbued explains why the United States's original "tobacco, corn, and pelts" colonial economy has transcended its once modest roots to become the mightiest economic power on earth.[31]

America did not rise to its current economic status because of the abundance of its natural resources, though they are substantial. Other regions, including the erstwhile Soviet Union, have had them in equal, if not greater, measure. To the contrary, the United States has prospered precisely because its people have energetically applied their capitalistic industriousness to its bountiful, but finite, natural resources in their quest for capital gain.[32]

"Utility" is the corollary to capitalistic industry and the prosperity that it engenders. For in Calvinist capitalistic eyes, nothing is important in and of itself. It still must be "good for something." Capitalists thus seek out accomplishment by employing multipurpose wrenches, integrating CAD-CAM (computer-aided design/computer-aided manufacturing) assembly lines, and creating multinational corporations.

They commit themselves to getting things done, and enjoy the fruits of getting them done—which are delivered to them in the form of capital gain. In this process, then, inefficiency is the moral equivalent of indolence, and hence, is "financial turpitude"—an unpardonable, ever-threatening secular sin.

Hence, while other, more aesthetic cultures admire the past and contemplate the future, the capitalist asks: What good will it do me now?—a penetrating question whose final answer provides the substance from which successful economies and civilizations have invariably been molded.

This insatiable drive for self-improvement explains why, in fact, America is richer than Africa, though it has fewer natural resources; more peaceful than the former Soviet empire, though it has more sects and creeds; and further at the cutting edge of technology than Europe, though it has a far less impressive intellectual tradition.

Indeed, America has built its national record of achievement far more through inspired economic values than through natural or human resources. Its citizens are integrally part of a "nation of immigrants." Its Founding Fathers were immigrants—and the ancestors of all its citizens, in one way or another, initially came here in immigrant status as well. The nation's economic preeminence has been built, in fact, directly upon the success of those who have come—entrepreneurs, factory workers, merchants, and farmers—all dedicated to the premise of diligent endeavor seeking a fair return.

Because it has opened its arms to immigrants, America has produced the most racially, ethnically, and religiously diverse country on the planet. Indeed, each time a new immigrant group has come, the nation's dominant culture has been both modified and enriched by their presence—as evidenced by the number of foreign words that creep into the English vernacular each year. In this process, its steadfast commitment to the precepts of free market economics has concurrently produced unparalleled upward mobility and a concomitant commitment to individualism and innovation.

Because America values merit, ambition, and achievement over legacy, inheritance, and tradition, new doors of opportunity continuously open to new talent and new energy rising from the bottom—rendering the nation uniquely suited to today's rapidly changing, knowledge-based economy. Thus, its legacy of ambient suburban residents is the embodiment of its ongoing successful experiment in realizing the American Dream via the free market ethic.

The United States hasn't always imported the planet's aristocratic elite. Indeed, it has more often received the world's disenfranchised citizens—people seeking refuge from perceived repression. Yet arriving, that great mosaic of humanity who did come—trusting the U.S. Constitution's failsafe guarantee of equal opportunity—have generally not been disappointed. For once here, they have embraced the nation's quite remarkable adaptation of historic capitalistic precepts embodied in free market democratic entrepreneurship—an ideology that has become the envy of the world.

Once here, they have thrived in an economic system underpinned by the rule of law—the freedom to contract with guaranteed enforcement, protection of private property, equality before the law, and, most importantly, a limitation of government that has long precluded the abject stifling of entrepreneurship through excessive taxation and regulation.

The American free market system is why New York Jews are not clamoring to go back to Budapest or Detroit Arabs to Beirut. America's democratic free markets are why the largest number of Iraqis outside of Iraq live in Dearborn, Michigan—productive citizens earning their livelihoods in U.S. service industries. It is why the largest concentration of Yemenis outside of Yemen are in Detroit, earning salaries a hundred times larger in the U.S. auto industry than they would in their original homelands.

It is why high-achieving Asian Americans now square off effectively against their native-born American counterparts in U.S. K–12 schools and why brilliant doctors, research scientists, and engineers from the Indian subcontinent are now prominent in prestigious U.S. university scientific departments—contributing to America's "free market miracle."

For despite its short-term strains, immigration has always brought dynamic new peoples to the U.S. shores—a million Germans in the wake of that country's 1848 revolution; another million Irish in that era fleeing famine; and many thousands of enterprising Cubans, Vietnamese, and Chinese within the past half century fleeing Communist repression.

Their results comprise the essence of America's spectacular economic success. For once here, they have continuously spawned innovative ideas, new products, and new growth areas for its economy. Indeed, the U.S. economy today remains the strongest in the world, in large part because of the hardworking immigrants who, for more than two centuries, have joined with their predecessors in establishing prosperous job-creating enterprises.

The American economic system works—and the world knows it—and is today "voting with its feet." Double or quadruple whatever may be "politically wrong" with America—its would-be immigrants say—and we will still be far better off economically in this country than in any other in the world.

America's entrepreneurial free market is, in fact, the defining commercial catalyst that underwrites its greatness. Her unique economic system—individuals seeking economic surplus won through profits to finance their ambitions and their dreams—is why peoples from every nation and ethnic background have come to the United States to forge their destinies and win fortunes on free market capitalism's bountiful and hospitable shores. It is a precious economic legacy that must not be sacrificed on the altar of public social experimentation funded by bureaucratic excess. It must not now be allowed to die.

NOTES

1. S. Clough (1951), pp. 6–7; E. Nell (1984), pp. 4–6.
2. S. Clough (1951), pp. 79–80.
3. S. Clough (1951), pp. 92–94: R. Sobel (2000), pp. 9 ff.
4. S. Clough (1951), pp. 94–97.
5. S. Clough (1951), pp. 100 ff.; J. O'Neill (1998), p. 29.
6. S. Clough (1951), pp. 126, 131 (quoted).
7. S. Clough (1951), pp. 132–34, 148; R. Sobel (2000), pp. 20 ff.
8. S. Clough (1951), pp.139–40, 149–51.
9. These developments are the focus of E. A. Gibbon (1969) and F. Lot (1931).
10. Bible, 1 Thessalonians 4:6; P. Hitti (1970), p. 315.
11. P. Hitti (1970), pp. 578 ff.
12. S. Clough (1951), pp. 167–69, 183.
13. Cited in R. Tawney (1926), p. 89; see also P. Kennedy (1987), p. 3.
14. S. Clough (1951), p. 166.
15. R. Crotty (2001), p. 113.
16. B. Croce (1927), vol. 2, p. 89; K. Phillips (1993), p. 200; Montesquieu quoted in R. Tawney (1926), p. 6.
17. W. Sombart (1916), vol. 1, p. 62.
18. Hence, the criticality of not confounding, in the words of Amintore Fanfani (2003, p. 48) "the relations between capitalism and the Catholic religion . . . with the

relations between capitalism and the Catholic Church as an organization" that represented formal legalistic bureaucracy.

19. M. Weber (1958), p. 35; idem. pp. 251–61, 587–88.

20. Similar reflections of Calvinistic doctrine would soon appear in Richard Steele's seminal seventeenth-century tract *The Tradesman's Calling*, wherein industry and trade were championed as both expedient and meritorious. They will, he claimed, help the tradesman from "frequent and needless frequenting of taverns," and "pin him to his shop, where you may expect the presence and blessings of God." (Steele quoted in R. Tawney (1970), pp. 245–46.)

21. L. Greenfield (2001), p. 19.

22. R. Tawney (1926), p. 194; see also M. Weber (1958), pp. 57, 139, 154.

23. R. Tawney (1960), p. 253; see also idem. (1926), pp. 96, 203–204.

24. A. Smith (1980a), vol. 1, ii, pp. 26–27, also cited in William Simon (1978), p. 21; Ibn Taymiyah (1976), pp. 100 ff.

25. Ibn Khaldun (1978), chap. 5:9, pp. 394–95.

26. On this, see A. Fanfani (2003), p. 115.

27. On this line of argumentation, see R. Brookhiser (1991), passim.

28. On this, see the rationales of historian Hugh Trever Roper synopsized in M. Novak (1982), pp. 276–79.

29. J. Calvin (1960/1986), vol. 2, p. 147; R. Tawney (1960), pp. 108–109; R. Grassby (1999), p. 13.

30. J. Calvin (1960/1986), vol. 2, p. 147; R. Tawney (1960), pp. 108–109 ff.; R. Brookhiser (1991), pp. 31 ff.

31. See sources cited in preceding endnote.

32. R. Brookhiser (1991), pp. 31 ff.

Part II

OVERARCHING ISSUES

A democracy cannot stand as a permanent form of government and will survive only until its citizens discover that largesse can be voted from the Public Treasury. Thereafter, the majority will always vote for candidates promising the most benefits from the Treasury, with the result that a democracy will always collapse over loose fiscal policy, always followed by a dictatorship.

—Alexander Trotter, British historian

The art of taxation consists of so plucking the goose as to attain the maximum amount of feathers with the minimum amount of hissing.

—Jean-Baptiste Colbert, finance minister of French King Louis XIV

Chapter Three

Why Bureaucracy Is Costly

The American republic will endure only until politicians learn they can bribe the people with their own money.

—Alexis de Toqueville

Preceding chapters have described the dramatic elevation of society over time powered by the pursuit of private profit motive within an unfettered free marketplace coursing a steady evolution that ranks among humankind's foremost monuments to economic progress. Yet today civilization's prized legacy of democratic capitalism—and with it, many of America's hard-won economic freedoms—stand threatened from within, challenged by the extravagances of an unconstrained public sector and the exorbitant costs they engender.

Such bureaucratic transaction costs, a product of public spending, matter because they vitiate the private profit motive that throughout history has been the primal force impelling social progress—the fuel that powers the economic engine that drives the march of civilizations. They matter because big government—regulation and other gratuitous public service—clearly has its price. Its toll comes in the form of excessive taxes and other governmental processes and systems that sap vigor from the productive private sector, while their financial multiplier effects erode the free economy in a variety of other ways.

Moreover, because bureaucratic transaction costs systematically attenuate the earnings of private businesses, thereby undermining their global trade deployment, the nation, through industrial out-migration and outsourcing, continues to lose higher-paying production jobs, which are, as the outsourcing phenomenon makes clear, too often replaced with lower-paying service ones.

In seeking prospective remedy to the resulting deteriorating job and income situation, it is critical to bear in mind that the facts of life remain largely economic. A healthy macroeconomy produces private economic well-being, whereas a deteriorating one precipitates correspondingly adverse socioeconomic consequences. Unemployment is economic. Welfare is economic. Crime is economic. Unaffordable health care is economic. The economy is where people live their lives.

American citizens seek—and expect—value for their tax investments. In seeking to meet this expectation, the key policy question thus becomes: How does government within a democracy, faced with the need to curry favor with voters by filling insatiable consumer demand, preserve private property earned through the pursuit of private profit while concurrently limiting the growth of government to keep the public debt and deficit under control?

This issue and its underlying dialogue are long-standing. John Locke, the early eighteenth-century British philosopher-politician whose political ideas inspired the Founding Fathers, believed that not debt but the "preservation of private property" should be the ultimate end of government, whereas his somewhat later eighteenth-century French counterpart, Montesquieu, in like manner, maintained that taxes were no more than part of a person's property relinquished in order to secure protection for the part that remained.[1]

Operating within the ideological framework of a profound sense of public need to protect private possessions, then, while the "republican" Alexander Hamilton espoused that "a national debt can be unto us a blessing," the "democrat" Thomas Jefferson believed that "limiting the purpose and size of government could best meet the private property needs of 'workers, farmers, and small businessmen'—the nation's citizens at large."[2]

Indeed, this was America's explicit social contract with its people, as delineated by Jefferson within the Declaration of Independence, the legally recognized principle that citizens were "created equal and endowed by their Creator with certain inalienable rights," among them "life, liberty, and the pursuit of happiness"—not happiness itself, per se, but the assurance of a level playing field in its pursuit.

That meant that they could not be bound by the sovereign will of the British king to pay taxes to sustain His Majesty's empire. For in the new United States, the people would be sovereign, and the government reduced to the role of a limited public servant set up with the consent of the governed to safeguard individual rights.[3]

Today, however, the demarcation of the respective ideological roles has become less clear. While Hamilton's Republican political heirs today preach, if not always practice, greater fiscal responsibility and balanced budgets, they nonetheless preside over record-breaking federal deficits. Jefferson's Democrats, on the other hand, despite his aspirations to limited government, have come to believe that larger, more assertive government is necessary to achieve their income redistribution goals.

Ironically, the programs the Democrats espouse are today devastating Jefferson's aspired prime constituency—those "workers, farmers, and small businessmen" who comprise the nation's productive citizens—as their tax costs increasingly undermine and destroy the abilities of the working middle class to help themselves. Instead, in a tragic spiral, as the tax burden occasioned by these costs grows ever more onerous, still more citizens are forced into public-sector dependency at the expense of those productive citizens who remain.

Benjamin Franklin once averred that "nothing is certain except death and taxes"—the modern response to which is: "At least death never gets any worse!" Yet tax-consuming big government has long historic precedent. Two millennia ago, the Roman statesman Cicero warned: "When a government becomes powerful, it is destructive, extravagant, and violent. It is a usurer that takes bread from innocent mouths and deprives honorable men of their substance for votes with which to perpetuate itself."[4]

The effects of such bloated government can be devastating. Throughout history, many of the world's supreme superpowers—third-century Rome, eighth-century Baghdad, sixteenth-century Spain, and nineteenth-century Britain—whose ascendancies were founded, without fail, upon the inherent strengths of durable private economies that enabled them to be net exporters of capital, eventually lost their global primacies due to the mounting taxes needed to cover burgeoning public debt produced by domestic fiscal excess.[5]

Excessive government, as noted, was likewise a clear concern of the nation's Founding Fathers—patriots who believed that all citizens possessed certain inalienable rights and freedoms, and that the prime purpose of government was to protect them from external threat. For they rightly recognized that regulation, by its very definition, is a diminution of freedom compelling citizens to do or not do certain things—and that every rule in itself is a loss of freedom because it restricts freedom of choice.

Indeed Jefferson, one of the Constitution's foremost architects, in one of many missives addressing the cost dimensions to excessive government, argued that "[l]oading up the nation with debt and leaving it for the following generation to pay is morally irresponsible. No nation has a right to contract debt for a period longer than the person contracting it can expect to live."

Upon reflection, he thus called upon the fledgling American democracy to

[d]eclare in the Constitution that they are forming that neither the legislature nor the nation can validly contract more debt than they can pay. . . .

The public debt is the greatest of dangers to be feared by a republican government. To preserve our independence, we must not let our rulers load us with perpetual debt. We must make our election between economy and liberty, or profusion and solitude. . . .

I wish it were possible to obtain a single amendment to our Constitution. I would be willing to depend upon that alone for reduction of administration of our government to the genuine principles of its Constitution. What I mean is an additional article taking from the federal government the power of borrowing.[6]

Accordingly, America's Founding Fathers explicitly designed the Constitution not to empower government but to limit it, for it was their intent that all power should repose in the people themselves. To this end, James Madison, a primary architect of the Constitution, argued that "[w]e have staked the whole future of civilization, not upon the power of government, far from it. We have staked the future . . . upon the capacity of each and all of us to govern ourselves, to control ourselves, to sustain ourselves, in accordance with the Ten Commandments of God."

In "Federalist #10," in fact, Madison expressly warned of the insidious dangers of "that old trick of turning every contingency into a new resource for accumulating force within government." Late in his career, Jefferson, in an equally despairing vein, likewise wrote, "Were we directed from Washington when to sow and when to reap, we would soon want for our bread!"

Similarly John Adams—like the Roman historian Polybius, whom he admired—argued that regulation was a mere way station on the road to tyranny. Indeed, a century ago even Woodrow Wilson—called by many "the father of modern public administration in America"—asserted: "Liberty has never come from government. The history of liberty is the history of the limitation of government, not the increase of it." Thus Wilson, like the Founding Fathers, was attuned to the lessons of economic history as well as to the scriptural admonition that "[a] good man leaveth an inheritance to his children's children."[7]

Historically, in fact, America has long honored an implicit social contract to leave a productive legacy for its offspring. But today, a permissive public-sector shortsightedness has set in that has left the American social contract in shambles. For in blithely passing off the burgeoning federal debt to its succeeding lineage, America stands in direct contravention of both historic warning and divine admonition—as many generations yet unborn will bear the burden of the current budgetary process. In so doing, a group is unabashedly being taxed that has no vote—an act that precipitated the Founding Fathers original political revolt: "taxation without representation," which they equated with tyranny.

America's current crisis of confidence in the effectiveness of expansive government and the taxation that underwrites it is thus sustained by the economic lessons of the past. For while government at all levels within the United States has undeniably grown big, it has concurrently grown weak—as today, the federal labor force alone exceeds 17 million workers administering a nation that contains nearly ninety thousand tax-levying governmental units.

At the top, there are the federal government and fifty state governments, and beneath them thousands of other cities, counties, townships, school districts, water and transportation districts, and other purpose-dedicated authorities. *Indeed, more people now work for government than in all types of manufacturing combined.* If government is failing in America today, then, it is not for want of adequate deployment.[8]

THE "BENEFICENCE" OF GOVERNMENT

Accordingly, because of its bureaucratic resources and sweeping assumed mandates, governmental spending today has become egregious—and it plays out in as many ways as creative bureaucrats can conjure up. There are four fundamental ways that the public sector can commandeer federal resources:

- tax and spend;
- borrow and spend;
- simply spend by printing money; and
- conscription and eminent domain.

Yet *legally*, the Constitution confines the spending authority of Congress to limited areas—mostly in Article I, Section 8—which includes the right to "establish Post Offices and post roads; raise and support Armies; provide and maintain a Navy; declare War"—and other mostly national-defense-related activities. The Tenth Amendment to the Constitution, in turn, further circumscribes these rights, asserting, "the powers not delegated to the United States by the Constitution nor prohibited by it are reserved to the states respectively or to the people."

Notwithstanding the Constitution's firm admonition and the Founding Fathers' clear intent, however, government has usurped circumventions around its constitutionally delineated revenue limitations—and its spending excesses have today become not only myriad but often equally malfeasant.

The Government Accountability Office recently found, for instance, that the Pentagon had reported an estimated $22 billion in disbursements that it has been unable to match with corresponding obligations. Its audit of Medicare also discovered that the federal government made $12.5 billion in erroneous payments in a single recent year. Another found that the food stamp program routinely sends out vouchers to ineligible "entitlement families."[9]

A recent Office of Management and Budget (OMB) assessment of 230 governmental programs rated the performance of 50.4 percent of them as "results not demonstrated." The OMB noted that it took Congress 101 years to spend $500 billion on such programs, but just ten years to spend the next $500 billion—and then just four years to spend the most recent $500 billion.

To perceive how government leavens everyday lives with just such largesse, one need only scan the "benevolent public service" embedded within programs approved in the FY 2004–2005 federal budget. In it, government spent about $2.3 trillion. Stripping out its core constitutionally mandated functions of national defense and justice, it still exhausted about $1.8 billion—some $17,000 for every household in the United States.

Among its financial commitments one finds outlays for such worthwhile *private* causes as subsidies for a DNA study of bears; Idaho weed control; Missouri wild hog control; the Pennsylvania Trolley Museum and the Punxsutawney Weather Activity Center; the Dennison Depot Railroad Museum and the Johnny Appleseed Heritage Center in Ohio; the International Coffee Organization; Beef Jerky television advertisements; "recreational improvements" in North Pole, Alaska; the California Pistachio Commission; the Popcorn Board; the Hop Growers of America; the National Preschool Anger Management Project; the Mohair Council of America; the Catfish Institute; the New York Wine and Grape Foundation; a study of brown tree snakes, development of the "Michigan byway story"; mariachi music courses in Nevada; and, quite naturally, Cleveland's Rock and Roll and Nashville's Country Music halls of fame—all the while worried parents are frantically raising money to buy Kevlar armored vests the Pentagon claims that it cannot afford to protect their sons and daughters stationed in Iraq.

To quote economist Stephen Moore: "Call it fiscal malpractice. Or call it the triumph of the special interest over the national interest. Call it whatever you wish, there is no denying this dismal fiscal reality: Washington is hemorrhaging money at a pace that one typically observes only in a bankrupt third world nation."[10]

Tragically, more than ten thousand such programs typically infest every federal budget at a cost approaching $25 billion every year. Yet to what end? Such spending does not benefit the economy. On the contrary, it simply crowds out an equivalent amount of private spending and thereby prevents resources from being employed more productively.

It is the profligate waste of precious publicly entrusted funds that has made taxpaying Americans today so wary of the motives of their government—

knowing that a large portion of their contributions goes not to promote that general welfare cherished by the Founding Fathers, but instead to special interest welfare groups that have secured pole positions at the public trough—farm subsidies, corporate subsidies, local pork, entitlements, and individual, not societal, public welfare.[11]

Yet all of this public sector "do-good-ism" ignores one fundamental economic truth—wherever something is subsidized, the need, over time, becomes self-generating and indeed multiplies—creating still more would-be *subsidees*, not fewer. The time-proven axiom thus holds true: Sanction some business subsidies and one merely gets more business supplicants. Give handouts to the derelict and one gets more derelicts.

INCIPIENT CAUSES OF BUREAUCRATIC EXCESS AND THE CALCULUS OF ITS ECONOMICS

Accordingly, while many criticize government for ineffectiveness, it is not for wont of inefficiency—as in many sectors today, the term "governmental performance" is deemed to be an oxymoron. Nor is it for lack of expenditure—as the incipient cause of inordinate bureaucratic transaction cost is excessive governmental spending. Indeed, within the past three decades, the tax consumption capacity of U.S. federal governance has risen to such gargantuan proportions that its extracts more than $2 trillion in direct taxes from American taxpayers each year.

While the total per capita spending at all levels of government stood at $331 per citizen in 1900, in fact, by 1980 it had grown to $4,115—and today, it stands at well over $8,000, whereas total annual household federal spending has grown from $1,651 to well over $23,000 within the last two decades.[12]

The prime cause? In 1963, just prior to the onset of the Great Society, entitlements accounted for just 22.7 percent of all federal spending and interest—leaving 67.3 percent of the remaining federal funds available for discretionary spending. Yet today, entitlements account for well over half the federal budget, with income transfer payments its fastest growing area.

Moreover, whereas total discretionary spending totaled 12.7 percent of GDP in 1963—primarily because of entitlements occasioned by the Great Society and its successor statist "rescue programs"—it has receded steadily but dramatically, falling to an average 10 percent in the 1970s, 9 percent in 1991, and 7.2 percent of GDP in FY 2005–2006.[13]

Consequently, while as late as 1970 total federal discretionary spending constituted 61.5 percent of the federal budget, by 1980 it had been reduced to 46.8 percent, by 1990 to 39.9 percent, and today, it hovers at around 34 percent—with nonmilitary discretionary spending at a historic low of around 19 percent. In 1930 the combined financial costs of government at all levels consumed 15 percent of total personal income. Today it has doubled to nearly 30 percent—excluding Social Security, Medicare, and the hidden costs of regulation.

Add into these totals the combined costs of Social Security and Medicare withholdings—a whopping 15.3 percent on the first $87,900 of all salaries and wages, constituting the equivalent of more than 8 percent of GDP—in fact, and government's total take of the average citizen's paycheck now exceeds 45 percent. Further add in the 10 percent of national income in hidden regulatory costs, and it becomes readily evident that government today consumes well over half of most average Americans' commitment to their economic daily lives, earnings, and well-being.[14]

As a result, the aggregate U.S. federal debt today exceeds $8 trillion, having reached that level in October 2005, and is growing exponentially. Three years ago, on January 1, 2004, it stood at $7,001,312,247,818.28, some 62 percent of GDP and $24,075 for every man, woman, and child in America. By January 1, 2006, it had soared to $8,153,881,581,212.99—$27,376.50 per capita—an increase to 64.7 percent of GDP, even though the national GDP has been growing at a very healthy average rate of more than 4 percent over the past three years—while profligate federal spending now adds to the federal debt at a rate that constitutes more than $23,000 per household for the first time since World War II.

It is not surprising, therefore, that in FY 2005 (October 2005 to September 2006), the U.S. government spent $22,039 per American household and collected $18,248 in taxes—with each household paying $1,582 in interest on the federal debt—a statistic meaning that federal debt service now takes 8.7 cents of every tax dollar. Indeed, the nation now spends two and a half times more on debt service ($627 per capita) than it does on education.[15]

Small wonder that Americans no longer believe that they receive value for their tax dollars. Small wonder that as early as the eighteenth century, economic philosopher David Hume determined that "[e]ither a nation must destroy public credit, or public credit will destroy the nation."[16]

As a consequence, when the costs of deficits are factored in, the typical American wage earner today must work nearly four months each year just to pay his or her total taxes to differing levels of government, as government takes the first and largest portion of the average citizens' wages, leaving them with steadily shrinking shares of the monies that they earn with labor and investments. Indeed, as noted, typical American taxpayers now work more than half a year just to pay for the aggregate costs of governmental taxes, fees, and regulations—and spend more on taxes than they do on food, clothing, and medical costs combined.[17]

Why? The answer is direct and simple. A liberal political elite that has for decades ruled from Washington has determined that they know how to spend the average American's earnings more wisely than he or she can. Hence, at their lead, tax dollars are squandered every day by thousands of faceless bureaucrats empowered by pandering politicians to finance their personal ambitions by catering to their small (but vocal) politically active special interest constituencies.

Consequently, while the federal government today spends unprecedented amounts on welfare, food stamps, and public housing, these monumental monetary outlays have proven to offer no humanitarian solution whatsoever. On the contrary, far too many Americans slip below the poverty line each year, as with its burgeoning market basket of handouts, the nation is creating an expanding and increasingly economically helpless underclass.[18]

Still Washington lurches mindlessly along, oblivious to the possibility that somewhere within the laws of economics there must be one that holds that incessant social experimentation, bred of infinite populist expectations, must be constrained by finite resources—that somewhere along the line this profligacy must stop—indeed, that it stands as the greatest threat to the nation's fiscal future, yet one for which there was ample forewarning two centuries ago.

While Adam Smith opined, "no one but a beggar chooses to depend upon the benevolence of his fellow citizens," de Toqueville in his *Democracy in America* similarly somberly observed, "The American republic will endure only until politicians learn they can bribe the people with their own money."[19]

Thus it is that America as a nation today finds itself financially imperiled by a liberal political crowd that seemingly cannot wait until 51 percent of the nation's populace becomes hooked on handouts—irrevocably addicted to the lure of so-called "social justice" blandishments. For thereafter, utopia for them becomes perpetual political empowerment by simply providing more nourishment to those already feeding at the public trough.

When nineteenth-century British economic philosopher John Stuart Mill compellingly argued that only taxpayers, and not governmental beneficiaries, should have the right to vote, he did so on the premise that to allow the tax recipients to vote would be tantamount to inviting them "to plunge their hands into their neighbors' pockets."[20] But that is precisely the essence of liberal economics—people voting themselves other people's earnings.

Yet liberals don't consider such "democratic confiscations" greed. They deem it to be greedy only when taxpayers seek to keep their hard-earned money for themselves. Conversely, redistributive economics, the act of randomly giving away other people's money, they define to be compassionate and generous—a free market analogue of the *Communist Manifesto*'s capstone maxim: "From each according to his ability; to each according to his need."

WHY DEFICITS MUST BE REDUCED
FROM THE BUDGETARY SPENDING SIDE

The compelling case for bureaucratic streamlining is made explicit by exploring the systemic reasons why the uncontrolled expansion of bureaucratic agencies into vast empires is invariably the case. The reasons are partly taxonomic—as the American public sector is a quite different economic animal from its private-sector counterpart. It is illuminating to explore the differences and reasons why.

The first incontrovertible reality is that the public sector is not—and perhaps cannot be—run like a business, as some corporate leaders and free market purists might expect and hope. For while businesses derive their profits from satisfied customers, governments get their revenues from often unhappy taxpayers. Businesses thrive on competition; but governments cannot exist except as monopolies. Business CEOs are driven by the need to show profit; politicians, by the need to generate votes. The public-sector management challenge, therefore, becomes that of attempting to measure productivity in sectors wherein, apart from regulation, there is no quantifiable output.

Two centuries ago, philosopher Honoré de Balzac blamed government's employees for its manifest incompetence—calling bureaucracy "a giant mechanism run by pygmies." But the fundamental "governmental-rightsizing" problem usually does not repose directly with the people who choose public service as their permanent careers, as often they are quite normal human beings—folks who mow their lawns, devoutly go to church, become members of the PTA, pay taxes, and, at times, even vote Republican.[21]

At the most basic level, then, the problem isn't them, but rather the system that compels them to become the problem. The problem's quintessence lies in the core corporate psychology that impacts directly upon every bureaucrat. For while all forms of organizational behavior are driven by incentives, those incentives are quite different in the government than they are in the private sector—as within the public sector, a bureaucrat can experience substantial and immediate rewards in the form of direct and indirect compensation by responding to its incentive structure. Indeed, by responding to such incentives over time, he or she can often identify individual personal success or failure with that of the program being managed.

But the public-private differences are often more profound than the mere natural bureaucratic response to the public sector "Skinner box." For in the private sector, individuals, households, and businesses must make tough economic choices in order to live within their means. Efficient spending makes higher living standards possible because more assets can be procured with fixed amounts of available income.

The bureaucrat, on the other hand, is incentivized by different stimuli. For governmental salaries are directly correlated with the size of a manager's staff and budget. If a public sector manager underspends his budget or utilizes his workers more productively so as to occasion the need for lesser numbers, he can later be penalized for failing to achieve the key professional benchmarks of bureaucratic success—resulting in career-threatening smaller budgets and smaller staffs in succeeding fiscal years. In other words, personal economic interests perforce become biased against professional economic interests.

Succinctly put, then, in the public sector managers are explicitly rewarded for financial inefficiency with greater funding, increased staffing, and enhanced career prospects—as bureaucratic rewards are awarded commensurate with higher levels of administrative and rule-making authority, larger staffs, bigger budgets, and an incessant quest for even greater working revenues.[22]

At the same time, the economic losses that result from this profligate spending process can readily be passed along to others—the taxpayers—as governments rule by "inputs," by the fiscal resources that they control. To this end, they immerse perceived social problems in tax dollars as signs of good public intent. Indeed, over time, their commitments become as boundless as their intents—for why should bureaucrats fight among each other for finite financial resources when they can get the taxpayers to pay for everything?

Still another key factor contributing to the inordinate price of government is that those cost controls induced by competition in the private sector are almost entirely absent in public service. The contrast is striking. In the competitive private marketplace, firms make decisions based equally upon costs and consumer preference. Customers know the specific unit prices of products and enjoy the freedom to buy from the competition, or not at all, if the prices of goods and services exceed their fair market values.

Market-driven competition, therefore, determines that higher product quality will benefit the firm financially, whereas poorer quality or service will generally cause it to fail. A private firm must thus be directly attuned to the particular needs and preferences of its market. It must concurrently ensure that its retail costs do not rise too far above those of its competitors, for unlike government, it cannot extract funding from customers who do not wish to buy.

Conversely, in the public sector, neither the bureaucrat nor the taxpayer knows the unit price of an agency's "products." Because governmental service offerings are a monopoly, moreover, taxpayers do not enjoy the freedom to purchase from the competition. As a result, customer-driven competitiveness does not shape governmental efficiency.

The resulting lack of market discipline, combined with government's unfettered ability to tax allows for the uncontrolled growth of ever larger bureaucratic staffs whose success is measured by the volumes of individuals and regulations over whom they preside. Consequently, the productivity of bureaucracy more often spirals downward rather than up. John Stuart Mill, in his 1861 book on public sector performance, described the process thusly: "The disease which afflicts bureaucratic government is *routine*. . . . Whatever becomes a routine loses its vital principle, and having no longer a mind acting within it, goes on revolving mechanically, though the work that it is intended to do remains undone."[23]

Regrettably, fiscal reality concurrently dictates that government cannot raise public spending absent tangible, perceptible results without diminishing the economy for all. For that which is paid to public employees must inevitably come at the expense of private-sector employees whose diminished earnings—and ability to productively spend—constitute the tax base.

Indeed, public employee unions, liberal proponents of larger government, and other self-appointed "keepers of the public trust" directly lobby for self-preservation. Bureaucrats have become masters, in fact, of the art of using red tape to defer measures they oppose—interpreting regulations in ways that directly serve their vested interests and dragging their feet on actions they disfavor, while at the same time expediting those that serve their particular ends and needs.

Over time, governmental employees become active lobbyists for the agencies that they serve—advocates for perpetuating those programs that perpetuate their own careers. Unfortunately, they too often concomitantly lose sight of who their employers really are—the services-seeking taxpayers who are their customers. The net result is that cost is not a readily evident concern to the typical public employee who is not compelled to directly confront the policy question: *Does government exist to serve the people or do the people merely exist to fund the government?*

The question that can evolve as a valid one, then, is: For whom do bureaucrats really work? Though citizens fund their payrolls, they rarely, if ever, take orders directly from them. Their performances are rated not by citizens but by fellow bureaucrats. Their careers are not funded by, or dependent upon, satisfied citizen-customers. Thus, from a career enhancement standpoint, they need not fix their mission objectives predicated upon citizens-customers' needs or desires, but rather merely upon pleasing other bureaucrats higher in the pecking order.

Whither, then, the attributes of honesty, integrity, accessibility, responsiveness, and concerned communication with the citizen-customer that were embedded in the original conceptualization of "honorable public service" so eloquently enunciated in the *Federalist Papers* at the nation's inception two centuries ago?

Arguably, bureaucrats, in principle at least, are responsible to elected officials as the people's representatives—but that assumption is often not perceived to be the case. For the public employee union axiom—"elected officials come and go, but bureaucrats are forever"—has been turned into a self-fulfilling prophecy by complex civil service regulations that public employees have devised to ensure that they seldom can be fired or even effectively monitored.

Yet by rendering it virtually impossible to fire nonperformers, mediocrities can be converted and promoted into deadwood through a natural selection process that punishes the creative in order to ensure the survival of the intellectually inert but bureaucratically entrenched.[24]

Where, then, do our *elected leaders* stand in this process of bureaucratic oversight? Essentially, they generally ignore it altogether in their endless quest to advance still more public agencies as proposed remedies for still more perceived socioeconomic problems.

Thus, stasis is built into America's administrative process. For the only true downside risk in public sector employment is that, though mediocrity is safe and tolerable, open failure can be deadly. Hence, the system discourages risk-takers and deliberately screens out creative thinkers. In government, performance incentive is directed not at forging new frontiers of success but instead at *not making a mistake.*

BUREAUCRATS AND THE QUEST FOR MORE ENTREPRENEURIAL GOVERNMENT

Given the on-the-ground realities of bureaucratic entrenchment, then, can America succeed in building more entrepreneurial government into its administrative system at all levels? Likely not—and certainly not as it is currently constituted—for its weeding and selective breeding processes, as noted, now too often preclude creative people from participating.

The system itself, in fact, is skewed specifically against the type of "beyond the envelope" thinking that creates that dynamic societal progress produced through private-sector innovation. For in most mid- to upper-level public-sector management positions, some level of security clearance almost invariably is required—conducted by fellow bureaucrats who, most often, have never themselves taken an entrepreneurial risk in their lives.

But private entrepreneurship, creativity in business, is by its very nature a risky undertaking. This is a normal part of doing business—it is free market capitalism carrying out its vital mission—founded on the axiomatic premise that it is better to have tried and lost than to not have tried at all.

Yet open, active participation in the free marketplace of creative destruction and reconstruction is likewise exactly what can cause the would-be bureaucrat to fail his or her security clearance background check. For in the eyes of the investigating bureaucrat, one who has tried and failed is immediately suspect.

Produced by a direct clash between the values of big bureaucracy and those of free market competition, this blanket indictment thus cuts a broad swath. This in itself, of course, is not a sinister process. Dun & Bradstreet data show that through just such "capitalistic weeding," well over half of all new capitalistic enterprises will fail within their first five years. But in so doing, they concurrently pave the way for the remaining, more durable, ventures to establish that vital economic base upon which all future private job and income growth are built.

Failure, then, is no more than healthy free market screening. For the nation's economic future is held directly in the hands of those not afraid to experiment even if failure is a possibility—not unwilling to commit that mortal crime of risking business loss that current bureaucratic cadres often see as a bar to public service.

Can the nation, then, continue to afford to deny its best and brightest the opportunity for public service just because of quite natural screening processes that are integral to the course of pursuing the American Dream—in so doing, consigning public service exclusively to those who have elected not to try at all? Can it continue to sort out its most inventive minds, to deny them access to the halls of government merely because they have knowingly participated in a capitalistic system that is now rightly held out as an exemplar to other nations—a process that is the very cornerstone of America's economic strengths and freedoms?

The public-sector performance problem is thus both structural and endemic. It cannot be solved by merely hiring "better" public servants, providing "better" management, or committing still more financial resources, precisely because of its inherent systemic flaw—the reality that the incentives and selection processes in government are skewed against the national interest.

As the public administration system now works in America, in fact, the purveyors of policy formulation have every possible incentive—and absolutely no disincentive—for making government bigger and more mediocre still. The folly of the reality is manifest in the results.

The results speak for themselves. The nation pays more for public school education than other countries do, but gets lower testing scores. It spends more on job training for the employment challenged, yet the number of citizens slipping below the poverty line each year remains inordinate. It commits increasing resources to police and corrections, yet crime rates rise faster still. Why? Because in the administrators' eyes, the results don't really matter. It is the rules, and the personal perks that characteristically attend them, that ultimately drive the process.[25]

Consequently, the price that Americans now pay for their present rules-driven form of government has become egregious. While it may retard some small measure of abuse, it simultaneously produces a monumental waste of resources, both public and private—as public programs today are too often driven by internal politics, not public policy; special interest constituencies, not taxpaying customers at large—producing results that are overlapping, at times fragmentary, and rarely precisely targeted. Hence, bureaucracies never die, are seldom self-correcting, and are invariably economically inefficient.[26]

Thus America today finds itself immersed in a public administration crisis rampant throughout its federal system—a circumstance in which rules have overpowered reason as the prime determinant of public action and one that, in the last analysis, can be cured only by a dramatic turn to a far more entrepreneurial, market-driven, customer-oriented approach to public-sector governance.

CAN GOVERNMENT ITSELF BE OUTSOURCED?

The foregoing realizations, however pessimistic, do nonetheless concurrently suggest a key approach to solving public-sector problems. To wit: when services of proximate or equal value can be provided by private vendors at costs lower than those of government, they can and should be submitted to a competitive bidding process wherein private service providers are allowed to compete on equal terms with the parent public agency.

Such competed services, it must be pointed out, are no less public services than those now provided by public agencies, since the programs themselves are still mandated by legislators and enforced by public servants. It is merely that service providers disciplined by free market forces, and thus more attuned to the needs of the customer base, are now in charge of field operations.

The approach, called "privatization" in contemporary political economics vernacular, is, in reality, governmental outsourcing—the process of turning over public-sector functions to private-sector companies in the quest to optimize public services delivery. It is predicated upon certain time-tested economic values holding that if government is to be made more economic and efficient, it must be forced to do the very thing that it has often forced private companies to do: divest itself of its monopoly stranglehold over the services it provides by fostering competition.

Its underlying premise, derived from private-sector models, is that a government should produce "value"—employing those assets entrusted to it by its constituents to produce things that are publicly sought. This goal thus mandates upon bureaucrats the challenge of accomplishing assigned missions as efficiently and effectively as possible—while exploiting the highest-value uses of the public-sector resources placed at their disposal.

"Privatization" is not an altogether novel concept. Municipal governments have been employing it for years, in the process often obtaining spectacular public-sector savings. Its underlying premise is that Americans will pay for quality services but that they resent taxes that pay for inefficient services delivered by their governments. As vested-interest taxpayers, while they believe that some governmental services are vital, they are simultaneously convinced that there is no excuse for governmental waste.

There are varied approaches to public-sector privatization. A bureaucratic operation may be sold outright to a buyer, it may be assumed by governmental employees, or government may contract with a private firm to provide services that it once offered directly. The new operator may be a commercial firm or a nonprofit corporation.

Alternately, vouchers may be given to governmental customers to purchase services from private vendors that they previously received from government, or government may subsidize private agencies performing previously public-sector functions through preferential tax treatment. Or it may engage in "load shedding"—simply announcing that it will no longer provide a public service while requiring that the function continue to be performed.

In these varied forms, privatization of a broad range of local governmental functions has gained significant momentum nationwide. Indeed, initially seen as a prime means for achieving cost savings in the public sector, it is now also playing an increasing role as a frontline tool for promoting economic expansion. Because of this dual advantage, compelling arguments can be made for its institutionalization as a formal part of the federal budgetary process.

The prime case for privatization is that because of its greater efficiency and economy of scale, the private sector can perform certain functions traditionally in the public domain in a more cost-effective manner. In so doing, it can likewise underwrite economic development in a variety of ways. First, it can reduce the nominal costs of public services, thereby encouraging economic growth. Second, it can promote development by more efficiently delivering public services, thereby promoting greater resource utilization.

Many examples of effective privatization support these contentions. Among them, the U.S. Postal Service, whose services have been deteriorating for years, now has strong competition from the private package delivery companies such as DHL, UPS, and Federal Express. So great are the actual cost and service differentials between public and private carriers, in fact, that the General Services Administration, an agency of the U.S. government, has frequently urged its sister agencies to reduce their mailing costs by employing private delivery companies.

Why are the cost savings of privatization dramatic? The economic rationales are evident. Service thrives on competition, but government, by its very nature, is a monopoly—and monopolies, by definition, preclude competition. Thus, because a government cannot be compelled to do what it does do in the most cost-effective manner, it cannot be expected to reach the competition-honed efficiency of the free market no matter how dedicated its employees.

But within the private sector, which must depend upon profits to survive, prompt customer service and sound resource management are essential elements of such competition. Hence, private firms almost invariably deliver their services more economically and efficiently than does government.

It must be emphasized, of course, that advocating privatization does not perforce mean that one is perceptually opposed to the actual provision of public services, but merely to their delivery mode. In reality, many people today have become so accustomed to governmental monopolies, or near monopolies, in such areas as fire and police protection, garbage collection, and the provision of water that it is often difficult for them to imagine that those same services could actually be provided by the free market.

Thus, when it is suggested that public services could indeed be offered with greater efficiency by private industry, the general reaction frequently tends to be one of skepticism. People want to know in precise detail just how such vital services could actually be handled by private-sector companies.

The answer is quite simple—they would be handled just as everything else is now handled within the free, competitive marketplace. Reflect for a moment upon a hypothetical scenario wherein government might have, for years, been providing the public with its personal automobiles.

If one were a privatization advocate, some might get the idea that he or she was somehow "against automobiles" in advancing the suggestion that government could effectively turn over its automobile monopoly to the private sector. How could the public be certain that private firms could handle such a project? How could citizens be assured that enough cars would be produced? Who would see to it that their quality was satisfactory? What if the selling price were too high?

The answer to all of these questions, of course, is that private enterprise now does, in fact, today turn out enough high-quality, low-priced cars to meet U.S. market needs. How? Simply through the healthy pursuit of profit in the competitive marketplace—through profit motive guided by trial and error, real-time competition, and the law of supply and demand—that "unseen hand" at work in the market that Adam Smith so eloquently defined more than two centuries ago.

Accordingly, in the last analysis, procompetition isn't antigovernment at all; it is simply the employment of market-based, price-driven means to ensure more cost-effective government.

NOTES

1. C. Adams (1998), p. 192.
2. J. Makin and N. Ornstein (1994), pp. 6, 265, 284, 303; R. Samuelson (1994), p. 41.
3. P. Drucker (1969), p. 198.
4. Cicero's *Orations*, quoted in "Thoughts on the Business of Life," *Forbes* (July 18, 1994): 340.
5. Proverbs 13:22. See also Ecclesiastes 18:33: "Be not made a beggar by banqueting on borrowing;" and 2 Corinthians 12:14: "Children should not save up for their parents but the parents for their children."
6. On this, see D. Calleo (1991), pp. xii; C. Edwards (2005), p. 12.
7. C. Edwards (June 2, 2004), p. 4.
8. S. Moore (January 13, 2004), p. 1.
9. C. Adams (1998), pp. 190–91.
10. See source cited in ibid.
11. C. Edwards (2005), p. 10.
12. *Budget of the United States* (2004), p. 8.
13. National Priorities Project (2004), pp. 1–2; B. Riedl (April 15, 2005), pp. 1–2.
14. D. Hume (1903), p. 366; D. Calleo (1991), pp. 39–40.
15. Tax Foundation (July 6, 2004), p. 3; idem. *Tax Features* (April 2004), pp. 1 ff.
16. P. Peterson (1993), p. 138; A. Gore (1993), passim.
17. A. Smith (1980a), vol. 1, ii, pp. 26–27; J. Muller (1993), p. 71; P. Peterson (1993), p. 312.
18. On this, see R. Dworak (1980), pp. 9 ff.
19. D. Osbourne and T. Gaebler (1993), pp. 14, 83; C. Edwards (2005), pp. 51–52.
20. J. Sobran, "Reflections on Elections," <www.sobran.com> (November 5, 2002).
21. Balzac quotation appears at <www.quotationsbook.com> (July 7, 2006); J. S. Mill, *Representative Government*, 1861, cited in C. Edwards (2005), p. 60.
22. D. Osbourne and T. Gaebler (1993), p. 140.
23. Ibid., pp. 112, 286–88.
24. Ibid., pp. 19, 165 ff., 180 ff., 288.
25. See J. Donahue and J. Nye (2002), pp. 297 ff., 301, 333.
26. Ibid., pp. 319–20.

Chapter Four

Why Regulatory Costs Matter

A wise and frugal government, which restricts men from injuring one another, must leave them otherwise fully free to regulate their own pursuits of industry and improvement, and shall not take from the mouths of men bread that they have earned.

—Thomas Jefferson

Regulation matters because it is the most tangible and invasive manifestation of bureaucratic excess. It matters too because, by decreasing competition, it destroys the incentives to be efficient. Conversely, *deregulation increases competition*, which, in turn, augments those incentives needed to innovate and provide better services at the lowest possible costs—benefits all lost with intense governmental control.

Public-sector regulatory costs likewise matter because, like tax costs, they drain the capital surplus, bred of the pursuit of profit motive, that is the lifeblood of productive enterprise. Preceding analysis has demonstrated the historic linkage between tax level and economic growth—a reality with direct modern extensions. Indeed, at the private-sector financial bottom line, the cost of public-sector regulatory compliance is itself an onerous tax.

For America's prime economic problem is not just overfunded government per se, but rather that its metastasizing outgrowths—pernicious regulation and inefficient spending—make higher taxes even more necessary to support their administrative overhead. Because taxes are mere outward manifestations of underlying festering public-sector excesses, then, it becomes critical to cast the quest for remedy clearly in such terms.

United States citizens today are regulated from dawn to dusk and from birth to death. An American awakening to a clock radio this morning likely rose to the dulcet tones of a radio station whose program content is fully licensed and regulated by the federal government. He showered with water provided by his local government. He ate a breakfast approved in substance by the Food and Drug Administration (FDA).

If he had a cigarette after breakfast, he not only bought from government, through cigarette taxes, the freedom to smoke, he also received a gratuitous public-sector reminder that "smoking is a main cause of lung cancer, lung diseases, and heart and arterial disease."

He drove to work on governmentally-owned streets; received his mail from a government-monopolized postal service; made his business decisions based on government-generated figures; left work for a happy hour drink likely sold at a governmentally licensed bar, which purchased it from a governmentally licensed wholesale outlet; and returned home to engage in an evening of TV watching equally sanctioned in most aspects by federal, state, and local government.

In short, big government pervades American lives in many direct ways as well as in a variety of ways that are not so readily evident. Productivity analysis makes clear that it saps national economic vigor. Indeed, by very definition, in a pure competition, laissez-faire economic model, anything a public agency does that diminishes prospects for profitability for a private-sector enterprise causes the economy to perform below its maximum efficiency.[1]

But humanity does not exist in a pure competition economic model, nor do citizen aspirations for a freer market obviate the compelling need to constantly seek out *more rational* government. Speaking precisely to this point, economist Milton Friedman asserts:

> The existence of a free market does not eliminate a need for government. To the contrary, government is essential both for determining "rules of the game" and as an umpire to interpret and enforce the rules decided upon. What the market does do is to greatly reduce the range of issues that must be decided upon through political means—and thereby minimizes the extent to which government needs to participate directly in the game.[2]

Civilized governance doubtless is a necessary, indeed desirable, framework for civil coexistence. Yet its regulatory approach is often highly intrusive and equally unwarranted—threatening industrial stasis at a time when greater entrepreneurial dynamism is needed to compete within the "new economy."

Uninformed and off-target rules preclude initiative and deny innovation. They reduce private companies to the efficiency levels of bureaucratic government—promoting economic dislocation while retarding innovation.

This unfortunate domino-like bureaucratic sequence and its economic impact are the focus and concern of the analysis that follows.

THE IRRATIONALITY OF REGULATION

Were the price of government not so costly, its results might be quite funny. Every four years, America trusts citizens in the street to elect the leader of the mightiest nation on earth. Yet most states don't trust them with discretionary decisions about, for example, whether to fasten their seat belts for personal well-being. The Consumer Product Safety Commission (CPSC) at one time had to recall ninety thousand buttons it had issued to promote toy safety. Why? Because they contained lead paint and posed a health hazard to the very children they were designed to protect.

Yet impossible as it may seem, some of the results of bureaucratic over-regulation are more egregious still. In a classic case some years ago, the CPSC ordered the Marlin Toy Products Company of Horicon, Wisconsin, to recall two of its special Christmas offerings that contained plastic pellets. If the toys cracked, it was alleged, the pellets could be swallowed by a child. The firm dutifully recalled its toys, redesigning them to eliminate the harmful pellets—thereby, in precept, legally entitling it to be removed from the banned products list.

Because of an "editorial error," however, the CPSC put Marlin on its subsequent banned products list, apparently incorporating an outdated previous circular. When the error was called to the commission's attention, its response was that it was not about to recall 250,000 lists just to remove two toys!

Marlin was forced to drastically restructure its business and lay off key employees at Christmas time. Why? Because the U.S. government agency that specializes in ordering companies to recall their products if any defective ones are found refused to recall its own products when there were defects in every single one. As Montesquieu said: "Even wisdom has its excesses!"

Thus regulatory excess proliferates. Indeed, at times, America's federal regulatory agencies even vie with each other for the same constituency. The U.S. Department of Agriculture, for instance, uses federal tax subsidies to promote the growing of tobacco, whereas the Office of the Surgeon General—dipping into the same federal revenue pot—uses its funds to condemn tobacco's use. In certain public buildings in Washington today, federal economists are diligently devising means to hold down prices to curb inflation, whereas in others, federal employees are equally busily at work sustaining agricultural commodity price supports.

Question: Who monitors the quality of meat sold in America: the Food and Drug Administration, the U.S. Department of Agriculture, or the CPSC? Answer: They all do, producing a confusing, almost invariably conflicting, patchwork of administrative rules.

The same three agencies also now vie with each other to monitor milk quality—producing an overlapping mosaic of regulation that the some cynics have called "udderly ridiculous." Yet today, more than a dozen similar federal agencies spend more than $1 billion each year to run some thirty-five other food safety and quality programs as well.[3]

Indeed, competing agencies of this nature throughout a multiplicity of business sectors proliferate the Washington Beltway. Most have long outlived their original intents but have survived by catering to the special interests that are their clientele—pressure groups who wouldn't dream of spending their own money on the bureau's particular functions, but are more than happy to have the taxpayers do it for them.

The utter hypocrisy of the big government cure stands in direct opposition to the solution that it promises to deliver—to the degree that were God to want today to part the Red Sea, he would readily run afoul of the Environmental Protection Agency (EPA) for violating the natural habitats of jellyfish. Were Jesus to want to feed the masses with "five loaves and two fishes," he would be busted by the FDA for improper ingredients labeling and running an unlicensed restaurant.

THE REGULATORY PARADIGM

Unfortunately, the economic losses caused by unwarranted governmental intrusion into the competitive marketplace go deeper than the mere squandering of tax dollars and private capital, arbitrary confiscations of private property, and widespread core inflation in providing quality goods and services to consumers. For the adverse impacts of governmental regulation as economic gatekeeper—raising new product market entry prices to a degree that regulatory costs actually determine which firms can and can't compete—ironically serve at direct cross-purposes to the antimonopoly safeguards that they were initially designed to protect.

One former business executive made this point persuasively in a speech some years ago when he said:

> We should be grateful that some of our "environmental intrusions" were predestined from on high. Imagine that today we had to deal with the bold new idea that "fire" somehow could be used to improve the lot of mankind. The

risks attendant to such a concept would be spread before the public in dreadful and sinister ways.

Investigations, regulatory authorities, and restrictions would be piled one upon the other to such depth that to even light a match would require at least four permits—renewable annually and backfitted quarterly. It seems quite likely that in today's environment, fire would not quite "make it" as an acceptable element of progress.[4]

In retrospect, it seems quite probable that soon after man discovered fire, some child actually may have accidentally burned his fingers—and at an early attempt at bureaucratic rule making, activist neighbors of that old Greek Prometheus did brandish their clubs and call for an early end to that vile force that scorches skin and emits billows of noxious smoke. Fortunately, economic reason prevailed and fire, over time, became one of man's most useful tools.

The automobile also is one of man's most useful tools, yet government has done little to enhance its market competitiveness. Indeed, it has bureaucratically encumbered it—with America's major industrial centers now paying an extremely heavy price in the severe economic restructuring ongoing within their vehicle manufacturing economies.

Thus, together with taxation, the onerous costs of public regulation impact dangerously upon economic growth. As much as 20 percent of the price of a new car today, for instance, is devoted to regulatory compliance—and a series of EPA requirements have also added more than twenty-five cents to the already highly taxed price of gasoline, making travel cost prohibitive for many.

In like manner, exorbitant gasoline prices today stem not from a shortage of oil, but because of public-sector gasoline taxes, and because federal regulations have precluded the licensing of new American refineries for decades, the last one coming online in 1976. The world suffers today not so much from a shortfall of crude oil production capacity as from the inability to produce sufficient quantities of refined petroleum products.

Regrettably, not only does government too often stand as regulatory gatekeeper—blocking market entry to would-be entrepreneurs—but the impact of its threat intensifies over time. Indeed, it is in the nature of bureaucracies to expand, and since rules are their only quantifiable productive output, regulation expands concomitantly. The bureaucratic algorithm is simple: Government says to the private sector, "You build a better mousetrap, and we'll build a bigger mouse!"

For this reason, some have argued that the proper definition of a "dinosaur" is a "governmentally owned lizard." Famed business analyst C. Northcotte Parkinson puts it more graphically still: "Government hires a rat catcher, and the first thing that you know, he has become a 'rat control officer.' But he has no intention of catching rats now. They have become his constituency!"[5]

As a consequence, because it is far easier to create bad public programs than it is to eliminate them once they have set root, many governmental agencies have grown to mammoth proportions—at times, even approaching the size of their client bases. Today, for example, an average thirty-nine layers of bureaucracy comprise the apex of the typical federal department—with the total strata reaching seventy to eighty layers in truly hierarchic organizations such as the Internal Revenue Service (IRS) and the U.S. Department of Commerce.

When the U.S. Department of Agriculture was originally established in Abraham Lincoln's administration in 1864, it had one employee for every 227,000 farms in the United States. In 1900 it had one employee for every 1,694 farms, and by 1935 it had one employee for every 315 farms. Today it has more than 7,400 field offices scattered throughout the country—occupying about 110,000 employees—one for less than every twenty of the 2,128,982 so-called farms identified in the 2000 federal agricultural census—the majority of which are mere hobby farms, typically earning less than $10,000 per year, and with more than 60 percent of their principal operators earning their primary livelihoods elsewhere.[6]

Presiding over some $17 to $18 billion in farm subsidies annually—paid to growers of wheat, corn, rice cotton, and soybeans, who constitute 36 percent of the value of all farm production, but not to growers of cattle, hogs, poultry, fruit, and vegetables, who constitute 64 percent of farm production—more than 72 percent of those subsidies go to just the largest 10 percent of the richest farmers, partnerships, corporations, and estates.[7]

Accordingly, despite the fact that the nation has been running agricultural surpluses for years, taxpayers continue to be bled financially to pay for the costs of, among other things, commodity price supports and enough "federally stored" powdered milk to meet total U.S. consumption needs for the next eighteen months. Speaking of the hypocritical irrationality of such farm subsidies on the U.S. House floor on June 25, 2006, Massachusetts Representative Barney Franks incisively proclaimed[8]:

> Mr. Chairman, I am here to confess my reading incomprehension. I have listened to many of my conservative friends talk about the wonders of the free market, of the importance of letting the consumers make their best choices, of keeping government out of economic activity, of the virtues of free trade, but then I look at various agricultural programs like this one. Now, it violates every principle of free market economics known to man and two or three not yet discovered.
>
> So I have been forced to conclude that in all of those great free market texts by Ludwig von Mises, Friedrich Hayek and all the others that there is a footnote that says, by the way, none of this applies to agriculture. Now, it may be written

in high German, and that may be why I have not been able to discern it, but there is no greater contrast in America today than between the free enterprise rhetoric of so many conservatives and the statist, subsidized, inflationary, protectionist, anti-consumer agricultural policies, and this is one of them.

So much committed to so few! Recall again that when governmental rural subsidy programs began in the late 1930s, there were more than 7 million farms, and 25 percent of the U.S. population lived on them. Today, there are 2 million farms—with less than half having annual income of more than $10,000—and just 2 percent of the populace lives on them.[9]

Reflecting that a proposed amendment to the U.S. Department of Agriculture's annual appropriation some years ago would have limited the number of employees in that department to no more than the total number of farmers in America, one is reminded of Reagan's recollection of going to the Bureau of Indian Affairs early in his first term and, upon seeing one disconsolate employee seated at his desk sobbing uncontrollably, inquiring as to the nature of his problem. The employee's response: "My Indian died!"[10]

Regrettably, the Bureau of Indian Affairs today still lives on—consuming some $2.4 billion in taxpayer dollars annually. It is perhaps the worst-run agency in all federal government, with even many of its former trustees calling it "incompetent" and "incapable of reform." In a series of recent court cases, in fact, its management has been described by Federal District Court Judge Royce Lambert as conducting "fiscal and governmental irresponsibility in its purest form"—and serving as "the 'gold standard' for mismanagement by government."[11]

THE PUBLIC SECTOR ACTION ALGORITHM

Analysis thus makes clear that the incipient cause of much governmentally administered private sector inefficiency stems from the traditionally reflexive patchwork and knee-jerk nature of the public policy formulation process itself. For public problems invariably emerge in the form of crises, and the remedies proposed address immediate symptoms rather than underlying causes. Mere manifestations are thus dealt with before systemic determinants are exhaustively explored, making the inopportune policy outcomes not surprising.

Can anyone look at the register of governmental oversight of private-sector activity to date and say: "Well done! We need more of this?" Can the performance of government lead anyone to believe that it deserves a still greater role in the competitive marketplace, that the nation needs still more public agencies to regulate free enterprise, or that government is even capable of managing itself?

Despite the woeful record of governmental intervention in the private marketplace, however, the social engineers of the liberal left continue in their contention that their policies have failed only because they haven't gone far enough. They persist in perpetuating the grand illusion that they can draft a law or rule to protect every right, defend every privilege, and anticipate every threat.

Even when regulation fails, as it invariably does, do they repeal their failed policies and programs? To the contrary, they continue to amend and expand them into infinite complexity until often the original purpose of the rule itself is lost. Like hard drugs to the addict, the excessive use of the "regulatory reflex" merely feeds an insatiable appetite on the part of an ever-expanding bureaucracy—as the cause of private-sector paralysis is forever resurrected as its cure.

As a consequence, the U.S. *Federal Register*—the compendium of all new federal regulations each year—which totaled 14,479 pages in the early 1960s and 53,376 pages in 1988, the final year of the Reagan administration—has now exploded to more than 75,000 new pages annually.[12]

Thus, the cause of the mushrooming of the regulatory process is both elemental and regenerating—as government is supremely capable of creating, but wholly incapable of abandoning, the obsolete. Pursuing the motto "nothing exceeds like excess," it knows how to add but not subtract, how to expand but not contract as its two principal products are bureaucratic structures and their attendant, repressive administrative rules. In the words of Reagan: "Governments don't solve problems; they just continually rearrange them."[13]

The net effect, then, is that the taxpayers and consumers are stuck paying for everything that the government ever tries, as public-sector bureaucracy devolves into an amalgam of the sum total of all pubic policy experimentation ever undertaken, whether good or bad—and, as shown in preceding analysis, its impact upon entrepreneurial economic activity can be devastating.

All of this frenetic activity, one is concurrently reminded, is expended in the noble effort to "protect" the individual taxpayer using his own tax dollars. Yet the process that this so-called protection entails is itself arcane, sinister, and ultimately self-defeating. Economist Walter Williams speaks precisely to this point:

> If a private person took money from one person and gave it to another, we would deem it theft, and as such, immoral. Does the same act become moral when the Congress takes the people's money to give to farmers, airline companies, or an impoverished family? No, it is still theft, but with a difference. It is legal, and the participants aren't jailed.[14]

In terms more graphic still, one is reminded of the pungent but nonetheless insightful observation of a former business analyst who, in arguing that the regimented mentality of government is no substitute for the efficiency of profit-driven management, allowed:

> I am always leery of any person or group compelled by a presumed greater wisdom to provide gratuitous service to the public . . . precisely because it is just such service that the bull has in mind when he contemplates the pretty heifer in the next pasture—and unfortunately, the results are almost invariably the same![15]

Such "gratuitous public service" likewise is what well-meaning bureaucrats have in mind when they plan yet another market role for government. But wouldn't their arguments be more compelling if government could manage its own affairs a little better? Is it sheer coincidence that those sectors of the economy habitually in the greatest trouble—railroads, farms, utilities, and financial services—are those that have traditionally been the focus of the most intensive governmental help?

For precisely this reason, Ronald Reagan, whose global assessment was that "[t]he liberal view of the economy is: 'If it moves tax it. If it keeps moving, regulate it. If it stops moving, subsidize it'" and "[g]overnment is not the solution to the problem; it is the problem," concurrently argued that "the most frightening words in the English language are: 'I'm from the federal government; I'm here to help!'"[16]

"Keeping government on the sidelines except when necessary and prudent" remains an important free market imperative—and must become a key component of much-needed balanced regulatory reform. For while limited, responsive government has historically served America well, it is its usurpation of functions that rightfully belong to—and have historically been performed by—families and the private sector that today cries out for remedy.

The "regulatory revolution" was not, of course, foreordained. Historically, the rule of law has been the foundation—and the pride—of America's national being. It has traditionally been a means, not an end—an administrative framework that sets the rules for economic fulfillment. Within it, careful public-sector oversight is often necessary and carefully meted out and, in fact, desirably so to preserve general social well-being, and is a legitimate function of government.

Indeed, the debate over the proper role of government in private economic lives is long-standing and was clearly a topic of concern at the time America was born. Adam Smith, who wrote his famed *Inquiry into the Nature and Causes of the Wealth of Nations* in 1776, the year that the United

States proclaimed itself to be sovereign, foresaw several distinct and vital, albeit limited, roles for government: To wit:

1) To perform those functions essential to the public welfare—such as defense, justice, education, and mass transportation—that are critical to the collective interest but uneconomic for the private sector to undertake. For by providing this public sector infrastructure, government creates the necessary preconditions for:

"that universal opulence which extends itself to the lowest ranks of people."

2) To provide for the stability and that security of person and prosperity necessary for private investment and the flourishing of commerce. To wit:

"promoting the prosperity of the commonwealth by establishing good discipline and discouraging every kind of vice and impropriety."

3) To provide a strong military to defend the nation, while nonetheless recognizing that the key to accruing wealth stems not from conquest but from commerce; and

4) Finally, to set the standards for, and provide a large measure of the cost of, education—while, letting the citizens purchase qualified education from the service provider of their choice.

Thus, Smith prescribed a holistic yet circumscribed role for government in contributing to economic prosperity—providing the legalistic crucible wherein free enterprise could flourish. So comprehensive, yet discrete, was the framework he detailed that when asked the proper role of government in contemporary lives, the great early twentieth-century economist Alfred Marshall responded, "It's all in Adam Smith."[17]

The nation thus had ample warning. For little did Adam Smith or the Founding Fathers know just how prophetic their words were—or how pervasive regulation would soon become. Indeed, foremost among them, John Adams, who argued passionately for a "government of laws instead of men," would doubtless be aggrieved, but not surprised, to learn that the United States has become a nation governed not by the rule of laws or men, but instead by rampant regulation anonymously, and without popular vote, promulgated in the name of the public good by a faceless sea of unelected bureaucrats.

THE LEGAL DYNAMIC OF THE REGULATORY REFLEX

The quest for remedy will not be easy—for the same proponents of the public-sector cure, who find market-driven natural monopolies so abhorrent, nonetheless have no problem whatsoever with the coercive artificial monopolies of government. Most states, for example, now "protect" their publics by limiting their access to a highly select, small number of telephone companies, electrical power distribution companies, state-run liquor distribution systems, and so forth. This limitation, they find, is "good" for the public.

Conversely, under the premise of antitrust law, the fact that a private company's products or services are overwhelmingly preferred by consumers and vastly outsell similar marketplace offerings is taken to mean that the market is "controlled" by the company capturing the bulk of the sales, so there is a lack of competition. As explained by economist Thomas Sowell, "If baseball were not exempt from the antitrust laws, the New York Yankees could be both fined and punished for having won so many World Series."[18]

But here the issue is more than one of mere semantics, as comprehending and addressing the economics of regulation require one to directly confront the market challenges posed by the "dualistic monopoly dichotomy." Perceiving the institutional distinction here is essential to properly capturing the dimension of the problem.

In economic terms, a monopoly occurs when a particular individual or enterprise exerts sufficient control over a product or service that it can set the terms whereby other people gain access to it. There are two types of such monopolies—natural and artificial—both of which are often perceived as problems for a free society. But in reality this is not the case, for in general, only the latter can metastasize into a true economic threat.

Natural monopolies are those that, by their very structures, are so operationally efficient and cost effective in delivering customer service that their competition cannot survive against them in the marketplace. By contrast, artificial monopolies are created not by competitive market forces but instead by denying competition via the threat of force—by criminals seeking to control drug trafficking through coercion, or by governments seeking to provide gratuitous, albeit mandatory, public services.

Most contemporary governmental functions could not exist, in fact, were they not monopolies—if there were real competition for their services, then better ways would have been found to do the job. Among them, America's public utilities and federal mail system are two classic examples of just such coercive artificial monopolies. Hence, it likewise comes as no surprise that they are habitually among the nation's foremost examples of industries in trouble.

Indeed, because of artificial price controls and other equally pernicious public-sector regulatory intrusions into operations of public utilities, they have for three decades been unable to raise the investment capital vitally needed to expand the national power grid—with electrical brownouts and otherwise intolerable service levels amongst the inexorable results.

The U.S. Postal Service is likewise in constant financial peril. Were it not for its ability to arbitrarily raise prices in a monopolistic market, it would never have survived. Yet while the federal postal service is in perennial danger of going broke, Federal Express, DHL, and other private carriers make millions of dollars in profits annually. How? Merely by employing that radical and subversive private-sector concept of offering more efficient, more reliable service to customers. Indeed, even the more conscientious U.S. government agencies now often turn to such private carriers when they need to get the job done right.[19]

In short, most artificial monopolies are coercive perforce—because they couldn't survive if compelled to compete in the free marketplace. Were government not an autocracy, in fact, it would soon price itself out of the market through its noncompetitive tax policies. It survives solely through brute force and not through natural market forces.

The bottom line on monopolies, then, is that natural private-sector monopolies are not inherently evil, nor artificial private-sector monopolies innately good. Nor is being a monopoly a guarantee of success. Penn Central's size did not save it from bankruptcy. In a free market system, wherein the customer can choose, size will survive only if it is efficient. Why? Precisely because of natural price-setting mechanisms of economy of scale.

Indeed, the American consumer's greatest market protection is the combination of free competition at home and free trade abroad—created equally by natural protection from the predatory practices of a single seller through the competition of another and by offering the best quality product or service at the optimal market price.

It is, in fact, precisely those regulatory remedies imposed by artificial monopolies intended as safeguards against the economies of scale of natural monopolies that are the greatest market threat to the consumer—and, in turn, to prosperity and economic freedom. In stifling acquisitive spirit, they thwart basic profit-driven processes that empower societies to advance.

As the antitrust process works in America today, if firms engage in pricing deemed by government to be too high, they are charged with monopolistic price gouging; if they set the prices too low, they can be charged with dumping; and if they charge the same amount in quest of a golden mean, they are susceptible to charges of collusion.

Imagine any business whose owners are admonished by the force of law that though they may compete, they must not prevail. To wit: You may continue to make your product but neither so well nor so cost effectively that you obtain a dominant market share. Yet if one can't play to win, why bother to compete? As customers, wouldn't people want their vendors to offer them the best possible good or service at the most economic price?

Wouldn't consumers want the best company to evolve that, through economy of scale, will produce the best for least? That's what the free market is all about. Still, if the company is truly successful in giving customers the best value for their dollar, that success in itself can lead to monopoly—and that's what proponents of big government now work so diligently to protect customers from!

That is why monopolistic public regulation in general is economically so pernicious—yet concurrently generally so unnecessary. It thrives only as a parasitic fungus sapping the vitality of the private economy in which it has set root and, in so doing, creating adversely noncompetitive market conditions that invoke the need for still further public sector intervention.

By contrast, a natural monopoly, by its very definition, cannot survive as a societal threat. If it is not delivering the best for least, it cannot endure—it will be driven out by ever-evolving competition. By way of illustration, it is useful here to paraphrase a hypothetical antitrust lawyer cross-examination recently conjured up by business analyst Humphrey McQueen:

Q: How did you become a monopoly?
A: We're innocent. Our machines did it!

Q: Did what?
A: Made our products the cheapest and the best.

Q: What can be done about your monopolistic power?
A: Technology will take it away.

Q: Where will it go?
A: To another monopoly![20]

In other words, the free market law of monopoly, as played today, is that someone has to be in charge of supply—and that if someone doesn't seize the advantage, then someone else will!

Indeed, only if the free market is eroded by artificial public controls will this quite remarkable, market-leveling "Darwinistic weeding-out" process cease to efficiently function. Only by undermining competition through needless regulation, in fact, can the disciples of big government turn their dire public protection predictions into self-fulfilling prophecies.

THE INORDINATE COSTS OF REGULATION

Today, the public-sector dimension to the global competitiveness challenge is not limited strictly to the direct costs of taxes. It is estimated that U.S.

regulations aimed at protecting health, environment, and safety alone now cost more than $200 billion annually—more than 2 percent of GDP—and that the aggregate cost of all new federal regulations issued each year increases by more than $50 billion.[21]

A recent National Association of Manufacturers trade competitiveness study has found, in fact, that "the total compliance burden of environmental, economic, workplace, and tax compliance upon the economy ranges in the order of $850 billion—with $160 billion levied upon manufacturers alone, equivalent to a 12 percent excise tax on manufacturing production. This figure represents an approximate 15 percent increase within the past half decade." The study further places the average firm's compliance costs at $2.2 million—or $1,700 per employee.[22]

Another study recently commissioned by the U.S. Small Business Administration similarly assessed federal regulation in direct costs alone across the national economy an estimated $8,264 each if apportioned across households—a total that also does not factor in indirect economic multiplier costs or the reduced economic growth that it occasions.[23]

This sum is in addition to the $19,613 tax share that, the study found, each household contributes, directly or indirectly, to federal revenues each year. The study also determined that firms employing fewer than twenty employees face an annual regulatory burden of $6,975 per employee, a levy nearly 60 percent above that facing a firm employing more than five hundred workers.[24] At the same time, the Small Business Administration estimates that the average household spends more than $8,000 per year in cost-inflated hidden regulatory costs in its purchases of goods and services.[25]

A 2005 Cato Institute study assesses the $843 billion federal regulatory cost bill at $869 billion in 2003—and $877 billion by 2006—an amount equal to 40 percent of all FY 2003 federal outlays, while constituting the equivalent of 7.9 percent of GDP. Indeed, combining this sum with total annual federal outlays brings the U.S. government's overall share of the economy to more than 27 percent—with more than seventy-five thousand pages of new federal regulation written every year![26] Consequently, by one estimate, more than $2 trillion is lost to the economy each year due to the cost of federal regulation.[27]

To enforce paying for just the regulation component to taxation, moreover, the Tax Foundation estimates that *compliance costs alone* afflict the economy with an annual levy that now approaches $300 billion—with the current federal tax code seventeen thousand pages long and including more than eleven hundred forms and publications. It further estimates that U.S. taxpayers spent an estimated 6 billion hours in 2005 at a cost of $265.1 billion complying with its arcane provisions—the equivalent of a twenty-two-cent surcharge for every dollar in taxes collected.[28]

The *Washington Times* recently calculated that with the IRS now sending more than 8 billion pages in forms and instructions to taxpayers each year, if all the paperwork it generates were laid end-to-end at the equator, it would encircle the earth thirty-six times! Small wonder that Albert Einstein famously said, "The hardest thing in the world to understand is the income tax"—and he died in 1955, before it got really complicated![29]

When the federal income tax amendment was ratified in 1913, the tax law was only sixteen pages in length. Today, as noted, the tax code approaches seventeen thousand pages and IRS implementing regulations alone comprise more than eighty thousand words. As a result, instructions for preparing the standard tax form 1040 have grown from 4 pages a half century ago to more than 130 by 2005—more than triple the size of 1975 and double the size of 1985—the year before taxes were "simplified."

Even the 1040 short form today, in fact, stands at forty-eight lines of calculation, more than double its size in 1945. Its typical preparation is now estimated by the IRS itself to take eleven hours and thirty-two minutes—just as long as its long form did just a decade ago—with the increase in the tax code's complexity estimated to have added a billion hours in annual compliance costs within that period.

Consequently, a myriad of highly paid professionals, with ever-increasing fees, now is required as a sine qua non to prepare most tax returns. For given the stark reality that IRS employees can make extraordinary demands upon taxpayers and take extraordinary actions against them—including a right to seize assets and close businesses without due process—they have no real alternative but to comply.

As with more than 115,000 employees, the IRS is a larger employer than all but three dozen of the largest U.S. corporations—and employs more investigative agents than the Federal Bureau of Investigation and Central Intelligence Agency combined.[30] Indeed, in oversight management alone, total federal budgetary outlays for administering and enforcing regulations more than doubled between 1990 and 2006.[31]

In sum, while regulations operate more as a "silent killer" than do direct taxes, they are nonetheless equally deadly. Constituting a huge, largely hidden tax that creates massive deadweight losses within the economy, regulations destroy productive jobs, torque commercial competitiveness, undermine self-government, and divert finite resources to unproductive uses.

REGULATION AS AN INSTRUMENT OF STATE

The chief threat to continuing U.S. global economic leadership thus issues not from Moscow or Beijing, Paris or Berlin, Tokyo or Seoul, but instead from right at home in Washington, D.C. Indeed, if government persists in its regulatory hostility toward innovation and entrepreneurship, it could soon readily doom the nation to the ranks of second-rate economic powers.

For as noted, industry pays a heavy price for its incessant regulation in the forms of higher production factor costs, diminished international trade competitiveness, and an eroding manufacturing jobs base—phenomena all now unfortunately leading to, and encapsulated in, the modern political buzzword: "outsourcing."

Yet there is no apparent bureaucratic cognizance of this competitiveness challenge that this crisis-driven reflexive use of regulation as a public sector algorithm poses, as governmental agencies persist in their policy of: when in doubt, don't equivocate—regulate! There is no private-sector problem that has no public-sector cure!

Thus it is that massive corpora of administrative laws accrue—piled one upon the other in the noble quest to serve the public good. But are they truly necessary? Do American consumers and taxpayers really need still more massive bureaucracy with the competence of the U.S. Postal Service or the compassion of the IRS? Tragically, the ultimate result is no real remedy at all, but rather that rampant bureaucratic inefficiency and institutional deadweight continue accrete within public-sector management systems.

Is it mere accident, then, that so many of the government's policies have gone awry, or that any real hopes for meaningful reform have turned instead into administrative disasters? Which, if any, of the federal government's social engineering initiatives has ever achieved its objective or its proponents' intent? Is the basic problem one of faulty programmatic design or that government simply is not the proper vehicle for effecting genuine socioeconomic change?

Accurate answers to these questions require careful formulation. For because of big government's adverse economic impacts, America's free market system now stands seriously at risk. Indeed, such ineffective, self-perpetuating public-sector approaches to quality job creation and advanced technology development cannot be tolerated if the nation is to ensure cutting edge global economic competitiveness.

But if the overregulation in which big government incessantly indulges is a clear and present danger, the impact of its overzealous, often mindless application has concurrently become progressively worse as the nation's liberal culture has evolved—and as a result, Americans are afflicted with bureaucratic excess in practically every aspect of their daily lives.

Yet remedy will not come easily. As explained in the previous chapter, bureaucracies everywhere are self-preserving and, once established, are highly impervious to change. The task is made the more difficult because the venerated public sector axiom—"You can lead a bureaucracy to slaughter, but you can't make it shrink"—is a featured hallmark of the nation's ever-expanding regulatory universe. This reality dictates that if the goal is to kill a needless governmental program, one must strike it in its infancy!

The quest to preserve economic freedom thus confronts not the mere abstraction of a pernicious public administration algorithm, but instead a direct assault upon the precept of a free society—as it is society itself that is today at risk. It is a process not only needless but one that makes a mockery of aspirations to public service—precisely the type of bureaucratic contravention that de Toqueville must have had in mind when he observed that Americans "would rather live equally in slavery than unequally in freedom."[32]

Notwithstanding, the peril evolves as innocuously as it is ultimately insidious. For as America's regulatory processes today continue to accelerate in their outreach and impact, the nation's economic base and economic freedoms continue to erode. This is not a sinister process, of course. It is not being orchestrated by mustachioed men wearing swastikas and shouting out: "Seig Heil!" Indeed, it is often carried out by those genuinely committed to serving an abstract "public good."

But as the early twentieth-century U.S. Supreme Court Justice Louis Brandeis, in a famous quote inscribed in the Cox Corridor on the House side of the U.S. Capitol, wrote: "Sometimes the most profound dangers to liberty lurk in the insidious encroachment of it by men of zeal, well meaning, but lacking understanding."

Though it is generally spoken of in platitudes, it is critical to clearly understand what the notion of "freedom" really means to the daily lives of Americans if its benefits are to be preserved. For though it is, at times, perceived to be an end unto itself, freedom is not an absolute. It is, in fact, as much a duty as it is a right—an obligation to act rationally within the latitude of responsible choice. Hence there can be no true freedom unless individuals are held responsible for their choices. Freedom becomes a tenable objective, then, only for citizens who are responsible.

To preserve the right of responsible individuals to choose thus invokes political and economic freedoms preserved by controlled, limited, and responsive governance. Indeed, it was America's Founding Fathers and such creative political geniuses as Edmund Burke in England who, more than two centuries ago, rightly recognized that it is the separation of social administration from the daily lives of citizens that is the cornerstone of both freedoms.[33]

The choice is simple, but crucial—and ultimately will decide what kind of nation America will become. In 1776 Adam Smith, the architect of the Western system of free enterprise, wrote: "Let there be no doubt that if government ever becomes a dominant part of our society, our economic freedoms will disappear—and when we lose them, our political freedoms will not be far behind."[34]

Modern Noble Prize–winning economist Milton Friedman renders Adam Smith prophetic in asserting: "Too many of us think that the threat to our freedoms is somewhere off in the distant future. A large fraction of our freedom has already been eroded, and to a significant extent, ours already is a controlled society."[35]

NOTES

1. M. Copeland (1965), p. 57.

2. M. Friedmann (1962), pp. 15, 25 ff.

3. D. Lambro (April 21, 1994), p. 6; see also R. Nelson (October 11, 1993), p. 50; C. Scrycki (2003), passim.

4. Walt Boris, Michigan Consumer Powers executive, speech in Jackson, Michigan, July 1973.

5. Cited in C. N. Parkinson (1958).

6. C. Edwards (June 2, 2004), p. 7; L. Thurow (2003), p. 103.

7. C. Edwards (June 2, 2004), pp. 3, 40; T. Sowell (March 31, 2004), p. 16.

8. Rep. Barney Frank quote posted on the "Club for Growth" website (www .clubforgrowth.org) June 26, 2006.

9. C. Edwards (June 2, 2004), p. 7.

10. Cited in M. K. Deaver (2003).

11. C. Edwards (June 2, 2004), p. 43; *Cobell v. Babbitt*, 91 F. Supp. 2d 1 (1999); *Cobell v. Norton*, 226 F. Supp. 2d 1 (2002).

12. C. Crews (2004), pp. 1, 8.

13. Quotation posted at <www.thefallschurch.com> (February 7, 2005).

14. W. Williams (May 7, 2003), p. 2.

15. Boris, speech, 1973.

16. Reagan speech to Republican local elected officials on March 22, 1988 in the Old Executive Office Building, Washington, D.C., <www.reagan.utexas.edu.com> (July 7, 2006); Ronald Reagan remarks to the White House Conference on Small Business, August 15, 1986, cited at www.presidentreagan.info/speeches/quotes; Ronald Reagan's principal policy contributions to deregulation were to apply cost benefit analysis as a test of all new regulations, put the Office of Management and Budget (OMB) in charge of federal regulatory oversight, and create a "Task Force on Regulatory Relief" chaired by the vice president. (On this, see M. Prasad [2006], pp. 62 ff.)

17. J. Schumpeter (1954), p. 835; J. Muller (1993), pp. 140, 177.

18. T. Sowell (July 21, 2003), p. 29.

19. C. Edwards (June 2, 2004), pp. 33, 35.

20. H. McQueen (2003), pp. 101–102.

21. R. Hahn and E. Layburn (2003), p. 16.

22. J. Leonard (2003), p. 19.

23. W. Crain and T. Hopkins (2003), passim, "Executive Summary" cited.

24. See source cited in preceding endnote.

25. S. Dudley (2004), p. 10.

26. C. Crews (2004), p. 2; C. Edwards (2005), p. 11.

27. See sources cited in preceding endnote.

28. National Taxpayers Union (April 14, 2004), p. 3; S. Moody (February 2002), passim; Tax Foundation (January 10, 2006), "Executive Summary"; C. Thomas (June 4, 2003), p. 1; T. Savage (April 15, 2004), p. 1. Other estimates place annual costs of tax compliance at more than $500 billion.

29. See sources cited in preceding endnote.

30. National Taxpayers Union (April 15, 2004), passim; W. Jett (2002), pp. 104–8.

31. J. Leonard (2003), pp.17–18.

32. A. de Toqueville, *Democracy in America*, part 2, book 2, chap. 1, cited in idem. (1982), pp. 351 ff.

33. On this, see P. Drucker (1965), pp. 109–13, 139 ff, 192.

34. Adam Smith in *The Wealth of Nations*, cited at en.wikiquote.org/wiki/Politics.

35. M. Friedman (1962), p. 33.

Chapter Five

Why Tax Levels Matter

In the end, more than they wanted freedom, they wanted security. But when the Athenians finally wanted not to give to society but for society to give to them—when the freedom that they wanted most was freedom from responsibility—then Athens ceased to be free.

—E. A. Gibbon, in epitaph to the ancient city state of Athens

When Ronald Reagan in the 1980 presidential debates said of Jimmy Carter: "He never met a tax he didn't like . . . or didn't hike!"—he was merely documenting an ideology typical of most statist politicians in which the American economy, and, by implication, its citizens, become ultimate losers. Under their leadership, the would-be achievers—those who believe in, and actively pursue, the American Dream—are rewarded not with success but with *punitive taxation*.

As analysis in preceding chapters has demonstrated, taxes matter because they are the price of public regulation and administration. They also matter because the results of bureaucratic intransigence and inefficiency unfailingly show up in ever-higher taxes. For taxes and spending are not separate fiscal domains that function in isolation but operate instead as reciprocals of each other. Taxes lead to public spending. Spending leads to further private-sector taxes.

Taxes likewise matter because they are the foremost determinants of economic growth within any jurisdiction—and because, when they become repressive, they destroy private economic surplus by stifling initiative through vitiating profit motive. They matter because they are singularly most responsible for destroying the incipient economic vitalities of nation-states.

Taxes matter because they defy the fundamental growth dynamic that makes a market-driven private economy work. Government is not a generator of economic growth—prudent businesspeople and diligent working men and women are. Vigorous expansion requires entrepreneurs able to create supported by investors willing to invest—and laborers willing to work harder in order to succeed. Precisely for this reason, then, the U.S. Congress Joint Economic Committee has estimated that for every additional dollar of tax raised, overall GDP growth is reduced by from between $1.20 to $1.60, while concluding that "[h]igh tax rates distort work and savings decisions and promote unproductive tax avoidance and evasive activities. These tax distortions thus create 'deadweight losses' which lower the nation's standard of living."[1]

The disincentive effects of such inordinate taxation are, in fact, worthy of special contemplation—for they underlie a fundamental economic reality that is too often ignored. Imagine for a moment that the government of a trillion-dollar economy has decided to increase its annual spending by $10 billion—1 percent of national income. Linear mathematics might suggest that it could accommodate this spending goal by raising its tax rate by 1 percent—from 10 percent to 11 percent.

Though seemingly a logical policy recourse, invariably this increased levy will not yield sufficient revenue. Why? Because an increase in the tax rate will cause at least some discouraged taxpayers to work less diligently, or to at least dedicate fewer hours to work. By diminishing the amount of income to be taxed, however, such a downsized work commitment shrinks the taxable income base—causing revenue yields to be reduced or even fall. In either event, then, it is clear that a 1 percent tax rate hike will not produce a corresponding 1 percent increased revenue yield from national income.

Hence, to raise the targeted additional $10 billion, taxes will have to be raised by significantly more than 1 percent—perhaps as much as 2 percent—thereby draining as much as $20 billion in financial capacity from the productive private economy while precipitating as much as a 3 percent drop in GDP growth. In short, in order to benefit government by a measure of one, the private sector must generally be disadvantaged by at least a measure of two!

Indeed, this is among the foremost fraudulent premises of the tax-and-spend approach. Because it empowers a government to do things it should not be doing, it deprives itself of the resources required for the things that it must do—the agenda it is constitutionally mandated to carry out, such as providing defense, ensuring equal access to educational opportunity, securing neighborhoods, fighting drugs and crime, and providing safe roads, infrastructure, and other public goods.

Eventually the price must be paid—as Santa Claus politics is no more than tooth fairy economics that ignores one simple economic truth: The more you tax of something, the less you have of it—a reflection of the reality that in the free marketplace, life is not a zero-sum game. There are indeed opportunity costs, as there is no such thing as an economic free lunch. To quote economist Walter Williams:

> How many times have we all heard of "free tuition," "free health care"—and free "you-name-it"? If a particular good or service is really free, then we can have as much of it without the sacrifice of other goods or services.
>
> Take a "free" library. Is it really "free"? The answer is no. Had the library not been built, that $50 million could have purchased something else. That something else sacrificed is the cost of the library.
>
> While users of the library might pay a zero price, "zero price" and "free" are not one and the same. So when the politicians talk about providing something for "free," ask them to identify the beneficent Santa or tooth fairy.[2]

Who, then, pays the price? The private sector, by its very definition, does. As Winston Churchill once observed, "Some see private enterprise as a predator to be shot, others as a cow to be milked; but far too few see it for what it is, a steady horse pulling the entire wagon."[3]

Yet no economy can survive if it continues to be treated as the cow that everyone is milking but no one cares to feed. Today it is too easy to forget that though some aspire to live at the expense of the state, it is actually the *state* that lives at the expense of everyone else—that no nation can ever hope to create productive jobs by expanding businesses when facing the Hobbesian choice of "heads, the government wins; tails, the taxpayers lose."

The fiscal bottom line, then, is that the more public revenue is spent, the less tax revenue can be collected from private-sector sources. This is precisely the flawed economic premise of the tax systems that support "Big Brother" government—they are antithetical to free market capitalism because they punish everything that decent citizens believe in: productivity, competition, and success.

Ronald Reagan was fond of telling the insightful story of a laborer working for a farmer who steals a ham from the farmer's pantry and takes it to the local grocer, selling it at wholesale for $35.00. With the $35.00, he puts $15.00 in his pocket and takes the remaining $20.00 down to the local welfare agency, where he buys $80.00 worth of food stamps. With the $80.00 in food stamps, he returns to the grocer, where he repurchases the ham, now at retail, for $45.00 and proceeds to restore it to the farmer's pantry shelf. So now the farmer has his ham back, the grocer has made a quick $10.00 profit, the laborer finds himself with $15.00 in cash and $35.00 in food stamps—and *no one* is the loser. No one—unless, of course, one considers the American taxpayer . . . but of course no one ever does!

One need only reflect upon the basic precepts of economic history to ascertain why taxes matter financially—for they impact in a multiplicity of ways. Not only do excessive tax rates stop poor people from getting rich, they actually destroy their opportunities for jobs in absolute terms. How? By lowering workplace productivity, limiting market access, and thereby destroying basic profit motivation, as inordinately high tax rates prevent entrepreneurs from investing in job-creating equipment that produces and supplies new, competitively priced goods and services that generate still more wealth and value and tax revenues.

Recall, for a moment, the lessons of Economics 101 respecting price, profits, and tax revenues, and the relationship among these three market phenomena. Prices aren't just made up—they evolve within the competitive marketplace. They are important market signals of the relative availability of any good or service. While rising prices imply a scarcity of product, declining prices imply the opposite.

Profits derived from income, in turn, are a direct function of prices and the reward of earning revenues. Though they are not a particularly large item within the national income accounts—typically accounting for about 6 percent of GDP contrasted with 60 percent for wages—like wages, interest, and rent, they are nonetheless vital components of a healthy economy and quintessential if dynamic entrepreneurship is to take place within it.

Entrepreneurship thus relies directly upon the surplus capital produced by profits for reinvestment into the development of still more new goods and services. Indeed, venture and mezzanine capital are the quintessential lifeblood of productive new business start-ups. Accordingly, if taxation becomes inordinate upon the private sector, reinvestment capital is not accumulated and innovation ceases.

Tax reduction becomes a necessary mandate, then, if economic dynamism is to ensue. The only alternative—the public sector—cannot drive productive growth. It lacks the local, tacit knowledge to first pick up the messages coming in from the market and then proceed with competence. Private entrepreneurs, by contrast, gain priceless detailed information by dealing directly in the marketplace. They can thus respond quickly to pricing and other market signals.

Lower taxes, on the other hand, promote entrepreneurship—and in so doing, they create productive jobs, even for those of lesser income status who, by virtue of them, are empowered to move upward into the ranks of the middle class. It thus is a cyclic win-win situation for all, for as the middle class gets richer, it moves into ever-higher tax brackets, thereby producing greater revenues for government.

By lowering taxes, therefore, democratic capitalism produces the opposite of feudalism. Instead of an upper class living off the labor of a lower class, the lower class within it lives off the capital of an upper class. It functions, and indeed derives its strength, from the premise that all of those who work are entitled to the fruits of their labors—for while governments may levy taxes to advance the common good, it is workers, not supplicants for public monies, who have the higher moral claim to their earnings.

Hence, in the last analysis, tax costs matter because they impact the market by punishing those who want to get ahead. They raise the price of earning more. They break up nuclear families by forcing both parents to work. They inhibit savings. They impede the flow of capital from declining old investments into more dynamic newer ones. Indeed, without the investable private capital that such flows produce, future economic progress would be stillborn.

The imperatives that these economic realities posit are thus both profound and relevant. Today the Reagan financial legacy is threatened. The top personal income tax rates are again 25 percent higher than the day he left higher office—with typical American taxpayers now having to work until April 26 in 2006 to pay governmental taxes and spending more on them than they do on food, clothing, and housing combined—with the emerging economic stress fractures today manifesting throughout the economy the inevitable results.

TAXATION AND THE RISE AND FALL OF NATION-STATES

The lessons of economic history thus are clear—as the imposing tax challenges confronting sound twenty-first-century economic governance date back to classic antiquity and continue to today. Since the dawn of history humankind has sought a proper tax and public service balance. Indeed, some have even said that taxes are the price of civility and order.

Such sentiments are attributed, in fact, to renowned former Supreme Court Justice Oliver Wendell Holmes—as inscribed in famous words upon the portals of the IRS headquarters in Washington, D.C.: "Taxes are the price we pay for a civilized society." Yet Holmes was later likewise moved to append the equally dire *warning*, curiously not immortalized on the IRS building, counseling that "[t]he power to tax is also the power to destroy!"[4]

These are not mere abstractions or idle contemplations. For the facts of life remain economic—and taxes are the singular factor that can make or break a productive economy. In moderation, they can fuel civilized progress—in excess, they can hasten, even precipitate, its demise.

For this reason, nations throughout the ages have wrestled with the proper balance between social responsibility and fiscal balance. The debate has been long-standing. The earliest literate civilizations of the Fertile Crescent of Mesopotamia—Lagash, Sumer, and Babylon—for instance, documented their tax-generated social spending upon stone. On one, describing tax collection, there is the poignant warning:

You may have a lord; you may have a king.
But the tax collector is the overlord to fear.[5]

In the Golden Age of Pericles in the fifth century BC, the Athenians in turn chiseled their expenditures on stone and set them into the walls of their treasury on the Acropolis. Tax collection itself was farmed out to private businessmen known as *telonai*, "buyers of taxes." One contemporary description depicts these *telonai* as "vulgar in character, lacking decency, and utterly without principle."[6]

The writings of Cato and Pliny the Elder indicate that the ancient Romans also kept detailed records documenting their civilization's concern for tax excess. Like the Athenians before them, the earliest Roman philosophers believed that in any conflict between taxation and liberty, tax tyranny would ultimately prevail. Unfortunately, their rulers far too often turned their greatest fears into self-fulfilling prophecies.

Ancient Egypt, whose Nilocentric economy was founded upon its annual river overflow, was, in like measure, predictable for its perennial outpouring of tax collectors in the flooding's wake. Indeed, there was little that escaped their ubiquitous grasp, as sales, slaves, imports, exports, agriculture, manufacturing, and commerce all were taxed.

Again, as in Greece and Rome, proceeds of those levies were precisely documented. Indeed, Egypt's famed Rosetta stone, inscribed circa 200 BC, was itself a tax instrument. The Russian economic historian M. Rostovzeff has convincingly argued, in fact, that the civilization of ancient Egypt ultimately died as a direct result of the system of repressive taxes that it endured.[7]

A millennium later, medieval Egypt's Fatimid empire would introduce an archetype of "double entry" book-keeping, in large part, to support collection of the eighty-three separate non-canonical taxes that, the Arab historian al-Maqrizi indicates, the dynasty found necessary to financially underwrite its imperial goals.[8]

Yet the economic multiplier impacts of such taxes, which ultimately hastened this Islamic dynasty's demise, were again quite predictable—standing in direct affirmation of the cogent warnings of the classic Islamic jurist Jacfar b.Yahya[9]:

> The quickest way to destroy a country,
> the abandonment of its cultivable
> lands, the destruction of its subjects,
> and the vitiation of its lands is through
> tyranny and extortion. The ruler who
> burdens his taxpayers until they cannot
> cultivate the land is like one who cuts
> off his own flesh and then eats it when
> he is hungry. . . . He who taxes his
> subjects beyond their capacities is like
> one who coats his roof from the foun-
> dation of his house.

Medieval and early modern Western civilization was likewise often characterized by deep-seated fiscal unrest, at times, leading to open tax revolt. In the sixth Gregorian century, when two children of Merovingian King Chilperic fell critically ill, his wife the Queen, pleaded with her spouse to "burn the wicked tax registers" in a desperate hope to invoke a Divine miraculous cure. Lady Godiva's famous "open air ride" also came in protest of her own ruling husband's tax oppression.[10]

Medieval England's Magna Carta, signed by England's King John at Runnymede on June 15, 1215, was similarly a binding pact explicitly designed to guarantee his subjects greater tax equity. Coming in response to taxpayer protests, it provided that the sovereign could not raise taxes without the consent of Parliament. The French rebellion, too, was essentially a protest against excessive levies, a tax revolt echoed in the contemporary writings of Voltaire, Rousseau, and Montesquieu that reached its culmination in the Revolution of 1789.[11]

In sum, the entire history of civilization is at once a history of taxation and reaction—of tax imposition and its popular resistance. Often levied modestly at first, such exactions would invariably grow progressively worse until ultimately some form of repressive tax farming became necessary to enforce collection.

Most often, as in the case of Rome, tax farming was accompanied by mounting tax evasion and the gradual abandonment of heretofore highly productive commercial and industrial properties. Such ubiquitous tax farming over time, in fact, would ultimately mutate into an unfortunate, albeit durable, coercive bureaucratic tool that survived globally for more than twenty-five hundred years and disappeared in the Near East only with the dissolution of the Ottoman Empire at the end of World War I.

TAXATION AND THE AMERICAN EXPERIMENT

Accordingly, just as every major empire throughout the course of Western history has felt the need for rising taxes, so, over time, those levies have invariably been accompanied by recurring complaints over exorbitant tax costs—a phenomenon that has been perpetuated until the present day.

Indeed, the American Revolution itself was founded upon the cresting wave of objection to taxes deemed to be unjust—as the Boston Tea Party, a protest against British commercial levies, was the catalyst that energized the momentous independence movement that would follow in its tide.

Encapsulated in Benjamin Franklin's famed exhortation in 1789 that "in this world, nothing is certain except death and taxes," the nonconformist spirit of the age was captured in a groundswell of contemporary commentary. In 1776, the exact year of the U.S. Declaration of Independence, for instance, Thomas Paine, in his pamphlet *Common Sense*, wrote: "Taxation, in its best state, is but a necessary evil; in its worst state, an intolerable one. . . . It is not the produces of riches only, but of hard earnings of labor and poverty—drawn from the bitterness of want and misery."[12]

In that same year, the great free market philosopher Adam Smith, author of *The Wealth of Nations*, similarly concluded that inordinate taxation "can obstruct the industry of peoples and discourage them from applying to certain branches of business which might give maintenance and employment to great multitudes."[13]

Smith, in an equally enlightened statement demonstrating his firm understanding of the fundamental precepts underlying supply-side economics, further contended that "[h]igh taxes, sometimes by diminishing a consumption of the taxed commodities, sometimes by encouraging smuggling, frequently afford a smaller revenue to government than what might be drawn from more moderate taxes."[14]

Accordingly, while Smith openly acknowledged that certain levels of taxation are necessary to cover essential costs of defense, justice, education, and public infrastructure, he concurrently recognized the fiscal dangers if those levels grew too high. "Each tax should be so contrived," he wrote, "as to both take out . . . of the pockets of the people as little as possible."[15]

The early history of taxation in America thus grew tumultuously. The thirteen colonies' independence movement first took form, in fact, when their leaders met in 1776 to protest the levies imposed by the British Stamp Act. Though the records show that this was in reality not an onerous levy, it was the very precept of seeking to impose foreign taxation upon an aspiring free people that triggered the revolt. Indeed, even many British opinion leaders, such as Pitt the Elder and Edmund Burke, sympathized with the colonies in their desire for tax remedy, with the latter asserting, "People must be governed in a manner that is agreeable to their tempers and dispositions."[16]

It is thus ironic that America, a nation born in 1776 in explicit protest over moderate British taxation of tea, now confronts exorbitant, ever-rising taxes of its own making—as the very factors that brought down the Greeks, Romans, Pharaohs, Muslims, and French monarchy in succession pose increasing threats to its own economic well-being as well.

Yet the nation had ample warning. Indeed, as early as its inception, James Madison, in "Federalist #10," wrote compellingly of the grave dangers arising within a democracy, of "over-taxation of the more productive few at the hands of the less productive many!"[17]

The remedies that issued from these concerns, then, came to be explicitly imbedded in Article I of the U.S. Constitution, as follows:

> Section 8: The Congress shall have Power to lay and collect Taxes, Duties, Imposts, and Excises, to pay Debts and provide for the common Defense and the general Welfare of the United States, but all Duties, Imposts, and Excises shall be uniform throughout the United States."
>
> Section 9: No Capitation or other direct Tax shall be laid, unless in proportion to the Census or Enumeration herein before directed to be taken.

The clear and present danger of tax dollar misuse—diverting public revenues to parochial purposes—was likewise clearly recognized by one of the Constitution's principal framers, Thomas Jefferson, when he wrote: "A wise and frugal government, which restricts men from injuring one another, must leave them otherwise free to regulate their own pursuits of industry, and shall not take from the mouths of men bread that they have earned."[18]

As Jefferson might well have concluded with benefit of further prospective analysis, when governments tax too much, they also steal from their own citizens the fruits of their labor—and when more rigorous collection methods become necessary to enforce compliance, they rob from them their economic liberties as well. For as Thomas Paine graphically wrote at the onset of the American Revolution in 1776:

> When we survey the wretched condition of man under systems of government, dragged from his home by one power or driven out by another, and impoverished by taxes more than by enemies, it becomes evident that those systems are bad, and that a real revolution in the principle and construction of governments is necessary.[19]

Yet history simultaneously makes clear that this was by no means a danger limited exclusively to the American experience. Throughout the course of history, tax laws have deprived more peoples of their liberties than have invading armies. The bottom line, then, is that taxation is no panacea. Because all taxes are paid by households, and not by corporations, all economic growth depends directly upon the consummate strength of a nation's productive private industrial base and reposes with the citizens who comprise it.

This is an axiom that must not be ignored if prosperity is to prevail. To paraphrase songwriter Willie Nelson: you must be careful what you dream because those dreams could soon be "dreaming you." The reason? Taxation, by its very nature, inevitably reduces the amount of money that would otherwise be employed in the private sector to increase production—and in so doing reduces the size of the collective "economic pie." As taxes come to consume ever-increasing proportions of private income, therefore, society is weakened economically.

WHY INTEMPERATE TAXATION IS BAD ECONOMIC POLICY

Little did Madison and his fellow Founding Fathers know just how prophetic their words, over time, would become. For until the onset of World War I, except for a small income tax levied from 1861 to 1872 to support the Civil War, most of the federal government's revenues came from tariffs. But from an initial 6 percent maximum marginal rate fixed when the federal income tax was instituted in 1913, the ceiling rapidly rose to a top rate of 94 percent within the next three decades to support the welfare programs of the Great Depression and the World War II mobilization effort. Indeed, even on incomes in the lowest bracket of less than $2,000 per year, the maximum rate was a hefty 23 percent![20]

While those exorbitant levies were, over time, substantially reduced, most notably through the Reagan tax cut of 1981—which, phased in over the next seven years, reduced the maximum rate to 28 percent by 1988—they have now again risen to 35 percent, a phenomenon also clearly anticipated by Madison when he warned that "[e]nlightened statesmen will not always be at the helm."[21]

The coalescing of such developments, replete with economic danger, must thus be fathomed in its full dimensions by the populace at large. For because big government is paid for by taxation—and because only individuals and households ultimately wind up remitting taxes, with business entities being no more than a levy "pass through"—it is the country's *citizens* who wind up paying the total tax bill.

Americans are generally willing to pay for worthwhile programs that preserve freedoms, ensure justice, serve the common good, and help the truly needy. They are committed to paying taxes if they are justly levied. It is at the frivolous waste of their tax dollars at the hands of cost-insensitive bureaucrats that they draw the compliance line.

The economic bottom line, then, is that from the perspective of taxpayers as public goods consumers, American's liberal tax package is a disastrously bad deal. Indeed, the consummate irony is—as shown—that even public welfare recipients themselves are not real beneficiaries.

Hence, though liberalism thrives politically through its unique ability to first force people from the workforce with mandatory higher employment costs, and then politically bribe their votes with compensatory public programs, those programs not only consign their recipients forever to the public dole, they concurrently fail all litmus tests of rational cost-effectiveness.

For because tax dollars pay for wasteful, inefficient public programs, they signal a failed approach that is antithetical to those fundamental free market processes engendered by democratic capitalism—punishing all those virtues in which decent Americans intrinsically believe: productivity, competition, and success.

Accordingly, it may be said that an overarching reason for present public disaffection with politicians and bureaucrats and their self-serving designs is that they, and the government they purport to represent, have alienated their customers. They have failed to provide value for their tax expenditures. They have failed to deliver cost-effective public goods.

Senator Hillary Rodham Clinton (D-NY), when first lady, went on record as asserting that Americans should accept gladly the 1993 increased levies made necessary to finance the Clintons' public-sector social experimentation agenda because "taxes are a moral issue."

Yet taxes are not a moral issue! At the most reasonable of rates, they are, at best, a necessary evil. At worst, they are a metastasizing cancer consuming the vital sinews of the nation's jobs and profit-producing private economic infrastructure. At no time in history, in fact, have higher taxes ever been responsible for greater economic growth.

Today, public spending at all levels approaches 40 percent of earned income—with nearly two-thirds of that total consumed by the federal government. In the past half century alone, total governmental spending as a proportion of national income has quadrupled—and federal spending has octupled from 3 percent to 24 percent. Such trends cannot be sustained lest America decline in a manner reminiscent of that of ancient Rome.

Yet the remedy is basic. Ronald Reagan's domestic policy was solidly founded upon the simple, yet irrefutable, economic precept that "no nation has ever taxed itself into prosperity"—a maxim that is clearly borne out in the economic data.

Indeed, the phenomenal success of tax revolts in recent years—whereby voters through their referenda have said, "We've had enough!"—leaves little doubt that tax levels and popular perceptions of prosperity are directly linked. In each and every instance within the past three decades when such referenda have succeeded, substantial tax reduction has been succeeded by sustained follow-on economic growth.

THE POSITIVE IMPACT OF
PRUDENT TAXATION WRIT LARGE

Ronald Reagan came to his presidency in January 1981 amid the worst recession the nation had endured since the nadir of the Great Depression that commenced in 1929. Gruesome economic numbers under the Carter administration had spawned the vividly descriptive hybrid term and concept of "stagflation"—11 percent unemployment, 15 percent inflation, 14 percent federal discount rates, and retail interest rates approaching 20 percent—which, combined with 70 percent top marginal income tax rates, were the economic order of the day. A scholar at the Brookings Institution coined the concept of a "misery index," connoting the combined inflation and unemployment rates, and soon everyone perceived its full and dire impact.[22]

Yet when Reagan left office in 1989, the top marginal tax rate had been sharply reduced from a 70 percent high to 28 percent, and he left behind an economic world transformed. Inflation had been brought down to 4.1 percent, unemployment to 5.2 percent, and the federal discount rate to 6.5 percent.

Under Reagan, the number of new jobs increased by more than 19 million and the median family income rose every year between 1982 and1989. Reagan's initial sweeping tax cuts, embedded in the Economic Recovery Tax Act of 1981, the largest U.S. tax cut in history, thus spawned a decade of robust economic growth throughout America. Indeed, it was greatest peacetime expansion in American history to that time.

In that same period, Proposition 13 in California, Proposition 2.5 in Massachusetts, and a major city income tax reduction in Philadelphia were producing similarly dramatic economic growth results. Yet this tax/growth linkage was no new phenomenon. John F. Kennedy's tax cut, the Revenue Act of 1964, also made the 1960s a prosperous era throughout all industrial sectors of America.[23]

Because of its documented spectacular results, the economic multiplier effects of the Reagan tax reduction are policy achievements that merit special scrutiny. Initiated in 1981, Reaganomics—first heralded in the incoming administration's call for a "New Beginning for the Economy"—represented the most serious attempt to change the course of U.S. industrial history since Franklin Roosevelt's New Deal.

Its theoretical essence held that the incentive effects of across-the-board cuts in personal tax rates would so stimulate the economy—so inspire individual work effort and new business initiatives—that the lower tax rates would actually yield higher tax revenues. Such tax rate reductions would, in turn, induce steadily rising levels of economic growth that would obviate the need for federal spending growth because of the resultant diminished need for welfare spending.[24]

The fulcrum underlying the philosophy was the so-called Laffer curve—a premise holding that there is a particular rate at which, moving up the curve, further tax increases become counterproductive. At that point, incentives diminish, production declines, and tax revenue intakes revert downward to zero.[25]

This was not a new economic insight, of course. It was instead a modern restatement of the famed fifteenth-century Arab historian-philosopher Ibn Khaldun's discovery, cited by no less than Ronald Reagan himself, that the volume of tax revenues produced by a fixed tax levy invariably declines as the levy matures over time—as higher tax rates increasingly attrite an economy to a point of tax exhaustion.

The Laffer curve was, at the same time, a contemporary embodiment of the nineteenth-century economist Jean-Baptiste Say's theory holding that "supply creates its own demand"—the premise from which modern supply-side economics derives its name. The notion that there is a certain ratio of tax take to GDP that tends to seek its own level—and above which, revenue yields actually diminish—was, in turn, developed into a full body of theory-based economic rationale by Australian economist Colin Clarke in the late 1930s.[26]

Supply-side taxation precepts, therefore, are not a new economic phenomenon, nor has their application been confined to U.S. borders. Applying them in the United Kingdom in the early 1980s, Prime Minister Margaret Thatcher likewise got that nation's lackluster economy dynamically moving forward once again—as from 1983 to 1990, its real annual GDP grew nearly twice as fast as it had from 1973 to 1980.

Its unemployment levels declined from over 11 percent to 6 percent in the same period, as between 1983 and 1990, the United Kingdom created more than 3 million new jobs, by far the best record among the major European nations. Indeed, due to such demonstrable successes, France, Canada, and a host of other nations subsequently followed suit in adapting a tax cut stimulus approach, producing strikingly similar salutary economic results.[27]

Thus the concept of supply-side economics, though not revolutionary, has resulted in dramatic industrial returns abroad wherever it has been applied—

and it worked within the United States through the 1920s, the 1960s, and the 1980s as well—as the economic stimuli of the Coolidge, Kennedy, and Reagan tax cuts, all supply-side variants, leave no doubt.[28]

Indeed, despite the ongoing desperate efforts by some seeking to rewrite the history of 1980s, recasting it as a callous "decade of greed," the results speak for themselves—revealing that the Reagan tax cuts, commencing in real-time impact in 1983, spectacularly restored economic growth both for the macroeconomy and for individuals. Indeed, after the effects of those steep tax reductions began to percolate throughout the U.S. private sector, America's economy took off in ascendant fashion!

Now, no longer was there the late-1970s recurring dismal talk of stagflation—nor of prospective reductions of inflation necessarily precipitating recession. No longer was there a president in office despondently wringing his hands and lamenting that the sorry economic state was entirely the people's fault—that they had inexplicably contracted chronic malaise.[29]

For unlike the Keynesian economic policy that it replaced—which employed easy monetary policy to stimulate employment and high tax rates to restrain inflation—the Reagan supply-side approach held that easy money drove up prices while high tax rates constrained output, and countered by controlling inflation with monetary policy and spurring real economic growth with significantly lower marginal tax rates.

To the great surprise of many, the policy produced precisely as promised. The economy expanded for seven years while inflation fell. Indeed, the 1981 Reagan tax reforms sparked a remarkable burst of GDP growth in the 3.5 to 4 percent range each and every one of the last seven years of his presidency.[30]

As a consequence, from 1983 to 1990 America experienced ninety-six consecutive months of sustained economic growth—the then longest peacetime expansion in U.S. history. The economy as a whole grew 34 percent—the equivalent of a West Germany—and nearly 19 million new jobs were added to its labor force. As a direct result, unemployment fell from 10.8 percent to 5.2 percent, and inflation declined to a mere one-seventh of its intolerable Carter administration highs. Real after-tax incomes concurrently rose by 15.5 percent, and real, pretax median incomes grew 12.5 percent![31]

Measuring the impact of the tax cut as a percentage of GDP is more illuminating still. For as America experienced its aforesaid solid 3.8 percent plus yearly GDP growth in the period between 1983 and 1989 as a result of robust income growth, federal expenditures as a percentage of national income declined from 24.3 percent to 22.3 percent (see table 5.1). At the same time, despite the sweeping marginal reductions of the Reagan income tax cut, its positive economic multiplier effects caused revenues to steadily increase as a percentage of a rapidly expanding GDP.

Table 5.1. Federal Fiscal Performance as a Percentage of GDP, 1983–1991 (Constant 1982 Dollars)

Year	Total GDP Growth	Total U.S. Outlays as a Percentage of GDP	Total U.S. Receipts as a Percentage of GDP	U.S. Budget Deficit as a Percentage of GDP
1983	3.6	24.3	18.1	6.3
1984	6.8	23.1	18.1	6.0
1985	3.4	23.9	18.6	5.4
1986	2.7	23.7	18.4	5.3
1987	3.4	22.7	19.3	3.4
1988	4.5	22.2	19.0	3.2
1989	2.5	22.3	19.3	2.9
1990	1.3	23.2	19.1	4.1
1991	−0.9	24.0	19.1	4.9

Source: Calculations performed on tabular data presented in the *Budget of the United States,* Fiscal Year (1983–1991), part 7–15.

Concurrently, the Laffer curve performed spectacularly, as the budget deficit was more than halved—from 6.3 percent of GDP in 1983 to 2.9 percent in 1989. Indeed, the national budget deficit now shrank to levels comparable to those of Canada, France, and Japan—with Japan's 1990 per capita debt actually standing at $14,049 contrasted with that of $12,433 in the United States.

In absolute terms, in fact, the sole reason that the federal budget deficit grew at all in the decade between 1982 and 1991 was that while federal revenues increased at a very healthy average rate of 5.8 percent per annum, federal spending expanded at an exorbitant 6.5 percent yearly rate—as a liberal Congress adamantly refused to adopt parallel requisite budget-balancing spending cuts.

Indeed, it was only after the recession-inducing tax increase of 1990 that America's annual GDP growth shrunk to less than one-third of its 1980s rate—to 1.3 percent in 1990 and an actual 0.9 percent decline in 1991—and that the deficit as a share of GDP began to climb dramatically once again.[32]

Granted, America's upper classes did well. Her ranks of millionaires more than doubled—from 574,000 to over 1.3 million during Reagan's two terms in office. But this was not strictly a rich man's boom. The nation's middle class likewise fared well, as the great growth and prosperity of suburban America became one of capitalism's greatest triumphs.

Indeed, the percentage of American families earning more than $50,000 per year increased from 25 percent to 31 percent of total households. At the same time, those families in the $10,000- to $50,000-per-year income range experienced a higher percentage of growth in net worth than did those earning in the top economic quintile.[33]

Real average family incomes of Americans living in the bottom economic quintile simultaneously grew by almost 12 percent, and the number of families making less than $15,000 per year actually decreased, while the national poverty rate declined from roughly 15.1 percent to 12.8 percent, as the total number of citizens officially classified as "poor" shrank by more than 3.8 million people.[34]

As a result of the incentives effect of the Reagan series of tax cuts, moreover, despite reducing the top income marginal rate from 70 percent to 28 percent, and with inflation generally in check, federal tax yields nearly doubled during the 1980s, from $517 billion in 1980 to $990 billion in 1990. Nearly half of the static losses from the Reagan tax rate reductions, in fact, were directly offset by increases in taxable income—and with the additional stimulatory effects of the tax cuts growing the economy, the U.S. Treasury collected an estimated $1.1 trillion more in total revenue in the decade than it would have had the pre-1980s rates remained in effect.[35]

In this process, the wealthy not only paid higher income taxes in real terms but also a greater share of income taxes as a percentage of their incomes than did any other income group. For while the top 1 percent of America's taxpayers in the 1980s saw their annual aggregate tax bills grow from $56 billion to $106 billion, a 60 percent increase; and the top 10 percent saw their total yearly tax contributions rise from $177 billion to $237 billion, a 34 percent increase; the remaining 90 percent of U.S. taxpayers actually paid $4 billion less in 1988 than they had in 1980, a 2.5 percent decrease—in dramatic affirmation of John Kennedy's oft-repeated maxim that "a rising tide lifts all boats."[36]

But this was by no means a wholly unique outcome. It likewise happened during the tax cuts of the 1920s—implemented in 1924 by Calvin Coolidge at the urging of his supply-side Treasury Secretary Andrew Mellon, thereby producing the Roaring Twenties—and the Kennedy tax cuts of the 1960s, enacted in 1964, which resulted in the equally prosperous Sixties.

The economic numbers thus leave no doubt that Kennedy and Reagan indulged in tax reduction effectively. Vowing to get the economy moving once again, Kennedy lowered the top marginal rate from 91 percent to 70 percent, producing the dramatic 1960s economic boom. Two decades later, Reagan transformed 1970s economic stagflation into a 1980s economic resurgence by further reducing the top marginal income tax rate from 70 percent to 28 percent.

Today, similar upward tax redistributions likewise are occurring as a result of the Bush II tax cuts. The most recent revenue data show, in fact, that whereas the highest-earning 20 percent of all households would have paid 78.4 percent of all federal income taxes based on the year 2000 tax law, their share rose to 82.1 percent by 2004 after the three Bush II tax cuts—yet every other income group now bears a smaller share of the total income tax burden

Hence, it is no accident that today, the top 1 percent of U.S. income earners pay 33 percent, the top 10 percent pay 67 percent, the top 20 percent pay 82 percent, the top 50 percent pay 97 percent, and the top 60 percent pay all U.S. federal income taxes—with the bottom 40 percent paying none at all, as the Bush II tax cuts have fully erased the income tax burden for more than 7.8 million families. The consequence is that after credits and deductions, a record 57.5 million Americans had no federal income tax liability whatsoever in 2004. Yet such results again come as no surprise. For as Kennedy himself said in 1962:

> An economy hampered by restrictive tax rates will never produce enough revenues to balance the budget, just as its trade will never produce enough jobs or profits. . . .
>
> It is a paradoxic truth that tax rates are too high and tax revenues are too low, and that the soundest way to raise revenues in the long run is to cut tax rates now.[37]

The subsequent revenue flows would prove Kennedy absolutely right. For after the economic effects of his reducing the top marginal tax rate from 91 percent to 70 percent began to officially register in the economic data in 1964, tax yields nearly doubled over the next four years—buoyant revenue streams consistent with a pattern that has attended most significant tax cuts over the past half century.

NOTES

1. Joint Economic Committee of Congress (April 2001), "Executive Summary" and pp. 12–13; likewise cited in L. Hunter (July 25, 2001), p. 22; W. Gentry and R. G. Hubbard (April 30, 2004), p. 21; idem. (June 2004), p. 39; idem. (November 2003), p. 26.

2. W. Williams (August 11, 2004), p. 1. Or as Reagan CBO director Rudy Penner puts it, "The good news is that they are doing a lot of good things with tax policy. The bad news is that we can't afford the 'good news!'" Rudy Penner, cited in M. Bearden (February 17, 2003), p. 1.

3. Winston Churchill quoted in "John Petrie's Collection of Political Quotes," cited at www.arches.uga.edu/~jpetrie/Political_Quotes.html.

4. Oliver Wendell Holmes, as cited in P. Drucker (1989), p. 70.

5. Cited in C. Adams 1993.

6. C. Adams (1993), pp. 3, 67.

7. Ibid., pp. 6–7, 21, 23; M. Rostevzeff (1926), vol. 2, p. 901.

8. al-Maqrizi (1957), pp. 16, 18–21, 72; idem. n.d., vol. 1, pp. 89, 103–11, 425–26.

9. Al-arush (1974), vol. 1, pp. 134–35; also cited in C. Adams (1993), pp. 132–33.

10. C. Adams (1993), pp. 153, 233–35, 441; B. Tierney and S. Painter (1970), pp. 73, 317; A. Wildavsky and C. Webber (1986), pp. 167, 175.

11. See sources cited in preceding endnote.

12. T. Paine (1969), p. 206, cited in C. Adams (1993), p. 275.

13. A. Smith (1909), p. 835, cited in C. Adams (1993), p. 286.

14. A. Smith (1937), p. 835, cited in B. Friedman (1989), p. 237.

15. A. Smith (1979), vol. 2, book 6, p. 826, as cited in J. Muller (1993), pp. 152–152.

16. *Burke: Selected Works*, 1881, pp. 95 ff., cited in C. Adams (1993), p. 302.

17. J. Madison, cited in C. Adams (1993), p. 365—making it doubly ironic that no monarchy in Western history *ever* taxed its subjects as heavily as *every* modern democracy does today. (On this, see J. Sobran [January 2, 2002], p. 7.)

18. Thomas Jefferson quoted in C. Katz (July 2002).

19. T. Paine, *Common Sense*, 1776, cited in C. Adams (1993), pp. 276 (cited), 448.

20. J. Makin and N. Ornstein (1994), pp. 104–105.

21. J. Madison, cited in C. Adams (1993), pp. 365 ff., 465.

22. *Budget of the United States: FY2004*, pp. 6–7.

23. See D. Kiefer (n.d.), vol. 5, pp. 12 ff.; J. R. Adams (1984), pp. 291 ff.; W. Brookes (1982), pp. 181 ff.; R. Grierson (April 1977), passim; M. White (1986), passim.

24. On this, see W. Niskanen (1988), pp. 3–4; B. Friedman (1989), pp. 20, 49.

25. So named after economist Arthur Laffer who has posited a reverse reciprocity between tax levels and revenue yields.

26. J. F. Bell (1985), pp. 285–86.

27. H. Figgie (1992), p. 157; J. Wanniski (1989), p. xiii.

28. On this, see L. Thurow (1983), pp. 126 ff.

29. R. Limbaugh (1993), pp. 123–24.

30. P. C. Roberts (March 17, 2004), p. 29; R. Rahn (August 26, 2004), p. 1.

31. C. Kolb (1983), p. 85; K. Phillips (1990), p. 6; R. Limbaugh (1993), pp. 113, 115.

32. See also R. Norton (October 19, 1992), p. 85.

33. C. Kolb (1983), p. 85; K. Phillips (1990), pp. 10 ff.; B. Jones (July 1994), p. 62.

34. See sources cited in previous endnote.

35. M. Forbes (March 14, 1994), p. 25.

36. C. Kolb (1983), pp. 92–93; K. Phillips (1990), p. xi.; W. Niskanen (1988), p. 313; G. Gilder (Summer 2004), p. 3; T. Savage (April 15, 2004), p. 2; D. Mitchell (August 13, 2003), p. 2; C. Edwards (2005), p. 151.

37. T. Savage (April 15, 2004), pp. 1–2; D. Luskin (August 27, 2004), pp. 1–2; D. Lambro (September 1, 2004), p. 13; Tax Foundation (August 17, 2004), pp. 1–4; idem. (August 5, 2004), pp. 1–3; idem. (August 2004), passim; idem. (June 9, 2005), pp. 1–2; idem. April 12, 2006, pp. 1ff.; W. Williams (September 8, 2004), p. 27.

Chapter Six

Why Global Trade Competitiveness Matters

We Romans have always shown more wisdom than the Greeks in all of their inventions or else improved what we took over from them—those key things, at least, that we thought worthy of attention.

—Cicero, the classic Roman orator-politician

Trade is a prime mode of civilization, creating wealth for individuals and nations. When it expands, employment and incomes concomitantly expand. On this reality, the lessons of economic history are both illuminating and vividly clear.

The first is that the great empires of the past have had at least two things in common: First, they had an ability to generate technological change to produce marketable goods and the ability to adapt to market change in that quest; and second, whenever they have lost either, they have generally lost their economic vitality as well.

Analysis has demonstrated that the prime key to securing any nation's economic future lies not in public infrastructure building financed by taxation but rather through strengthening its productive private sector and improving the financial factors of its trade competitiveness to empower it to compete within international markets. It is by no means a tautology to say that the world today lives in a global economy and that the only way durable net wealth can be created within it is through some variable combination of the processes of discovery and external trade.

These are critical imperatives. Indeed, all of the great civilizations of the past were founded upon the cornerstone of global commerce made possible by technological advance.

The economy of ancient Greece was greatly dependent upon trade with overseas areas, and the success of that trade was largely a function of its efficiency in maritime shipping. Adopting the trireme—a large ship with three banks of rowers capable of transporting as much as 250 tons—as their prime shipping mode, the Greeks devoted vast resources to docks and other infrastructural developments in such key ports as Athens, Corinth, Miletus, and Delos.[1]

With these dramatic new technological developments, Greeks ships were soon able to wend their ways all around, and out of, the Mediterranean basin, not only to the proximate Egyptian and Syrian ports but equally to France and Spain and regions bordering on the North and Black seas. Products involved in this trade included indigenous iron weapons, tools and other industrial products, jewelry, leather goods, pottery, and works of art in exchange for metals and other raw materials, amber, ivory, lumber, wood, grains, salt fish, and dried fruits.[2]

The Greek economy, as described in chapter 2, was essentially laissez-faire—and nowhere was its firm adherence to free market precepts more readily evident than in its commitment to external commerce. Free trade was avidly pursued, as due to the Greeks' well-acknowledged maritime technological superiority, the country's exports competed on highly favorable terms with goods of foreign origin.

Because the Grecian economy was reliant upon strategic metals and other principal raw-materials imports, unimpeded flows of commerce were quintessential for its industrial well-being. Such state intervention as did exist, therefore, was designed to facilitate trade, not frustrate it—including minting a stable currency, establishing uniform weights and measures, and steadfastly enforcing the sanctity of binding commercial contracts.[3]

Rome too rose on the inherent strengths of her superior techniques of production and trade. Indeed, a major economic consequence of its vast, far-flung conquests was a monumental growth of commerce, as trade diligently followed the Roman flag. The ports of Rome, Puteoli, Ostica, and Brindisi were greatly expanded. Roads were extended throughout the Italian Peninsula as well as across southern Gaul—and long-standing caravan routes to the Near East were likewise significantly improved.[4]

In exchange for timber, pottery, metal products, and other manufactured goods, Rome imported copper, tin, and silver from Europe; grains from Sicily and North Africa; textiles and dyestuffs from the Near East; and spices, perfumes, and carpets from the Orient. With its balance of trade against it, Rome requited its trade deficit with tributes, taxes, and earnings extracted from conquered foreign properties.[5]

The subsequent sudden rise of the Islamic Empire as imperial Rome's successor in dominating the commerce of the Mediterranean was meteoric, yet also not surprising. Arab merchants of antiquity had long been key links in the trade that provided the markets of Syria and the Roman Empire with merchandise from South Arabia and Africa—the legendary ivory, gold, frankincense, and myrrh trade—as well as commodities from India and the Orient.[6]

Indeed, many medieval Arab merchants owed their livelihoods and prosperity to the upper classes of the late Roman Empire gathered around the Mediterranean—and to their insatiable appetites for luxury items: ivory, horn, spices, aromatics, silk, slaves, precious metals jewelry, and other blandishments.

The Arabian Peninsula, located at the nexus of three continents—Europe, Asia, and Africa—was an ideal locale for conducting trade. Economically dominated by three cities in its western region—Makkah, Madinah, and al-Tā'if—its littoral was a veritable "concourse of commerce" possessing both Eastern and Western tributary markets. A variety of land- and seaports connected it with the outside world, which concurrently interlinked with an intricate network of internal overland routes that traversed the peninsula and connected it with Asia as well as much of central Europe.

Like the Romans before them, the Arabs created one of the largest landmasses ever assembled under a single administration—extending from the Oxus River in the east to Morocco and the Iberian Peninsula in the west; and from Yemen in the south to the Caucuses in the north. And like its Roman predecessor, Arab trade likewise followed the troops. Indeed, burgeoning commerce made the Islamic Empire the economic superpower of medieval times.[7]

Renaissance Europe's dramatic geopolitical expansion in the period between AD 1500 and 1800—an era known as the Golden Age of Exploration—was similarly attended by a dynamic expansion of trade. Beside the preeminent names of such explorers as Prince Henry the Navigator, Vasco da Gama, Ferdinand Magellan, Hernándo Cortés, Francis Drake, Francisco Pizarro, and Christopher Columbus, therefore, must go those of the Dutch East India Company, the English East India Company, the French West India Company, the Virginia Company, the Massachusetts Bay Company, and the Hudson's Bay Company.[8]

In each instance wherein global commerce came to serve as a prime instrument of imperial policy, moreover, the attendant expansion of export trade was accompanied, and stimulated, by the advance of technology-driven workplace productivity—and by surging market demands for new products made possible by technological advance. Indeed, the constant search for ever-greater economic prosperity through enhanced industrial productivity dates back to the very dawn of history—to Stone Age efforts to forge new and better stone, and later copper, tools to enable economic man to better cope with his environment.

The Greeks ushered in the Iron Age, which enabled them to transcend the progress of the Copper Age. Revolutionary iron weapons, instruments, and tools—shovels, spades, plows, forks, axes, scythes, plows, mattocks, adzes, saws, shears, chisels, anvils, drills, chains, and blocks and tackles—now came to be manufactured from wrought iron, which was infinitely more durable than either bronze or copper. The automated rotary quern for grinding grain into flour likewise came about at this time because of breakthroughs in ironsmithing technologies.[9]

Capitalizing upon this avalanche of technological breakthroughs, Greek engineers in the six centuries preceding Christ soon perfected them into industries that were at manufacturing's then "cutting edge." It was in this era that Hero of Alexandria produced a prototypic "steam engine" and Archimedes of Syracuse introduced hydrostatics and principles of the lever, screw, wedge, ratchet, cam, and compound pulley.[10]

Greek entrepreneurs, in turn, so organized the production from these technologies, and Greek merchants promoted them to such degree, that their nation soon advanced to the forefront of contemporary industrial achievement—indeed, becoming the "workshop to the ancient world."[11]

At the onset of the Christian era, Roman engineers likewise strove diligently to translate Greek theory and its rudimentary practice into more pragmatic application. Indeed, their leading contemporary Latin work on mechanics and architecture, written by Vitruvius circa AD 1, displays an intricate and sophisticated knowledge of the workings of pumps, waterwheels, windmills, cranes, and the transmission of power by gears.[12]

The engineering of catapults and battering rams further added to military capacity, as well as to the vital private industrial strengths of imperial Rome. The military and economic significance of the empire's widespread road network must also not be underestimated—and the construction of massive aqueducts, coliseums, and amphitheaters are yet another premier tribute to the sterling achievements of Roman engineers. Indeed, many of their monuments still stand today in recognition of their architectural ingenuity.[13]

The era of Islamic economic dynamism between the seventh and tenth centuries built upon the scientific achievements of its Greek and Roman predecessors, thereby enabling the Arab Empire to become the premier commercial power of the Middle Ages. It was now that Muslim savants pioneered the disciplines of algebra, astronomy, and chemistry; invented naphtha, alkali, and numerous other chemical compounds; and developed the astrolabe and a wide variety of optical and surgical instruments.[14]

Muslim scientists at the courts of 'Abbasid caliphal rulers likewise made numerous breakthroughs in the field of physics—with one particularly enterprising family of engineers, the banu Musa, leaving for posterity a remarkable work titled the *Book of Ingenious Devices*—a detailed compendium of innovative mechanical equipment and precepts that are today deemed modern—complete with precise drawings depicting automated valves and controls as well as hydrostatic and hydromechanical instruments. The developments of the lateen sail, the tidal mill, and sophisticated clocks are also attributed to medieval Muslims of this era.[15]

Renaissance Europe's First Industrial Revolution was likewise precipitated by intellectuals intrigued by new technology. The more than five thousand pages contained in the *Notebooks* of Leonardo da Vinci, for instance, are devoted to sketches and descriptions of "interesting things"—taps, dies, shafts, presses, pulleys, belts, sprockets, chain-drives, gears, bearings, hoists, springs, propellers, windmills, wedges, pumps, a variety of guns and cannons, and even helicopters.[16]

While improved horseshoes, stirrups, bridles, and whippletrees directly contributed to more effective harnessing of animate energy in this age, technological advance was not confined to the domain of animals alone. Indeed, the effective capture of coal, wind, and water power; the use of the canal lift and other feats of hydraulic engineering; the development of the suction pump and flywheel; the automation of textile spinning and weaving; the invention of the telescope and other precision-ground lenses; the mechanized printing press, the screw-cutting lathe, and similar technical instruments; as well as sundry mechanical agricultural equipment—all were forward-leaning by-products of this quite remarkable industrial era.[17]

Europe's Second Industrial Revolution, commencing circa 1750, in turn, put many of these innovative technologies directly into mass production. It was in this era that weaving's flying shuttle, the power loom, the cotton gin, the coke-fired blast furnace, the perfection of cast iron, the Bessemer converter used in steel production, the grain reaper, the horse-drawn mower, the steam-driven piston engine, the gasoline engine, the locomotive, the harnessing of electricity, the lightbulb, the telegraph, and countless other innovative machines were now conventionalized and commercialized.

For this was an age when man's insatiable quest for progress conveniently coalesced with his ever-expanding understanding of mechanics and hydraulics, ready capital availability, abundant raw materials, burgeoning market demand, and improving transportation modes to manufacture, market, and then deliver increasingly more technology-intensive products to the four corners of the globe. It was by the middle of this period, circa 1850, in fact, that Britain became widely known as the "workshop of the modern world"—only to later be eclipsed by America in the twentieth century, as previously described.[18]

PRODUCTIVITY AND TRADE COMPETITIVENESS: A CONTEMPORARY PERSPECTIVE

The steady advance of technology over the span of history, and its role in shaping civilizations, has been both impressive and unprecedented. Yet the reality that technological superiority has traditionally underpinned economic supremacy and global trade competitiveness is concurrently an ominous foreboding for America's industrial future.

For today, because of the inordinate price drag of bureaucratic overburden, the nation's traditional technological trade competitiveness edge within the expanding world market has narrowed dangerously—and indeed, may well have disappeared. This reality impacts profoundly upon the key qualitative dimensions to its future industrial and job development.

The truth lies in the commercial numbers. Despite the fact that in recent years America has created a plethora of jobs of sundry types, cursory review of the employment mix typically reveals that almost all of the principal gains are occurring in low-tech sectors that normally do not generate exports earnings or incur import competition.[19] Reviewing such job growth performance, economist Paul Craig Roberts notes:

> This is not the profile of a high tech, knowledge-based economy. It is not even the profile of a low tech developing economy. It's the profile of an economy in serious trouble. Where are the new jobs for skilled workers or university graduates in engineering or in R&D for scientists? Where are the jobs in export and import competitive sectors to close the massive U.S. trade deficit?[20]

Reflecting that while as late as 1997 the United States enjoyed a $60 billion trade surplus in advanced technologies, for the first time on record, commencing in the last half of 2003 and continuing today, it is running an actual trade deficit in advanced technology products and services, Roberts asserts that "[w]hat is happening is not 'free trade' in the Adam Smith sense whereby Portugal produces wine and Britain makes textiles and ships. What is happening is the mass transfer of the basic 'factors of production' from the First World countries to Third World countries."[21]

He concludes that "[i]t has been years since the U.S. economy has created any net new jobs in export- or import-competitive industries. Obviously trade and our massive trade deficit are not the stimuli to our export sector that some economists claim."[22]

The net result? Since 1974 the United States has endured a chronic and increasing trade deficit. The deficit exceeded $725 billion in 2005, representing 5.7 percent of GDP, and extends to all sectors of U.S. merchandise trade. Only in services does the nation enjoy a slight trade surplus. In aggregate economic contribution, U.S. exports annually account for less than 10 percent of GDP. In Germany and Italy, they account for 40 percent of GDP, and in China nearly 50 percent of GDP. Indeed, of the top seven exporting countries accounting for more than 50 percent of all global trade, while the United States exports about $4,000 per capita, other nations dispatch two to three times that—ranging from more than $5,000 in Japan to $13,000 in Germany.

These disparate trade trends must perforce constitute an issue of vital national security concern—as evidence is mounting that the global technological playing field is gradually being leveled in a commercial world that, columnist Thomas Friedman has asserted, is becoming more "economically flat." In concurrence, economist Charles McMillan similarly determines that "the superiority that the United States has held in technology trade has suddenly vanished."[23]

For these reasons, with America's long-standing technological trade competitiveness having been hamstrung by excessive bureaucratic transaction costs, her most recent export data suggest that apart from high-tech aircraft, the nation's prime source of international comparative advantage today lies in the production of soybeans, metal scrap, hides, skins, and other semi-processed materials.

Accordingly, given that the nation's economy is creating no net jobs in the production of semiconductors, electronic components, communications equipment, computer and peripherals equipment, and chemicals—and is actually losing jobs in the electrical equipment, appliances, and transportation sectors—it becomes critical to assess how the job generation process works in the face of the mounting bureaucratic drag that imprudent public policy places upon it.

For one cannot view either the annualized trade statistics time series, or outsourcing, to the extent that it is ongoing, in isolation—as they are immediate by-products of the business environments within which they operate. In some aspects, as subsequent sections reveal, the current depressing export data notwithstanding, American industry does continue to be in the vanguard of actually developing and manufacturing many superior high tech goods and services.

How, then, may these trade and production anomalies be reconciled? The findings of this inquiry leave little doubt that America's primary trade competitiveness problem is not that premier high-tech goods and services are not being produced, but that combined with cheaper unit labor costs overseas, they are being priced out of the international market by bureaucratic over-burden—financial phenomena that render understanding the operational dy-namics of contemporary job creation essential.

THE DYNAMICS OF THE JOB GENERATION
PROCESS WITHIN AMERICA TODAY

To explore the full dimension of America's contemporary global trade com-petitiveness challenges, it is constructive to reflect upon just how the job cre-ation process within a free market system really works. First and foremost, it is imperative to comprehend that change is an inescapable part of industrial development through entrepreneurial advance.

Entrepreneurs succeed through innovation. In so doing, they destroy the old while creating the new, as economic construction is based upon a priori economic deconstruction—and in the resulting displacement, some will lose while others will realize significant economic gains. To free up capital and la-bor for productive new industrial uses, then, they must first be withdrawn from older, nonproductive ones. Such disinvestment, by definition, invariably causes someone's economic loss.[24]

This act of "creative destruction," in the words of early twentieth-century economist Joseph Schumpeter, is the "essential fact of capitalism."[25] Business employment research at the state level indicates, in fact, that in this dynamic process, every area in the country invariably loses about 8 percent of its em-ployment base annually and about half of it every five years. Even regions that are experiencing high rates of net employment growth often simultane-ously incur higher than average rates of job loss.[26]

At the national level, this economic reality is demonstrated in the findings of trade policy analyst Brink Lindsey in his longitudinal analyses of the U.S. employment base:

> Even in good times, job losses are an inescapable fact of life in dynamic market economies. Old jobs are constantly being eliminated as new positions are created. Total U.S. private sector jobs increased by 17.8 million between 1993 and 2002. To produce that healthy net increase, a breathtaking total of 327.7 million jobs were added, while 309.8 million jobs were lost. In other words, *for every net new private sector job created during that period, 18.4 gross job additions had to offset 17.4 gross job losses* (emphasis mine).[27]

Accordingly, while the U.S. manufacturing economy, and its durable goods industry in particular, are now undergoing a dramatic cycle of industrial re-cycling, it is not the recycling itself that is the prime public policy dilemma.

Indeed, it is part of natural, healthy structural development. For job generation is a dynamic process, and all economies are constantly undergoing evolutionary change.

Rather, the dilemma is that most Western industrial nations, America among them, have lagged behind in traditional production job growth since the late 1980s primarily because of varying combinations of the economic realities that (a) rapid technological development is producing dynamic new workplace productivity that is displacing older-paradigm assembly jobs; and (b) their in-house job-generating mechanisms are not optimally competitive in meeting next-generation job requirements.

Ultimately, twenty-first-century development success within any jurisdiction hinges not upon the actual magnitude of its job erosion but upon the quantitative and qualitative functions of its job replacement. It is these dimensions to employment growth that can best be impacted by the workings of targeted, effective public development policies and systems.

In the ongoing quest for full employment in the highest-quality jobs, therefore, innovation-generated productivity is not the primary threat to the nation's existing industrial base; instead, it is its last, best hope. To again quote Lindsey: "There is no significant difference between those jobs lost because of trade and those lost because of technologies or work processes. All of those job losses are a painful but necessary part of the much larger process of innovation and productivity increases that is the source of all new wealth and rising living standards."[28]

Hence the foremost development reality of the twenty-first century is that the evolving "new economy" is one far more entrepreneurial than was its industrial predecessor—rendering traditional public-sector economic stimuli largely ineffective in the emerging Information Age.

Because of the ongoing economic misconceptions constantly being fomented in political rhetoric about jobless recoveries resulting from outsourcing, therefore, it becomes instructive in critical analysis that seeks remedy to keep the actual magnitude of the challenge it poses in perspective. For the charges, if true, are indeed alarming.

The key questions thus are: Are they real? And if so, are they statistically significant? Forrester Research, Inc., a trend analysis firm, in early 2004 produced a controversial study, often cited by liberal political economists, which projects that some 3.3 million U.S. jobs will be shipped overseas in the period between 2003 and 2115—an average of 275,000 jobs per year that would constitute about 19 percent of the net average annual job creation realized in the decade between 1994 and 2003.[29]

That sum, while undeniably staggering, however, is not particularly meaningful in light of the twin realities that the American economy, on average, for the past decade, has created 8.1 million jobs and shed 7.7 million jobs, for a net gain of four hundred thousand jobs *every quarter*—and that the Forrester methodology is predicated upon a static, zero-sum global view of employment—to wit, for one jurisdiction to have gained employment, someone else had to lose it.

This is a myopic analytic philosophy that ignores economic gains produced by the production efficiencies that result from new technology. Historic examples are abundant. When Lyman Blake automated shoemaking in 1858—and when General Electric introduced Frigidaire "electric ice boxes" in 1919—these innovations eliminated millions of manual jobs in the shoe-cutting and ice-handling sectors, but they did not reduce employment. To the contrary, they augmented the workforce with massive numbers of new, higher-quality ones.

When Henry Ford's assembly lines in Detroit created massive high-quality employment opportunities in Michigan starting in the 1920s, did that development concurrently precipitate corresponding numbers of job losses in Massachusetts or Ohio? There is no evidence of such anywhere in the economic data. In 1970 the U.S. telecommunications industry employed 421,000 switchboard operators to process 9.8 billion long-distance calls. A quarter century later, just 78,000 operators were required to transmit 98 billion calls.[30] Where did those jobs go?

Others contend, on the other hand, that the actual annual job out-migration due to outsourcing is no more than 2.5 percent. But if true, even that outcome would not be inconsequential. For even a 2.5 percent increase in employment means 3.5 million jobs in a civilian labor force 140 million strong—the statistical difference between 3.2 percent frictional unemployment and the 2005 borderline structural unemployment rate of 5 percent—in other words, the defining statistical difference between prosperity and the beginnings of perceived recession.

But the real problem with even that flawed hypothesis is that those who would go to Youngstown, Pittsburgh, Detroit, and other economically challenged cities of the nation's industrial heartland lamenting an ongoing loss of quality manufacturing jobs through out-migration have missed one stark economic reality—that massive amounts of U.S. production employment cannot have possibly moved to another country. For every year since 1995, conventional job statistics reveal, *every* major industrial power has lost manufacturing jobs, and especially Germany, Japan, South Korea, and China—as economist Alan Reynolds has demonstrated:

> Manufacturing cannot have moved to another country, since every industrial country has lost manufacturing jobs since 1995—particularly Japan, China, and South Korea. . . .

Manufacturing jobs declined in all three countries, and most others, but industrial job losses were much greater in Japan and Germany. From 1990 to 1995, total manufacturing jobs fell 1.6 percent a year in Japan and 4.2 percent a year in Germany, yet only 0.6 percent in the United States.

. . . anyone who now wonders where U.S. manufacturing jobs have gone in recent years need not bother looking for them in Germany, China, Japan, Hong Kong, or South Korea. All those countries suffered much larger percentage declines in manufacturing jobs than the United States.[31]

Politically inexpedient, perhaps, but true. Or, as the late Senator Daniel Patrick Moynihan aptly put it, "Everyone is entitled to their own opinions, but they are not entitled to their own facts."[32]

A greater problem, however, is the ongoing perpetuation of the specious notion that quality U.S. jobs are somehow being "pirated." The economic evolution of rural America illustrates the issue, as over the past two centuries, farming has gradually declined from more than 90 percent to just 2 percent of the aggregate U.S. employment base. Indeed, at the onset of the twentieth century, 10 million American farmers and laborers produced the food needed to feed a population of 76 million.[33]

Does that mean that agriculture is in decline? On the contrary, today, fewer than 2 million people on America's farms are producing the bounty to feed a population that now approaches 300 million U.S. citizens—as well as exporting a significant surplus to the world. That's a net "loss" of well over 8 million in farm employment in the last hundred years. Who "stole" that wealth of agricultural jobs?

Of course, no one did. They were merely overtaken by productivity-driven industrial progress. For employment creation is not a zero-sum development game that posits that if jobs are lost in one place, they must have perforce been gained somewhere else—an industrial reality that puts economist Walter Williams squarely on the mark in saying:

A job is not a good or service. It cannot be imported or exported. A job is an action, an act of performing a task. The next time any politician or union leader complains about exporting jobs overseas, maybe we should ask him whether he thinks that Congress should enact a law that mandates U.S. Customs Service seizure of all shipping containers filled with American jobs![34]

If, then, no actual great numbers of manufacturing jobs are being lost, because there are not a great number of them to steal, the vast majority of such job exporting through outsourcing must perforce be coming from the services sector—which would be quite logical since that is where 83 percent of the American employment base actually now lies—and the United States is indeed, by far, the world's largest exporter of services, selling much more outsourcing of them to other countries than it buys in return.

In this process, therefore, job creation is also a very busy, healthy two-way street. For while some erstwhile U.S. jobs undeniably do move overseas as they transition from the product-driven to the cost-driven phase of their industrial life cycle, there are likewise foreign jobs simultaneously moving to America in droves. In the words of Peter Drucker, "No one seems to realize that we import twice or three times as many jobs as we export. I am talking about the jobs created by foreign companies coming to America."[35]

Hence, bilateral flows of investment do produce very healthy bilateral flows of trade. The reason is fundamental. The global economy is a mutually interdependent world. The United States cannot sell everything and buy nothing. The rest of the world can't sell something to the United States if it doesn't, in return, buy something from it to provide the cash flow needed to make the reciprocal purchase.

The trade balance key thus is to offset high unit value technology-driven sales with lower unit value semiprocessed, production input purchases—the exact reverse of what is happening in America today. This is a point clearly recognized by eighteenth-century Scottish economic philosopher David Hume, who asserts: "A kingdom that has very large import and export must abound with industry, and that employed upon delicacies and luxuries, more than a kingdom which rests contented with native commodities. It is, therefore, more powerful, as well as richer and happier."[36]

In the present case, however, there still remains one greater problem— one of serious misdiagnosis that makes "outsourcing" a misnomer—for Information Age jobs are, as noted, for the most part, ones engaged in services production—as today, with CAD-CAM manufacturing, production primarily has become high-tech design and process control services.

Accordingly, in a dynamically expanding economic environment, higher imports (net of exports) are a clear sign of emerging industrial strength. Indeed, much of what the alarmists of outsourcing today identify as job migration is actually services importing—and such imports only increase in a buoyant economy experiencing rapidly increasing inputs demands that exceed indigenous supply—as America's robust H-1B and L-1 foreign technician visa programs now indelibly attest.[37]

Precisely because imports always grow most rapidly when production is expanding and conversely shrink when it is in decline, then, the economic record predictably reflects that U.S. trade was in balance in the 1979–1982 and 1991–1992 recessions—but also that in each instance, the national current account balance fell back into serious deficit as soon as recovery had set in.[38]

Indeed, this financial reality invariably occurs in *all* free market economies. Yet the problem is that if those who are now indeed serious about actually fixing the illusory phenomenon they would call "outsourcing," the only true time-proven solution to a dynamically expanding market would be to induce recession to stanch incipient marketplace demand.[39]

This realization that the nation is incurring greatly enhanced service import growth because of a bustling economy, of course, also far better comports with the domestic product growth records, production indices, unemployment rates, and other economic performance measures which, since 2003, have been robust and positive.

Indeed, if trade deficits are direct functions of a combination of high governmentally-levied bureaucratic transaction costs, together with higher governmentally mandated unit labor costs—and taxes and regulation are, in fact, economically *good*—what is the solution: raise taxes further still and make current proposals for a $7.00 per hour minimum "living wage" a ceiling rather than a floor? The intuitive response to that question suggests that the quest for better answers must go further still.

The composite of the foregoing realities, however, is why business journalist Lou Dobbs's recent book—*Exporting Jobs: Why Corporate Greed is Shipping American Jobs Overseas*—is not at all constructive. For if the economic evidence that most of the American manufacturing jobs now disappearing are not being lost due to outsourcing, because, in fact, there are so few of them to steal—and also because what some erroneously identify as outsourcing is actually service imports generated by an expanding economy—then not only is his work flawed in logic, he has confounded cause and effect in that he has his arguments exactly upside down.[40]

Dobbs passionately contends, for instance, that "the shipment of American jobs to cheap foreign labor markets threatens not only millions of workers and their families, but also the basic American way of life." He continues, "There are winners and losers in our global economy, and the scorecard is there for all to see. . . . Germany, Japan, Russia, Canada, Brazil, and China have enormous trade surpluses and are the clear winners. Turkey, Australia, Israel, and the United States are the clear losers."[41]

The only problems with this hypothesis, however, are that the United States today produces about 31 percent of the world's GDP and its share has been growing each year in recent years, and that since the initial incidence of impact of the 2001–2003 federal tax cuts, non-farm productivity has consistently been growing at more than a 4 percent annual rate as well.[42]

Turkey, Australia, and Egypt have also generated a larger share of the world's GDP in recent years than they did in 1990. The Germany, Japan, Russia, and Brazil shares, on the other hand, shrank within that period, whereas

Canada's remained constant. Only China's share, among Dobbs's anointed "winners," has grown.[43]

In other words, in terms of net wealth generation, Dobbs's "losers" are actually the winners and his "winners" are actually the losers—belying the notion that nations with trade surpluses in the twenty-first century are doing better economically than those with trade deficits. In this case, in fact, exactly the opposite is true in that the nations that are incurring deficits are doing so, in no small part, precisely because their economies are expanding so rapidly that their production service input demands are outpacing in-house supply.

The economic bottom line, then—while it may be politically useful for some to continue to frame the ongoing state-of-the-political-economy debate in twentieth-century industrial paradigm terms, since many of their constituents are trapped in them, their approach actually does their constituents a grave disservice—shifting needed focus away from the quest to create those dynamic twenty-first-century jobs that would actually empower them to escape their entrapment.

Their would-be solutions ignore one basic marketplace reality—that any notion that the free market can somehow be governmentally managed is an oxymoron. Either one commits to protecting obsolescent jobs of the past or instead to preparing people to position themselves for the jobs of the future.

Opportunities exist. As the American economy continues to transition from the industrial age into the Information Age, it is undergoing structural change as profound as that that attended the shift from the Agrarian Age to the Industrial Age at the onset of the twentieth century.

In this ongoing transformational process, moreover, it is axiomatic that every time an economic activity increases productivity, less labor input is required. Therefore, given the powerful productivities that new information age technologies are capable of unleashing, *the nation's manufacturing labor force in the future will always continue to shrink in favor of service jobs.*

Acknowledging this reality, former Federal Reserve Board Chairman Alan Greenspan aptly observes, "Ideas, not physical goods, are increasingly becoming the predominant means with which we create wealth. I think that's good, not bad, for the economy as a whole. But if you are a maker of stuff, it isn't."[44]

Yet only in a "zero-sum" static global view is this development a bad thing. For as the marginal costs of production fall, prices fall concomitantly, making goods and services more affordable, which increases demand and consumer purchases, which, in turn, creates new and better jobs. Only a Luddite would seek to reverse this progressive industrial course.[45]

These realities are clearly borne out in the economic numbers. Economist Alan Reynolds has demonstrated that from 1995 to 2001, total manufacturing jobs declined by 2.5 percent a year in Germany, 1.8 percent a year in Japan, and 0.4 percent in the United States. In that same period, annual productivity increases were 2.8 percent in Germany and Japan and 3.8 percent in the United States. Accordingly, the country with by far the greatest productivity gains also endured the least traumatic loss of manufacturing jobs.[46]

Indeed, U.S. productivity growth has increased by more than 3 percent per year throughout the past decade—more than double the average of the previous two decades—and has exceeded 4 percent per annum growth since 2002. This shop floor economic reality of rapidly increasing productivity means that with a labor force growing at a yearly rate of 1 percent, every 1 percent increase in productivity eliminates the need for about 1.3 million old jobs, and that when factoring in population growth, the U.S. economy, by definition, will have to grow at least 5 percent each year before any substantial *payroll* growth, in absolute terms, will occur.[47] As Morton Zuckerman has editorialized:

> We have already seen this movie before. Productivity has brought huge job losses in manufacturing, not just in America but worldwide where 22 million manufacturing jobs vanished between 1995 and 2002. In the 1990s, we began outsourcing memory chips, laptops, and other high tech equipment manufacturing to China and Taiwan.
>
> The fear was then that this might lead to the loss of our technological edge. But U.S. semiconductor makers then shifted into higher value microprocessors and sparked a new productivity boom. All sorts of new businesses found new ways to apply this technology, resulting in multi-million dollar new Internet markets and thousands of new jobs. The same is happening again.[48]

Labor force data reveal, in fact, that U.S. manufacturing employment peaked in mid-1979 at 19.5 million jobs. Today, that total stands at about 14.5 million jobs, a 5-million-job loss. But concurrently, through 2004, aggregate employment grew by more than 40 million net new jobs and manufacturing output rose by over 80 percent—as American companies are becoming ever more productive and shifting to even more value-added output.[49]

It is intuitively logical, therefore, that when an economy is undergoing profound structural change, as is happening throughout the United States today, it is unrealistic to expect the preponderance of robust employment growth to occur within industrial sectors that are losing out—those being displaced and in continuous decline—and a malfeasant waste of public revenue to seek to reverse the course of powerful natural market forces that the trend represents.

Indeed, it is tantamount to attempting to assess the current health of the U.S. auto industry by inventorying the total number of horse-and-buggy teams actively at work on American streets today. For job eclipse and attendant sectoral employment stasis are symptomatically inherent in mature and aging industrial economies. In the last two decades of the twentieth century, for instance, while the U.S. Census Bureau Establishment Data reveal that the American economy created more than 41 million nonfarm jobs, the whole of the much older European Union production base did not net a single one![50]

Accordingly, while it is certainly accurate to conclude that obsolescent twentieth-century type of job creation isn't keeping pace with present population growth, the twenty-first-century "new economy" entrepreneurial and individual ownership types of job creation are blossoming in profusion.

The bottom-line economic reality, then, is not whether jobs are being created—as the current low and steadily decreasing unemployment rate shows that they clearly are—but instead that they are not evolving within those anachronistic declining industrial sectors traditionally captured in conventional twentieth-century paradigm assembly payroll sectors data.

Accordingly, within the modern job generation process, while divergent, readily evident industrial trends today have threatened the economic well-being of those whose old-line jobs have been displaced, they have not threatened the economy as a whole. In fact, they may well have been good for it—producing far better goods and services at more affordable prices

In the ongoing quest for full employment in the highest quality of jobs, therefore, innovation-generated productivity is certainly not an overarching threat to the nation's existing industrial base. To the contrary, it is its best hope. To quote economist Brink Lindsey: "There is no significant difference between those jobs lost because of trade and those lost because of technologies or work processes. All of those job losses are a painful but necessary part of the much larger process of innovation and productivity increases that is the prime source of all new wealth and rising living standards."[51]

Hence, the foremost new development reality of the twenty-first century is that the evolving "new economy" is one more entrepreneurial than was its industrial predecessor—rendering traditional public-sector economic stimuli largely ineffective in the emerging Information Age.

Indeed, many archaic would-be public-sector remedies have ceased to work entirely. As across the span of policy options, the message from the federal wage and employment data aggregates reveals that within the past half century, *only* the Kennedy tax cut of 1964 and the Reagan tax cut of 1981 erased national manufacturing job growth erosion in real terms.

MODERN JOB GROWTH WITHIN THE
MATRICES OF INTERNATIONAL TRADE

The real economic lesson learned, then, is that those who would effectively dabble in producing policy within the political economy must have an a priori understanding of how the modern industrial job creation system really works. It is not rocket science, nor is it new. It is instead merely a function of the workings of free market process—with the impact of bureaucratic transaction costs upon entrepreneurship its most formidable determinant.

For a nation promotes the creation of net wealth not by implementing new public programs per se, but instead by stimulating new private investment—and usually this goal is best reached by reducing, not increasing, public-sector intervention into the competitive private-sector marketplace.

In those success scenarios where public-sector intervention has actually made a significant impact on economic growth, in fact, that success has come largely because local public policy makers have energetically sought to create the political environment most propitious for new private-sector entrepreneurship and innovation to evolve. Relaxation of prevailing public tax and regulatory milieu has usually been the focus of such productive policy efforts.

But again, these findings are neither truly new nor radical. Indeed, as early as the eighteenth century, the aforesaid Scottish philosopher David Hume, in his master work *On the Principles of Political Economy and Taxation*, wrote, "It should be the policy of governments . . . never to lay such taxes as will inevitably fall on capital, since in so doing, they will impair funds needed for the maintenance of labor, and thereby diminish the future production of the country."[52]

Accordingly, it bears reiterating that high bureaucratic transaction costs—among them inordinate taxation and regulation—are the foremost deterrent to vibrant and sustained jurisdiction-wide economic growth. That was the conclusion of such profound classic political economists as Hume and David Ricardo; that is also the conclusion of the two most articulate and creative free market thinkers of modern times: Milton Friedman and George Gilder.

It was likewise the conclusion of the three most successful modern political leaders operating within the realm of developmental economics—reached by John F. Kennedy in the prosperous 1960s, again by Ronald Reagan, and yet again by Margaret Thatcher in the equally prosperous 1980s—and as the findings of this inquiry demonstrate, it is an economic development calculus that, without fail, clearly works.

The reason why most advanced industrial countries are today all losing jobs, then, is not a function of who happens to be sitting in the U.S. White House or its overseas equivalent at any given time. It is instead a function of how those leaders formulate economically-friendly public policies designed to promote dynamically surging industrial productivities powered by new information age technologies.

Today's industrial transformation, therefore, is not a sign of industrial weakness but instead one of evolving economic strength—as productivity

commences by initially producing lower input costs, which are then se-
quentially transformed into more competitive pricing, increased sales, and
ultimately higher wages—and it is a prime reason why, not coincidentally,
the U.S. automotive industry produces 25 percent more cars today than it
did in 1990.[53]

The crucial policy question thus becomes: How can prudent public policy
best serve to ensure that the nation's job-generating machine is optimally
maintained so that the qualitative dimensions to futuristic job creation in
America are best promoted and preserved?

NOTES

1. S. Clough (1951), pp. 89–90.
2. Ibid., p. 90.
3. Ibid., pp. 93 ff.
4. Ibid., p. 131.
5. Ibid., pp. 131ff.
6. On this trade, see Diodorus Siculus (1933–1967), book 2, chap. 49, sections
2–3, and chap. 50, section 1.
7. B. Spuler (1970), pp. 17–19.
8. S. Clough (1959/1968), pp. 125 ff.
9. Ibid., pp. 36 ff. The succession of technological advances that characterized the
Bronze and Iron Ages, in fact, spearheaded concurrent development of the Babylonian, Pharaonic, and Greek civilizations. These advances were accompanied by dramatic extensions of trade, expansions of the operating scales of business, greater di-
visions of labor, and, more importantly, the deepening of investment. Such increases
in investment per worker, and the attendant acquisitions of more, newer, and better
tools, thus made enhanced productivity an inevitable reality.

The ziggurats of Babylon, the Parthenon that still crowns Athens, and the pyramids
of Egypt today remain as spectacular monuments to the profound results. Herodotus estimated that setting the 2.3 million stone blocks, each averaging 2.5 tons in weight, that
constitute the Great Pyramid of Cheops in Egypt took over one hundred thousand men
working continuously over a two-decade period—standing in magnificent testimony to
the efficacy of contemporary pulleys, hoists, fulcrums, and levers. Indeed some of the
stones at its base weigh as much as 350 tons. More remarkable still, that base, which
measures 777.7 feet on each side, has less than one inch of deviation in either length or
level.

10. S. Clough (1951), pp. 78 ff.; idem. (1959/1968), p. 39; J. Mokyr (1990), p. 21.
11. S. Clough (1951), pp. 126 ff.; idem. (1959/1968), pp. 39, 43; M. Cary and
T. J. Haarhof (1940), pp. 221 ff.
12. See sources cited in n. 11.
13. Ibid.
14. J. Mokyr (1990), pp. 41–42.

15. See A. A. al-Hassan (1980), passim.

16. S. Clough (1959/1968), pp.174 ff.; J. Mokyr (1990), p. 34.

17. S. Clough (1959), pp.174 ff.; J. Mokyr (1990), pp. 35 ff., 51, 65–66,71–72.

18. S. Clough (1959), pp. 260 ff.; J. Mokyr (1990), pp. 62, 84 ff., 93,116 ff., 122 ff.,131 ff.

19. P. C. Roberts (April 14, 2004), p. 26.

20. Ibid., p. 26; see also P. Buchanan (March 3, 2004), p. 4.

21. P. C. Roberts, cited by P. Buchanan (March 17, 2004), p. 4.

22. P. C. Roberts (March 17, 2004), p. 26.

23. C. McMillan (April 2, 2004), p. 1.

24. L. Thurow (1985), pp. 22, 77.

25. See J. Schumpeter (1950), pp. 82 ff.

26. On this phenomenon, see D. Birch (1979), pp. 21 ff.; C. Harris (September 1984), pp. 21–27; R. Meyer (1984), passim.

27. B. Lindsey (March 17, 2004), p. 1. A net total of about 1.8 million new jobs must be added to the U.S. economy each year just to accommodate new labor force entrants.

28. B. Lindsey (March 19, 2004), p. 1.

29. J. Weisman (September 13–21, 2003), p. 19; S. Coleman (March 3, 2004), p. 14; calculations performed on the BLS Current Population Survey: "Civilian Non-Institutional Employment by Age and Sex" database; B. Bartlett (October 12, 2004), pp. 1–3.

30. T. Kane (June 30, 2004), p. 5; W. Williams (December 3, 2003), p. 10.

31. A. Reynolds (March 21, 2004), passim; idem. (March 14, 2004), passim; S. Chapman (March 24, 2004), p. 8; M. Zuckerman (February 9, 2004), pp. 67–68; idem. (September 20, 2004), p. 76. Reynolds's findings are replicated in an Alliance Capital Management study which found that from 1995–2002, 22 million factory jobs disappeared worldwide—with Brazil losing 20 percent, Japan 16 percent, China 15 percent, and the United States 11 percent of their manufacturing employment bases. Notwithstanding, within that same period, global industrial *output* grew by more than 30 percent.

32. A. Reynolds (March 21, 2004), pp.3–4. This statistic is somewhat illusory, however, because in contemporary high-performance manufacturing, CAD-CAM has shifted the paradigms of production away from rote assembly into *services*. This industrial reality does not mean that manufacturing is any less important within the economy than it was a half century ago, merely that it has operationally reconfigured, and hence is reflected in the data sets in different, less apparent, formats.

33. T. Sowell (January 21, 2004), p. 27.

34. W. Williams (August 20, 2003), p. 1; idem. (May 21, 2003), p. 30.

35. P. Drucker, quoted in T. Sowell (January 21, 2004).

36. D. Hume, *Essays on Economics*, cited in E. Rotwein (1955), p. 13.

37. The way to cure outsourcing, then, is to simply train workers who are more capable.

38. A. Reynolds (March 14, 2004), p. 1; idem. (March 21, 2004), p. 2.

39. A. Reynolds (November 16, 2003), pp. 1–2.

40. L. Dobbs (2004), passim; see also idem. (May 2, 2004), passim.
41. See sources cited in n. 41.
42. R. Lowry (March 10, 2004), p. 1.
43. On this, see T. Walsh (August 25, 2004), p. 1.
44. Alan Greenspan, quoted in the *Washington Post*, September 8–14, 2003, p. 24.
45. B. Wesbury (February 2004), p. 2. Luddites were an early nineteenth-century worker cabal named after a mythical leader, Ned Ludd, that would forcibly invade British textile factories to destroy knitting needles and mechanized weaving equipment by throwing wrenches into their gears in a belief that technological progress was depriving people of their jobs.
46. A. Reynolds (March 21, 2004), p. 1; idem. (August 31, 2003), p. 2.
47. M. Zuckerman (February 6, 2004), p. 67; idem. (September 20, 2004), p. 76.
48. M. Zuckerman (March 29, 2004), p. 96.
49. R. Samuelson (January 19–25, 2004), p. 26.
50. B. Lindsey (2002), p. 240.
51. B. Lindsey (March 19, 2004), p. 1.
52. D. Hume, quoted in R. Kuttner (1984), p. 188.
53. S. Chapman (March 24, 2004), p. 8.

Chapter Seven

Why Technology-Based Development Matters

Successful innovations exploit changes that have already happened. They exploit the time lag—in science, often twenty or thirty years, between the change itself and the perception and final acceptance.

—Peter Drucker

Among the twenty-first century's great economic realities is that civilization has progressed to the degree that its advance is no longer predicated solely upon the free market's ability to adapt to its environment but instead upon its ability to adapt its environment to it. Technology advance has made such progress possible, and societies that succeed in capturing it are those concurrently destined to be the most socially advanced on earth—as economic winners invariably catch and ride the next technological wave.

Accordingly, as the twenty-first century continues to unfold, America is confronted by heretofore unimaginable global market opportunities and equally imposing commercial challenges—with only the span of its economic reach defining the boundaries of its potential. In this quest, technology-based development is critical—creating a need for greater understanding of both its operating synergies and the public policy strategies needed to support it.

The case for a policy focus on advanced technology-based development is perhaps best made by developing an accurate understanding of the indispensable role that it plays in sustaining balanced industrial growth. For analysis of economic development strategies executed at state, national, and international levels over the past two decades clearly reveals that those successful—the best job and profit generators—are built around high-performance technology reflecting the reality that innovation is the most important resource in the knowledge-based economy.

Given these new realities, dramatically new public policy approaches are invoked. For as the global economy has undergone its radical transformation within the past three decades, so industrial production has changed with it—gradually evolving from more traditional large-scale assembly-line types of operations into knowledge-based systems built upon much smaller companies specialized in technology-specific innovation.

Several factors underlie this profound transformation. Foremost among them, in the new paradigms of production, workers' knowledge and skills have been rendered a more valuable commodity as previous ways of working, based on blue-collar factory jobs, are being replaced by ever-more-sophisticated ones involving white-collar specialists in the knowledge-based economy applying human logic, as well as mechanical tools, to operations of manufacturing.

Consequently, yesterday's remote outputs churned out by high-production assembly lines are giving way to highly customized robotics, machine vision, and computer-aided design/computer-aided-manufacturing (CAD/CAM) operations. With this evolution, in turn, markets that traditionally have been local, or regional at best, are now becoming far more international in their scope, and historic strategic raw materials—oil, coal, electricity, and steel—are being supplanted by knowledge-based services as the most critical input in manufacturing processes.

Concurrently, within the workplace itself, dramatic revolutions in the throughputs of high-performance manufacturing process have complemented this microeconomic evolution—combining low overhead, innovation, quality management, and rising productivity to turn out the world-class products that twenty-first-century society demands. New technologies and ever more formidable global competition are the prime forces impelling this transformation.

The ubiquitous computer drives both—empowering workers with information, automated factories, and more decentralized primary businesses. Computerized telecommunications, working in tandem, has simultaneously made real-time international trade transactions a marketplace reality—ushering in a new era of intense commercial competitiveness.

Such a computer-driven, technology-based society, of course, dramatically changes how people approach their lives as well as the development needed to sustain their lifestyles. For unlike a traditional manufacturing economy, capital does not directly substitute for labor in a knowledge-based one. Nor does new technology necessarily generate higher productivities in knowledge-based service employment.

While in the twentieth century paradigms of "making and moving things," moreover, capital and technology were basic factors of production, in the technocentric industrial sectors now evolving, they have become the actual tools of production. These realities explain why many long-standing public-sector economic development strategies, because they impact upon the wrong determinants, no longer work—and why so many of America's traditional mainline industries have been among the hardest hit in this evolving new age of international trade competitiveness.

Clearly, the rules of competition have changed—indeed, much faster than America's industry—as the nation's traditional manufacturing base is now being devastated by competition playing by different rules. As a consequence, the nation no longer enjoys its once-formidable advantages of education, training, technology, and capital over its foreign competitors.

For in Information Age "new economics," production capability and competitiveness are functions of acquired knowledge that operate in the same manner regardless of their location. There is, then, no necessary reason for the relative costs of manufacturing goods to vary substantially from one country to another—save only as functions of disparate bureaucratic transaction and labor costs.

Yet these "new age" shop floor realities come as no surprise. Indeed, they embed a long-standing, well acknowledged economic precept. To wit: when the economic theorist David Ricardo in the nineteenth century revealed his principle of comparative advantage, he also correctly concluded that it did not hold if certain fundamental factors of production were "internationally mobile."[1] For then, those mobile factors of production would migrate to countries that enjoyed the greatest absolute advantage. It was they who would ultimately win, whereas all others would lose—prevailing commercially by seizing the competitive advantage.

That is, in fact, precisely what is happening throughout the global economy today—as the reality that computer programming and engineering and similar knowledge-driven high-skilled jobs are migrating to China, India, and elsewhere throughout East Asia in a process of what might be called "white-collar outsourcing" seemingly stands in direct conflict with the two-century-long understanding of the comparative advantage doctrine.[2]

The reason is rudimentary. Advances in telecommunications such as the Internet and broadband have led to new methods of commercial operation that do not fully mesh with traditional trade theory. For now that brainpower—human capital—can rapidly move anywhere around the world at relatively low cost, a more *global* labor market for skilled workers is evolving—a development that clearly possesses the potential to overturn long-standing concepts of national specialization.

Indeed, with many of the countries of East Asia now turning out increasingly more quality college graduates, it is unclear whether America still enjoys a comparative advantage within information technology industrial sectors—or whether long-standing understandings of globalization any longer apply in this new age of white-collar outsourcing.

These new economic realities, in turn, almost by definition invoke a need to reevaluate long-practiced precepts that govern the economic development process in the ongoing quest for better ways to generate meaningful, rewarding jobs whose productive output is marketable within the global marketplace—and thereby preserve prosperity.

The policy challenge presented, therefore, is that of navigating the transition between a mechanistic industrial past and a knowledge-based, high-tech economic future. The challenges that such a task poses are obvious. The key question is: Can a more prudent, visionary government actively help? Answers to that question are the focus of analysis in the remaining portions of this inquiry.

THE PRODUCTIVITY DEVELOPMENT IMPERATIVE

To commence approaching answers, it is constructive to take recourse to the lessons of economic history. As preceding analysis has made clear, in the East and West alike, humankind's quest for economic progress through improved technologies made possible through greater industrial productivity began with its very first appearance on the planet and has continued ever since. This is an evolutionary process pregnant with profound implications for the formulation of future U.S. industrial policy.

It also is an economic reality that carries with it the implication that if the United States is to retain a living standard envied and emulated by the world, it must strive to compete in the global marketplace not on the basis of comparable wage but on the basis of consummate productivity.

Though in reality this workplace axiom is no more than economic common sense, for the West it is a relatively recent realization. Indeed, as late as half a century ago, the modern concept of "productivity" was not even reflected in the most definitive authority of the English language, the *Oxford English Dictionary*. But though it has always implicitly been so, now more than ever, industrial productivity is the primal force that drives the world economy.[3]

The reason is axiomatic. There is today nearly universal consensus that technology is the clearest-cut determinant of economic progress. The most commonly accepted measure of such progress, in turn, is productivity, usually defined as "unit of output per unit of time." Productivity growth, by definition, thus occurs only when higher production efficiency is achieved.

Presently, therefore, while productivity continues to be the principal force driving the global economy, it is likewise the foremost factor establishing any modern society's ability to generate and sustain a world-class lifestyle. It is the determinant that singularly affords competitive advantage in the expanding global economy. Indeed, the only way in which sustained growth in ambient living standards can be achieved is by increasing productivity. It is no accident, therefore, that as the world's consumption has quadrupled over the past century, so has productivity.[4]

Macroeconomically, with productivity increasing, employment levels can rise without increasing inflation. So powerful is its impact, in fact, that any twenty-first-century nation's quality of life has become a direct function of its private sector's capacity to harness industry to achieve higher productivity and to increase it over time.

By way of illustration, in normal economic times, were a jurisdiction to succeed in adding just 1 percent to expansion in worker output per year, its per capita gross domestic product would become four times greater than it will at current economic growth rates.[5] Conversely from a microeconomic perspective, under rapid productivity growth, wage increases also can more effectively be absorbed without increasing production costs. The increased consumption demands generated by rising real wages, in turn, can be met by expanding productive capacity.

Rapid technological progress and attendant lower production costs likewise are directly linked to the abilities of modern manufacturing industries to more effectively compete in export markets. In addition, contrary to traditional economic contention, it has become undeniably evident that higher productivity does not promote, but rather can reduce, chronically high unemployment.

The dynamic progress of the advanced Western economies over the past three decades makes evident, in fact, that rapid productivity growth and low unemployment rates go together—and that it is invariably easier to sustain full employment when technological advance is rapid than when it is slow. These market-driven realities thus combine to create a compelling need for greater understanding of the operating synergies of the most critical twenty-first-century advanced technologies—and the public policy development strategies needed to foster and support them in the quest to build balanced economic growth.

America's principal trade rivals fully recognize the reality that enhanced productivity is at the cutting edge of commercial competitiveness. Because of superior productivity, Japanese automakers can now come to America and compete within the paradigms of U.S. production costs at a time when indigenous automakers are rationalizing, downsizing, or moving offshore in an effort to cope with those same costs. Equally critically, for reasons that will soon be evident, the nation today is likewise rapidly losing its machine tool manufacturing base—its vital process technologies—because of many of the same cost issues.

It is not surprising, then, that the relative production inefficiencies of large segments of traditional U.S. durable goods manufacturing sectors continue to create industrial imbalances that must be remedied expeditiously. For in an age of global competition, strategic national interest can no longer be viewed exclusively in just military or moralistic terms. Economic security and industrial competitiveness must perforce be factored in.

Sustaining productivity growth thus requires a jurisdiction's economic base to strive constantly to regenerate itself—raising product quality while improving process technologies and boosting production efficiencies, as these are the only means whereby individual firms, and indeed entire industries, can effectively compete.

Productivity, however, is inexorably linked with capital—with the fundamental factors of production—capital, human resources, physical resources, and time—costly, albeit necessary, components of the ongoing quest to apply human knowledge to material resources to stimulate productivity advance.

Hence, future capital formation must be equal to that required to sustain and enhance technological progress. For in the dynamic modern economy now rapidly unfolding, tomorrow's jobs will inevitably require much higher capital investment than those of today do—which will require greater capital formation, which can only come from that economic surplus produced from the profits of productive enterprises and creative entrepreneurs.

To this end, then, though the American economy is currently undergoing a structural transition unrivaled since the onset of the nineteenth-century Industrial Revolution—producing a dramatic employment shift from manufacturing to the services sector—preserving the ongoing vibrancy and competitive vitality of the nation's production facilities is nonetheless critical for maintaining a balanced, expanding industrial foundation.

Manufacturing is the cornerstone of economic base—remaining its prime engine of both vibrant growth and wealth creation. Accordingly, if America is to prosper, factories must continue to be in its future. If U.S. employees are not to be left behind in the quest to optimize market advantage, then the nation's private sector must strive constantly to achieve accelerated development and distribution of its innovative manufacturing processes and systems.

To these ends, capital investment in factors of production that are jurisdictionally unique are of paramount importance if any nation is to effectively purge itself of industrial stasis within the increasingly competitive global economy. Here process technologies—incorporating into line production the buildings and machinery that most efficiently combine with labor to optimize output—become the key to sustaining dynamic economic growth.

Indeed, process technologies have become of such paramount importance in the quest for global commercial supremacy that industrial comparative advantage in forthcoming decades will derive directly from a nation's foresight and success in developing them. To ensure true marketplace competitive advantage, it will not be sufficient that a product is unique; the producer must also develop a unique way of making it.

But while investments in modernized process equipment are a demonstrably key factor in upgrading factory productivity, America's gross industrial investment for developing process technologies within the past several decades has consistently represented a smaller share of GDP than that of any other modern, technologically advanced nation.

Compounding the development challenge is that its principal trade competitors' attention to the power of productivity is manifest in their levels of commitment to the engineering disciplines. Despite having less than half the population of the United States, for instance, Japan graduates more scientists and engineers—giving them an average of 5 scientists and engineers per thousand people, compared with just 3.3 in the United States. The net result is that the average major Japanese industrial firm now has more than twice the number of engineers on its payroll than does its American counterpart.[6]

The percentage of undergraduate engineering degrees awarded in Germany also typically constitutes more than one-third of the student body, contrasted with slightly more than one-twentieth within the United States. This factor explains why each year there are usually at least three times as many patents issued in Japan and more than twice as many issued in Germany as in the United States.[7]

Accordingly, to effectively raise productivity, ever-increasing direct investments in both new capital equipment and training will be required. For no technician is better than his tools or his training. But better tools can be built and better training can be bought—and with carefully targeted productivity-enhancing investments in the workplace, employee output levels and attendant unit labor costs can simultaneously be dramatically improved.

Hence, with the United States's principal trade competitors continuing to gain in their across-the-board industrial production capabilities, creative means to sustain more buoyant U.S. productivity growth are no longer a discretionary option, but are instead indispensably invoked if the twenty-first century is to be another American Century.

THE TRADE DEVELOPMENT IMPERATIVE

Addressing the Trade Competitiveness Phenomenon

In the quest for better answers, there likewise undeniably are certain public policy changes that America can, and indeed must, undertake to enhance its global commercial competitiveness as competitive foreign trade becomes even more vital to sustaining national economic health.

The ultimate economic goal of any jurisdiction must be to create net wealth—and such wealth is optimally created through a combination of inventiveness and expanding exports mixed with influxes of reverse investments from external sources. To this end, therefore, the most productive path to wealth generation is through the development of dynamic industrial and service sectors fueled by increased private investment. This goal can best be reached, in turn, through

1. enticing external investment to promote development designed to expand and diversify the domestic economy; combined with
2. funneling that new investment into exportable goods and services industries that augment the wealth of the domestic base.

Foreign trade is vital to both initiatives—as well as to the American economy at large. Today, it accounts for 27 percent of the $12 trillion U.S. economy—supporting at least 12 million domestic jobs that on average, pay 18 percent more than other jobs. In so doing, they account for one in every five manufacturing jobs and 20 percent of the profits of all American corporations. Accordingly, international sales contribute mightily to U.S. gross domestic product (GDP) formation and indeed, until recently at least, have been growing steadily.

While the export share of GDP formation appears to have been leveling off in recent years, however, it is the specific composition of U.S. merchandise exports that must be of equal, if not greater, concern. For as analysis has revealed, bureaucratic transaction costs—taxation and regulation—combined with high labor costs, are now rendering American-made products increasingly noncompetitive.

This concern becomes all the more critical with the ongoing relative demise of publicly funded defense and space-related research and development (R&D) and the commercialized product and process spin-offs that they have historically engendered. For except for a very few select technology-intensive sectors wherein the nation still enjoys technological advantage, such as commercial and fighter aircraft and satellites, it has become primarily an exporter of unprocessed raw materials.

As noted in chapter 6, no longer is the United States the foremost exporter of computers, telecommunications equipment, and other high-tech electronics gear for which it was once known. Indeed, after aircraft, its number-one export is soybeans—followed by "corn, wheat, animal feeds, cotton, meat, metal ore, scrap, gold, hides and skins, pulp and waste paper, cigarettes, mineral fuels, rice, printed materials, coal, tobacco, crude fertilizer, and glass."[8]

Hence, with a large trade deficit in manufactured goods and a large trade surplus in agricultural goods, in the sobering words of Patrick Buchanan: "Airplanes aside, the United States has the export profile of an agricultural colony." Yet this commercial reality, in a way, makes sense. For if the incidence of impact of bureaucratic cost overburden upon industrial production reduces one's export options to the federally subsidized production of soybeans, then soybeans are perforce going to become one's number-one export.[9]

If America is to restore its erstwhile trade preeminence, these are realities that clearly cannot stand. For the twenty-first century is an age of global economic interdependence wherein less than 20 percent of the world's citizens live in the industrialized countries of the West, yet their aggregate share of global consumption—including high-tech applications—exceeds 65 percent of the world's resources.

The disparities in production and consumption are even more distinct for America, the planet's hegemonic economic engine, in particular—a nation that possesses less than 5 percent of the world's populace, yet produces nearly one-third of its $35 trillion GDP—an output total greater than the next five major industrialized countries combined—and its share is constantly rising. In so doing, while adding more than 1.5 percent to the world's aggregate growth rate each time its own economy grows by 5 percent, it imports nearly half of all of the raw materials that it consumes.[10]

Accordingly, while the advanced Western industrial nations may wield enormous technological power, they are, at the same time, rendered economically vulnerable because of it. For though their productive capacities are phenomenal, they cannot exercise them without key external services inputs, energy, and other vital raw materials. In a global economy, therefore, to paraphrase the seventeenth-century English metaphysical poet John Donne, "no nation is an island"—and within any nation destined to prevail, economic security must come to parallel military security as a paramount sovereignty concern.

External trade thus holds the key to both national security and domestic prosperity. Any jurisdiction that seeks to generate net wealth and investment strictly from within is merely indulging in a zero-sum shell game, redistributing existing internal assets among its members, but without any true net wealth being created in the process. More succinctly put, rising exports bring in new wealth while domestic sales merely recycle it. This is an economic reality replete with socioeconomic policy implications—as before any government can redistribute wealth, it implies, its economy must first earn it.

Increased exports abroad, bred of enhanced marketplace competitiveness, on the other hand, can create the wealth that will ensure economic prosperity at home. They are essential in America's quest to create full employment in high-quality, productive jobs—and are critically needed at the very time that ongoing global restructuring is playing devastating havoc with the nation's manufacturing workforce, drastically reducing its long-standing demand for traditional assembly line jobs.

This blue-collar work reduction, as noted, is due in large part to the ongoing shift to capital-intensive, labor-saving high-performance manufacturing throughout the workplaces of industrially advanced countries, and particularly those of the United States. For in the past four decades—since 1960, in fact—durable goods production employment has declined both in absolute terms and as a percentage of the total workforce.

Hence, expandable exports production is vitally needed to gain American access to new job-creating international market demand. The employment-generating potential of such foreign trade can be significant. The U.S. Department of Commerce estimates that the direct and indirect economic multiplier effects of every $1 billion in increased exports is that some fifteen thousand new domestic jobs will result. Consequently, roughly one in every five American jobs is today either directly or indirectly related to exports.

The vivid economic lesson, therefore, is that in the increasingly global marketplace, firms need to think and act more globally to survive. Yet today, fewer than 10 percent of American manufacturing firms export and some 80 percent of the total value of all U.S. exports is produced by only 250 companies, with more than a quarter of that produced by the 15 largest firms. The export ratios within the home bases of the nation's principal trade competitors, on the other hand, are often three to four times higher.[11]

Yet business experience indicates that the export market need not be limited to big businesses. Because of the dramatic, ongoing shift away from raw materials and heavy manufacturing goods toward high-tech, knowledge-based product and service industries, smaller firms likewise can increasingly become significant players in international trade.

Indeed, because they are frequently at the cutting edge of innovation, such smaller firms often enjoy a unique ability to move in swiftly to capitalize on new windows of market opportunity as they emerge. The key to their success, then, is the challenge of getting them into a more proactive exporting mode. For increased exports are not merely a private-sector commercial mother lode, they are a national economic imperative—as the United States has not run a significant foreign trade surplus since 1975!

Thus, to provide more vigorous trade expansion, it is vital that America focus upon enhanced commercial competitiveness for all firms across the board as the quintessential course to increased international market share. For within the intensely competitive global economy, the path to ultimate success lies not in profit maximization but in export quality and volume to create *market maximization* with products matched to emerging demand.[12]

In the last analysis, then, international trade must be both opportunity driven and market driven. Each evolving market enjoys its own tastes and preferences. Hence, if a firm is going to succeed within it, it is going to have to custom tailor. It must produce precisely those goods and services that the consumers within a given market want to buy—high-quality goods distinguished not by where they are produced, but because their production is world-class. The time-tested market axiom remains: "If you want to be a true world-class exporter, you must first become a world-class producer!"

Addressing the Jobless Recovery Phenomenon

The Statistical Anomalies Issue

As noted in analysis, critical to understanding what some in 2002–2003 were erroniously wont to call a "jobless recovery" economy is an a priori understanding that the concept is quite illusory and often statistically greatly overvalued—as more than 90 percent of ongoing mistargeted political hyperbole derives directly from the reality that the mechanics of economic data trends have not yet caught up with the operational realities of twenty-first-century production of goods and services.

Today, for instance, three statistical anomalies contribute significantly to the notion that the U.S. foreign trade deficit appears, superficially at least, to have substantially increased within recent decades. In reality, however, the hard economic data show that such is not entirely the case. For the problem evident is that current U.S. trade accounting methodologies are now so badly out of date that they capture a large part of only half of the international commerce stream—merchandise exports—while simultaneously ignoring a parallel surging tide of invisible service exports.

Six decades ago, when much of the nation's primary workforce was engaged in manufacturing, this was not an overtly serious problem. But today, over 83 percent of all U.S. workers are engaged in the production of services—including many highly exportable services—and with the proportion continuing to grow, the current fastest growing trade is not in merchandise at all but instead in ideas and money.

When America's banks, architectural and engineering, construction, accounting, and consulting firms set up offices overseas—repatriating vast sums of income and tax dollars to the United States—this is a vital export, yet one that is often missed by conventional trade data. This represents a major trade-reporting gap.

By way of illustration, the 1993 American sale of seventy-two F-15 fighter jets to Saudi Arabia produced about $5.3 billion in direct income benefits and $8 billion in indirect income benefits to the U.S. economy. Yet only the $5.3 billion purchase price of the aircraft ever substantially appeared in U.S. export statistics. The remaining $8 billion was produced primarily by the economic multiplier effects of "after sales service," that is, "invisible" service exports combined with the repatriated wage and profits earnings of Americans. Indeed the tuitions paid by foreign students on U.S. university campuses, which should also be counted as "exports of educational services," in themselves exceed the value of U.S. arms exports to the entire world!

Hence, when service exports are fully factored back into the commercial equation, combined with the well-documented chronic underreporting in the merchandise trade data, the nation's annual export total and its overall mercantile picture become substantially brighter.

The statistical bottom line, then, is that while the American labor force has decidedly shifted from an overwhelming manufacturing labor force to one predominantly engaged in services, such structural employment shifts should be far better reflected in the export data bases as well. Yet this hasn't fully happened, leaving the illusion of a massive overall trade deficit far larger than does, in reality, obtain.

Yet another factor contributing to misleading trade perceptions, moreover, is the ever-increasing globalization of manufacturing, as the law of supply and demand no longer respects international borders. Upward of two million "Japanese" cars, for instance, are manufactured in the United States each year. Honda is now making vehicles in Ohio, Mazda in Michigan, Nissan in Tennessee, and Isuzu in California.

In the process, corporate ownership has been obscured as well. Daimler, for example, has bought into Chrysler, which has bought part of Mitsubishi. Ford owns part of Mazda, and General Motors owns parts of Japan's Isuzu and South Korea's Daewoo. Ford produces a Mazda-designed car in Mexico for global export. General Motors makes automotive robots in a manufacturing joint venture with Fanuc of Japan—and countless other Japanese technology-based companies have correspondingly set up throughout America to engage in a wide variety of assembly operations.

Quite naturally, these phenomena drastically complicate accurate documentation of global trade flows—as today, more than one-quarter of all "American exports" bear the labels of foreign-owned companies. Auto spare parts, in particular, know no borders. DaimlerChrysler gets transaxles and engines from Mitsubishi. GM buys diesel engines from Isuzu. Ford buys key parts from Mazda. As a result of the global homogenization of auto ownership, in fact, there is now more American-made component value in a Honda or Toyota than there is in certain General Motors models.

Is Honda, then, actually a Japanese firm or an American firm when it makes and sells more cars in the United States than it does in Japan? When Bill Clinton was promoting Boeing aircraft sales abroad a decade ago, did he mention that he was simultaneously promoting Mitsubishi, Kawasaki, and Fuji, suppliers of substantial components on Boeing planes? A half century from now, in fact, very few people will be able to say that they work within either an American or a Japanese economy—instead they will work within the world economy.[13]

Are these occurrences ominous perforce? Not necessarily. For if corporate America can manufacture more efficiently elsewhere, this outsourcing adds to productivity, while, in the process, substituting for lower-paying blue-collar jobs more highly paid domestic white-collar ones involved in the future planning and managing of the work of others.

It also adds to new product development. In recent decades, for instance, foreign-owned companies have invested more R&D money per employee in the United States than have their U.S. counterparts. Indeed, more than five hundred of them today finance applied research at domestic academic institutions. Because such foreign capital adds to America's problem-solving capability, the U.S. economy will, of necessity, unfailingly be better off in the long term.[14]

The Downsizing Dilemma

The downsizing dilemma, on the other hand, is painfully real, as the industrial workplace has moved into its fourth transformation within the past century in the form of a global "new economy" empowered by the knowledge-based technologies of the Information Age—an industrial evolution pregnant with public policy implications and with striking cyclic parallels rooted in the past.

When the mechanization of agriculture reduced rural job opportunities at the turn of the twentieth century, for example, Henry Ford's urban assembly lines moved in to meet employment needs. Then, when industrial automation eliminated assembly jobs at a prodigious rate in the 1930s, contributing to the Great Depression, government readily moved in with New Deal public-sector jobs to fill the resulting workplace void. When market saturation and economic and financial rationalization diminished public-sector employment prospects in the 1970s and 1980s, in turn, private-service sector jobs evolved to meet employment needs.

But today, the evolution of quality jobs within the sundry service sectors is likewise starting to slow down. The transformation is profound—as airline clerks and bank tellers, among others, are rapidly disappearing because of paperless airline tickets, ATM machines, and analogous forms of electronic customer transactions.

The same downsizing, moreover, is ongoing among sales clerks, accounting staffs, and other documenters of routine customer transactions—as shopping by computer becomes an ever more dominant factor within the retail marketplace. It is also likely why the U.S. Capitol Building is probably the only one in America today that still retains human elevator operators. For the economic facts of life include that, due to the realpolitik of ongoing marketplace demands and consumer preferences, most jobs *do* eventually become obsolete over time.

Just as the formerly dynamic service sector is decelerating in its ability to provide increased work opportunities, moreover, evolving information age automation is reducing the need for workers across other key broad sectors of the *production* employment spectrum—automated communications, CAD-CAM, sensor-guided adaptive controls, and the like—and though one likely eventually will, for one always has, so far, no new post–information age employment sector has evolved to provide jobs for those now being industrially displaced as the "post–Information Age" economy has not yet evolved.

The Outsourcing Anomaly

The outsourcing anomaly is also portrayed by some as very real and the reality of employment downsizing is said to be attended and compounded by an ongoing exporting of jobs, making the need for constant economic regeneration a national policy imperative.

Outsourcing is not a new economic phenomenon looming on the American public policy scene, of course. Indeed, it explicitly underlies the traditional north-south dichotomy that for much of the twentieth century characterized America's industrial development. Historically, the northern states have provided the modern research agglomerations, technical know-how, business infrastructure, and highly trained labor force that underlie the nation's technological superiority.

But when the products of that technology have become more prevalent within the marketplace and are copied by others, price competition enters into the selling process—with the technology life cycle moving from being product driven to being cost driven. It is at this stage, then, that for a long time, first the U.S. southern states, and then the more entrepreneurial third world countries such as Korea, Taiwan, Mexico, and Brazil, have offered "low-wage/low-benefit" havens for those industries that no longer require those finely honed skills and portfolios of expertise that have historically been available in the industrially sophisticated, but also more expensive, north.[15]

Accordingly, because much traditional twentieth-century-style manufacturing has today moved into the cost-driven stage of its technological life cycle, and because of an attendant American failure to expeditiously address its bureaucratic overburden–bred production cost trade obstacles — the identical reasons why the nation has been reduced, in large part, to being an exporter of semiprocessed materials — the United States today does, in fact, face mounting cost competition challenges within the international trade arena.

Indeed, such realities coalesce to make the economic bottom line on outsourcing that yes, some measure of it is transpiring, though it exists primarily at the margin and its prevalence is vastly overrated in most contemporary political debate. In many advanced technology sectors, in fact, the third world simply doesn't have enough high-tech workers to pose an employment alternative threat.

Lower-end information technologies are a noteworthy exception. The Internet doesn't require expensive, complex physical infrastructures. It exists more within the recesses of human minds and hence is more labor cost-driven and can migrate anywhere in the world, as the Bangalore, India, development model reveals. This phenomenon has somewhat amplified the magnitude of service imports in that production input demand is being generated by America's current buoyant economic recovery.[16]

Also ongoing is the outsourcing of certain low-end, old-line manufacturing jobs characteristic of aging production sectors that have transitioned from product-driven phases and are moving through the final cost-driven stages of their industrial life cycles. In the quest for more competitively priced goods and services, absent the embedded costs of excessive bureaucratic overburden, in fact, such a recourse can often can often be a rational business decision and, to the degree that it empowers productive bilateral trade, even good for the domestic economy.

Yet the movement of such jobs from America to lower-wage regions of the world is not unusual. Indeed, it is for the identical reasons that caused those earlier out-migrations that took place from the more expensive unionized shops of the northern states to the less expensive right-to-work southern states in the second half of the twentieth century. Hence, as the aggregates of manufacturing jobs throughout the planet are now everywhere retrenching, certain employment based on the twentieth-century production paradigms is undeniably concurrently relocating from the United States to Asia and elsewhere to serve out its declining years.[17]

The ongoing job erosion problem is further compounded by the reality that service jobs typically generate far fewer economic multiplier effects than does production employment—for whereas each manufacturing job has historically created more than four jobs derived from it, its 4:1 job percolation ratio is more than double the 1.5:1 ratio of business and personal services jobs, and more than quadruple the less than 1:1 ratio of retail trade jobs.[18]

Make no mistake: outsourcing, to the extent that it is occurring, is a serious economic challenge. For the past half century, American strategic policy has directly hinged upon sustaining a strong science and engineering workforce producing cutting-edge technological products that reduce national economic vulnerability. Indeed, with its world-leading research universities, the country is secure precisely because of its technological superiority. To the extent that this competitive edge is eroded and lost to foreigners, that security is undermined.

The nation has traditionally benefited tremendously in that process, moreover, by its "brain drain" from other countries—as the planet's best and brightest are attracted to America and the job and research opportunities that it affords. To the extent that this flow of talent is slowed by the emergence of similarly attractive opportunities at home, then, the nation is the poorer for it.

Such outsourcing can seriously impact upon the nation's indigenous development of talent as well. For as the country's brightest students increasingly shy away from specializing in the migrating technology disciplines because of waning job security, America's prospective talent pool is correspondingly reduced.

In addition, whereas in the past, as noted, major new technologies have typically emerged to replace the job losses caused by migrating ones, this time these replacements are not readily apparent. These are industrial challenges that must be fully comprehended and addressed, as their impact will reverberate sharply at the national level with long-term economic consequences if corrective actions are not expeditiously taken.[19]

Downsizing and outsourcing—each is a compelling twenty-first-century imperative whose causes must be more precisely defined and understood if the challenges that now confront modern manufacturing are to be effectively addressed by carefully formulated and targeted public policy.

For it is clear that in each instance, it is operating cost factors, not any particular trade or administrative policy, that is driving American jobs away, making it again highly instructive to ascertain precisely what the culprit truly is. Such factor costs, of course, consist of two prime components: first, market factors, disparate unit labor costs; and second, public policy factors, inordinate bureaucratic transaction costs—making two policy options potentially possible, but only one pragmatic.

Genuine free market systems do not invoke public policy solutions that dictate the actual levels of relative wage rates in the quest for enhanced trade competitiveness. Instead, natural free market forces will, over time, automatically adjust the imbalances as they have in the case of the United Auto Workers and the American auto industry.

In the search for short-term redress, however, what enlightened public policy effectively can do is moderate disparate market price differentials by modulating the business costs of public-sector bureaucratic overburden—which is precisely what the subsequent recommendations of this inquiry propose to do.

In the longer term, however, such new global realities concurrently suggest that the ultimate key to successful expansion in an industrially mature economy is to refocus development efforts onto regenerative high-tech R&D and investment incentives, rather than on conventional locational inducements, in the quest to develop dynamic new technology-intensive processes, goods, and services that cannot readily be replicated and mass produced by lower-cost foreign producers elsewhere.

In this quest, workplace training is also vital. With Information Age industrialization continuing to progress, the preponderance of all new employment that it creates will invariably continue to be concentrated in more highly skilled employment—sectors inappropriate for those relatively uneducated routine service providers whose jobs now are being lost—as in the emerging high-tech global marketplace, what one learns is what he earns.

These new economic realities—mounting high-tech job displacement combined with attendant weakened consumer demand resulting from the loss of purchasing power of those employees so displaced—are precisely why the key to America's continuing future economic prosperity lies neither with trade protectionism nor with still more stopgap remedial federal domestic programs but rather with (1) public fiscal responsibility to accelerate creation of that vital economic surplus that underwrites leading-edge industrial development through education and research, and (2) the vital training needed to optimize its potential.

NOTES

1. P. C. Roberts (March 4, 2004a), p. 29.
2. On this, see P. C. Roberts (August 13, 2003), p. 27.
3. See P. Drucker (1992), p. 94.
4. P. Krugman (1994b), p. 1.
5. P. Peterson (1993), pp. 218–219; P. C. Roberts, quoted in R. Limbaugh (1993), pp. 89–90.

6. On this phenomenon, see L. Thurow (1985), pp. 207 ff.; idem. (1992), pp. 160 ff.

7. See sources cited in preceding endnote.

8. P. Buchanan (March 3, 2004), p. 2. See also P. C. Roberts (May 8, 2002), p. 19.

9. See source cited in preceding endnote.

10. L. Dobbs (November 24, 2003), p. 48.

11. W. Grieder (1997), p. 216.

12. R. Kuttner (1991), p. 30; M. Jacobs (1991), p. 68.

13. L. Thurow (2003), pp. 12–13, 15; W. Grieder (1997), p. 212.

14. On this, see R. Reich (1991), pp. 127 ff., 244 ff.; idem. (1987), pp. 81–84; G. Brockway (1993), pp. 243 ff.; P. Drucker (1992), p. 38.

15. R. Ady (1983), pp. 9–10; R. Vaughan (1979), p. 44; W. Thompson (1982), pp. 222 ff.

16. At the upper end, of course, America has historically endured a chronic shortage of IT technicians, necessitating the importation of foreign expertise entering on H-1B and L-1 visas.

17. On this, see W. Peterson (2003), pp. 81 ff., 93; W. Grieder (1997), p. 30. Such industrial out-migration is not a new phenomenon, of course. French economic historian Fernand Braudel, in his epic three-volume history of modern capitalism, has documented in compelling terms how the global center of productive dominance in the early to mid-Renaissance moved around for a half millennium in Europe before migrating to the United States—commencing within the Italian city state of Venice, "Western capitalism's progenitor," in the late fourteenth century, moving to Antwerp in the fifteenth century, to Genoa in the sixteenth century, to Amsterdam in the seventeenth and eighteenth centuries, and to London in the nineteenth century, before moving on to New York and points west in the twentieth century—with the twenty-first century seeing it again looking westward to the Pacific Rim. (See F. Braudel [1981], passim.)

18. See sources cited in the preceding endnote; D. Lambro. September 8, 2004, p. 8.

19. On these challenges, see R. and A. Hira (2004), pp. 117 ff., 137 ff., 143.

Chapter Eight

Education and the Technology Development Process

The government should be capable of offering greater education and better instruction to people than they would demand from it. Education, therefore, is one of those things that a government should provide for the people. The case is one to which the reasons of the non-interference principle do not apply.

—John Stuart Mill

Education matters because it is the impetus that propels the technological progress that powers the advance of civilizations. It matters because it epitomizes the fruits of those cultural blessings that issue from a free society. Education forges the future of a nation and is a prime beneficiary of the capital surplus that derives from prudent tax and regulatory policies. It is the catalyst that creates the vanguard of cultural progress.

Civilization, as preceding analysis has shown, flows from freedoms: freedom from political oppression, freedom from the subjugation of economic regulation, freedom from the need to devote the totality of one's energies to the exigencies of sheer survival so that they may be redirected to the arts and sciences.

Liberal dogma not withstanding, then, it is not the state that is the wellhead fount of societal advance. Indeed, name a single statist society that enjoys a rich cultural heritage? There are none. Milton Friedman speaks precisely to this point:

Great advances of civilization, whether in architecture or painting, in science or literature, industry or agriculture, have never come from centralized government. Columbus did not set out to seek a new route to China in response to a majority directive of parliament. . . .

No government can duplicate the variety and diversity of individual action. At any moment in time . . . by imposing uniform standards in schooling, road construction, or sanitation, central government could undoubtedly improve the level of performance in many localities and perhaps even the average of all communities.

But in the process, government would replace progress with stagnation, it would substitute a uniform mediocrity for that variety essential for experimentation that can bring tomorrow's laggards above today's mean.[1]

These, then, are the limits to what may otherwise be the boundless span of human progress. At best, government can establish preconditions and provide incentives for individual motivation. Alternately, it can destroy both if its power grows too great. A delicate balance—carefully maintaining a milieu that fosters creative thought—therefore must be struck if government is to ultimately serve the public good.

It all begins with education—the creative art of teaching people how to learn. "Education," in the words of historians Will and Ariel Durant, "is the transmission of civilization."[2] H. G. Wells, in his *Outline of History*, declared, "history is a race between education and catastrophe."[3] Franklin D. Roosevelt, echoing Plato, called learning the "foundation of democracy."[4] As Henry David Thoreau put it, "I know of no fact more encouraging than that of man's unquestioned ability to elevate his life through conscious endeavor."[5]

Certainly, a strong educational infrastructure and the research and development infrastructure that it engenders are the prime progenitors of economic progress—and are indispensable if any nation is to elevate its quality of life through technological advance. For education and technological and cultural advance are inexorably intertwined. Thus, in educating its next generation, society secures both its industrial future and its intellectual legacy.

The starting point for such progress has always been simple curiosity—the quest for learning, which then proceeds through economic building blocks. Wonder leads to knowledge, which is transformable into productivity. Productivity spurs trade competitiveness, which generates exports. Exports, in turn, create economic surplus, which underwrites the cultural advance that is at once the supreme goal of knowledge and the sublime reward for diligence in the quest of learning.

"Wonder," said Plato, "is the beginning of philosophy"—an assertion that destined him and his colleagues to become early champions of the quest for knowledge. From his master, Socrates, he learned that "the unexamined life is not worth living"—a mindset that, in his age, would empower man's search for learning and enable it to transcend esoteric priesthood up into the open marketplace of human interaction.[6]

The ancient Greeks thus emancipated the search for truth from its all-enveloping miasma of ancient superstition—and in so doing they pioneered in turning the science of philosophy, the "love of wisdom," into a useful tool for furthering the intellect of mankind. Such pursuits, in fact, would ultimately lead them to the apogee of civilized learning, ushering in the Golden Age of Pericles.

The biologist-philosopher Aristotle, the geographer Herodotus, astronomers Hipparchus and Eratosthenes, the mathematician Pythagoras, and the geometrician Euclid—all were products of that ongoing quest for theoretical knowledge so ably articulated by Plato, himself a mathematician and philosopher.[7]

The greatest contribution of imperial Rome to the planetary realm of knowledge, in turn, was to harness and mobilize the brilliance of Greek theory and put it to pragmatic use in the real world. In the aforesaid words of Cicero:

> The Greeks held the geometer in the highest honor, and in their esteem, none came before the mathematicians. But we Romans have established, as the limit of this art, its usefulness. . . . We Romans have always shown more wisdom than the Greeks in all of their inventions or else improved what we took over from them—those things, at least that we thought worthy of attention.[8]

This utilitarian approach to the ongoing quest for knowledge soon produced such inquisitive and inventive luminaries as the explorer Hippalus, the cartographer Ptolemy, the geographer Strabo, the agronomist Cato, the natural scientist/historian Pliny the Elder, the astronomer/mathematician Varro, the medical researcher Galen, the pharmacologist Dioscorides, and other scientists of similar pragmatic ilk. Concurrently, Roman architects and engineers were designing and producing a dramatically new style of majestic columns, domes, arches, and vaults that survives until this day.[9]

Medieval Islamic rulers similarly promoted intellectual progress both by directly patronizing the acquisition of learning and by creating a private economic dynamic capable of creating that social overhead critical for productive scientific inquiry to take place. The analysis in chapter 2 demonstrated how Islamic civilization—which emerged in the seventh century and developed prodigiously in the eighth to tenth centuries—provided the requisite ideological leaven needed to generate renewed entrepreneurial and intellectual curiosity in Christian Europe commencing from the eleventh century forward.

In this cross-cultural transfer process, in addition to original Islamic scientific and philosophic contributions, much pragmatic acquired Greek and Roman knowledge, as well as the theoretical works of such acknowledged classic savants as Aristotle, Euclid, Galen, and Hippocrates—which had been lost

in the West yet preserved in translation by the Arabs during Europe's prolonged Dark Ages—was now reexported, via retranslation from Arabic to
Latin, into the cultural heritage of the West.

It was now too that the intellectual base of Christian Europe was deeply enriched by the scientific research of Muslim *original scholars* delving into
such highly utilitarian fields as astronomy, biology, chemistry, geography,
medicine, optics, physics, and mathematics—the latter including algebra,
trigonometry, and Arabic numerals.

Indeed, such numerals, and the decimal point that attended them—freeing
scholarship from the baggage of cumbersome Roman numerals—in the Western Renaissance enabled the astronomic calculations of Johannes Kepler,
Isaac Newton, and Galileo, as well as the computations of modern physics
and the documentation of commercial transactions. Lessons of economic history thus converge in compelling ways to suggest the unique utility of education as a foremost instrument of human progress.[10]

EDUCATION AND THE
TWENTY-FIRST-CENTURY GLOBAL ECONOMY

Education, as noted, is a vital—indeed, essential—public sector function if
the course of civilization is to advance. Reflecting this reality, the U.S. Constitution, Article I, Section 8 makes "progress in the arts and useful science"
an explicit mandate of government—again making manifest the Founder Fathers' abiding foresight and intent.

Education is also an intangible building block whose long-term repayment
horizon puts it beyond the grasp of most private-sector investment models.
The reason lies in its fungibility. While physical capital can always be repos-
sessed and resold, such is not the case for human capital; yet it is indispensable for long-term success in the economic development process.[11]

Research, an integral by-product of education, is likewise an essential element of progressive economic development. As such, debate over its public-sector role in advancing national technological development mirrors that of defining the proper governmental role in promoting the more broad-based economic
development technologies described in the analyses of preceding chapters.

More specifically, the public interest questions become: How can society's
need for prompt, pragmatic policy responses be reconciled with the operational dynamics of free market process? Should government intervene to promote the more promising, strategically vital research sectors? If so, what form
should such intervention take? What key areas should be singled out for pub-

lic support? How should governmental policies and institutions be structured to facilitate technology-based development?

This challenge of creating more advanced productive processes and systems is long-standing and deep rooted. For even in areas where American firms today enjoy a clear advantage in inventing cutting-edge technologies, they frequently encounter structural disadvantages in rapidly bringing them to market in the form of leading-edge innovative products. The prime policy question, in this case, becomes: How can basic research be transformed into products and processes that yield public economic benefits more readily?

A particular present structural gap is that America lacks the effective policies and institutions needed to successfully commercialize the products of basic and applied research into useful technology. This is a serious process shortcoming whose solution must be holistic. For to be effective, public policy initiatives must promote domestic private investment in futuristic industrial systems through policies that encourage not only greater capital formation, as described in chapter 7, but also through research, training, education, and entrepreneurship.

There is a powerful concomitant need to strengthen those dimensions to the nation's educational systems that constitute its technological research infrastructure. Indeed, there is a long and strong tradition of governmental involvement in ensuring that its jurisdictional science- and technology-based R&D facilities remain soundly founded, well funded, and dynamic. For pioneering government R&D programs contribute mightily to educating research scientists and engineers while providing them with requisite facilities and equipment and promoting that underlying theoretical research needed by private industry to develop follow-on applied commercial technologies.

Yet over the past several decades, America's once commanding global advantage in forward-leaning technology development has eroded. Within that period, while many foreign competitors have been building up their technological R&D infrastructures, U.S. funding for university research, plant, and facilities has, in real terms, been downsized by more than 90 percent. As a consequence, while the nation's research universities remain among the best in the world, making them one of America's foremost development assets, its share of global patents is declining, just as that of the Asian universities is rising.[12]

The present decline in America's federal R&D commitment thus makes clear that the quest to diversify the nation's technological base must commence at the doorsteps of its major colleges and universities. For a prime prerequisite in implementing any truly dynamic innovation-based development strategy is the creation of effective university-sponsored industrial research and engineering systems.

Indeed, it is such efforts aimed at technological innovation that spawn new processes and products, minimizing production inefficiencies while reducing production costs so that a jurisdiction's economic base can compete and expand. But if innovation is, in fact, the key to accelerated economic growth, it is the prior development of state-of-the-art research agglomerates that generate new advanced technologies that sets the quality jobs creation process into motion.

Such premier R&D facilities are, in fact, a technological development sine qua non. For without the proximate presence of a strong research base with fully equipped laboratories and well-trained scientists and engineers, any economic expansion effort founded upon the job-generating potentials of a high-technology industrial base is ultimately doomed to fail.

Conversely, the rewards from an effective higher-education technology development program can be immense. Some 480 graduates of the Massachusetts Institute of Technology (MIT), for instance, created the firms that now account for more than 50 percent of the sales of that state's largest industrial corporations. Indeed, studies indicate that a single square mile in Cambridge, where MIT's research laboratories are housed, created more jobs in the 1980s decade than did thirteen major industrial states, including Michigan, Illinois, and Pennsylvania.[13]

Not only did these stellar achievements produce strong investment stimuli to the Massachusetts economy, moreover, they represented significant importation of skills and job producers. For while more than 85 percent of MIT's students come from out-of-state, less than 20 percent of the all new business spin-offs that result from MIT industrial research typically move more than twenty-five miles away from the laboratories that spawned them.[14]

Hence, the MIT data make vividly clear that the stakes are extremely high in the higher-education technology development process—and that public investments in a jurisdiction's higher-education technological R&D infrastructures are concomitantly sound investments in its economic future. For their quality job generation returns have no match with the entire domain of economic development science.

Indeed, because of the unparalleled R&D output quality of such research universities as MIT, Stanford, California Polytech, Michigan, and others—as evidenced by the great number of foreign engineering students who flock to them each year—research is an area wherein America already enjoys a significant comparative global advantage. For whatever the manufacturing secrets and pragmatically engineered adaptations of its principal trade competitors—the Japanese foremost among them—while they are great emulators, they are generally notoriously poor innovators.[15]

While America tends to win the scientific Nobel Prizes in physics, chemistry, and medicine—177 separate awards or coawards in the period between 1950 and 2004, contrasted with 50 for Britain, 32 for Germany, and just 8 each for France and Japan—the Japanese readily borrow the output of that impressive R&D, assimilate it into their manufacturing processes, and then ship it back to the advanced Western countries in boatloads.[16]

Hence, just as major U.S. firms reap profits transferring advanced technology to the Japanese, the latter reciprocate by selling its concepts back packaged as practical, affordable merchandise. Indeed, the synergies produced by this strategic industrial development approach may well be worthy of reverse emulation in America as well.

The bottom line is that while all great industrial concepts do not necessarily originate within the United States, the good concepts of others can nonetheless be assimilated, adapted, perfected, and put to work to contribute to national economic well-being here—as a strong applied research base holds important keys to both indigenous innovation and the pragmatic adaptation of the imported technological advances of others. While it may be said that America currently retains a commanding edge in advanced R&D infrastructure, therefore, this is a critical source of relative advantage that must be painstakingly preserved.[17]

Unless the nation places much greater emphasis upon its higher educational priorities, and dedicates far greater resources to both basic and applied research, its long-standing advanced technology lead over its global trade competitors could well dissipate as their educational infrastructures are perfected over time. Indeed, emerging signs of R&D decline in the United States are already readily apparent—making paramount the need to create those research infrastructures that will provide the new knowledge-based solutions needed in the evolving Information Age.

THE LIFELONG TOP-TO-BOTTOM WORK FORCE TRAINING IMPERATIVE

Such knowledge-based imperatives thus become critical as America moves further still into the twenty-first century; as within the "new economy," successful technological development strategy will be founded squarely upon state-of-the-art education and top-to-bottom workforce training; as within the twenty-first-century development process, education's potential is limited only by the horizons of humankind's creativity.

In its most pragmatic context, education sets into motion a cyclic progression—fostering applied research, which leads to new products and processes, which result in new businesses, which provide jobs, which create economic surpluses produced by wages and profits, which contribute public revenues for further funding education—all of which impel civil progress.

Knowledge is likewise a prime source of global hegemony. It has always conferred power upon those who have it and know how to properly use it. For education fuels an economy by shaping society at the hands of its productive people. Unlike a tool or a machine, which can be used by only one person at any given time, moreover, the same body of knowledge can be employed by many different users simultaneously—and when optimally productively employed, can generate still more new knowledge and information.

Knowledge is no longer just a resource, then, it is *the prime resource* that powers modern civilization—shaping America's society while driving its economy. Indeed, the proliferation and dissemination of knowledge to increasingly greater numbers concurrently holds the crucial key to both political sovereignty and future economic progress. For just as the last century's industrial age required horsepower, so the "new economy" requires brainpower. But in planning its development, its road map must be carefully crafted to national strengths and values.

Knowledge in any society is no less than the collective corpus of those individual ideas and philosophies that forge its distinct character, and in the ongoing quest for economic and societal success, individual ideas matter. Recall the words of John Maynard Keynes, who, cognizant of this reality, in his famed *General Theory of Employment*, concluded: "Sooner or later, it is ideas, not vested interests, that are dangerous for good or evil."[18]

In the modern era, Pakistan, Japan, and Taiwan stand as exemplars of the classic art of capturing ideas—using their acquired knowledge to develop indigenous human capital and mobilizing the resulting talents as prime instruments of societal advance. Nations blessed with relatively modest natural resources, they have nonetheless mastered the techniques of developing their indigenous economies by exporting human resources in exchange for repatriated earnings.

Thus, in addition to the lessons of economic history, those offered by key prospective global competition also provide keen insight into how America's future development efforts should be focused. To wit, any truly effective initiative to sustain its industrial preeminence must be firmly founded upon the abilities of its greatest development asset: the remarkable resourcefulness of its people.

The inherent strength of any nation lies in the capacity of its productive populace to produce, employing skills that are at once upgradable and renewable. The talents of a nation's workforce are thus what make it unique—and can make it uniquely successful in the evolving world economy—as it is sound, in-depth education that is the prime catalyst that makes productivity enhanced through technology possible. Education thereby serves the industrial economy by making it more efficient, linking future ability to prosper with present ability to educate and empower a workforce.

Human resource development must therefore become of paramount importance in any comprehensive twenty-first-century public economic development strategy. This imperative arises both because returns on human capital are now constantly on the rise relative to those on financial capital and because such investments aid the efforts of a jurisdiction's citizens in adding value to the global economy.

As in the international marketplace, workers can command higher wages and better jobs only by adding more value to their products and services than do their counterparts abroad—thereby offsetting much higher earnings with greater productivities to produce those necessarily balanced unit labor costs that preclude inflation from engulfing the domestic economy and destroying global trade competitiveness.[19]

While in the Industrial Revolution the economic balance of power dramatically shifted from labor to financial capital, moreover, within the "Knowledge-Based Revolution," the value of human capital is rapidly ascending, replacing monetary assets as the prime vehicle for prosperity and growth. Because it reduces the need for raw materials, labor, space, time, and dollar capital, acquired knowledge is, in fact, the force singularly driving economic advance as the nation moves further into the twenty-first century.

Today, six sophisticated technologies are often projected as the future key market leaders in net wealth and quality job production potential for the next several decades: biotechnologies, computers and attendant software, telecommunications, artificial intelligence and robotics, microelectronics and analogous nanotechnologies, and ceramics, biomaterials, and similar synthetic materials.[20]

These are the cerebral industries, all of which could settle anywhere on the planet. Yet the jurisdictions that ultimately succeed in capturing them will be those that train and mobilize their indigenous brainpower to pioneer their future development and application.[21]

The key to success in mobilizing indigenous talent, therefore, clearly lies in workforce training, as in the successful economy of this new production age, competitive advantage and productivity growth will issue increasingly from skill, not scale. But workers can be more productive only by bringing newer and higher skills and knowledge to their work, thereby requiring a labor force comprehensively trained from top to bottom.

While brainpower can create the new technologies, skilled labor complements intellectual contributions by providing the trained arms and legs that allow them to deploy, thereby empowering a jurisdiction to take quick and flexible advantage of emerging engineering breakthroughs to become the low-cost masters of the new process and product technologies that they generate.

In the cogent words of former Federal Reserve Chairman Alan Greenspan, "Skill has taken on a much broader meaning than it had only a decade or two ago. For today's workers must be prepared along many dimensions—not only with their technical know-how but also with their ability to create, analyze, and transform information, and with the capacity to effectively interact with others."[22]

To these ends, then, continuing investment in people and workplace infrastructures become critically important. For creative people need challenging places to work—and to create. But capturing their latent talents also requires a dramatic redefinition of the way they work as well as a restructuring of the settings in which their work takes place.

While capital and new technologies are capable of migrating anywhere around the world, highly trained manpower generally moves in search of specific economic opportunity. Hence, in the last analysis, skilled people become the only *sustainable* modern source of relative comparative advantage, and creating economic opportunity becomes key to their attraction.

Accordingly, if America is to preserve its preeminence in the contemporary global market, its greatest industrial challenge is that of increasing what its workers can productively contribute to the world economy—first by enhancing their skills and capabilities, and then by directly linking those evolved capacities to emerging needs of the international marketplace.

When human investments become the prime engines of economic growth, moreover, *everyone gets to play the economic game.* For human-resource-based development policies are those most likely to narrow widening income gaps by bringing the lower strata up, not dragging the upper strata down.

THE ECONOMICS OF EDUCATION

This latter imperative thus is of foremost economic development importance. For today America stands as a people divided, as those who now earn their livelihoods from *work* are too often losing income ground. For many, failure of policy is snatching economic defeat from the jaws of technological victory, causing needless financial pain.

These workplace realities dictate that in the "new economy" there can be but one cure—a top-to-bottom focus upon the national education system. For earnings are education's principal by-product, and to effectively compete within the paradigms of the twenty-first-century job market, anyone who would earn must constantly relearn.

The United States remains a land of dynamic opportunity, and there is no denying that for many, recent results have been spectacular. Thousands of enterprising citizens have become millionaires within the past three decades. Millions of others, in middle management and the skilled trades, have likewise become increasingly affluent, as evidenced by the luxury vehicles parked beside the impressive homes in the lush ambience of many suburbs.

But prosperity also has its price, with mounting hopes for some now tempered by declining opportunities for others. As today's millions of formerly productive and dedicated employees have simultaneously been economically displaced by the technological revolution, production workers' wages have stagnated and others have been educationally unable to find or keep industrial jobs—motivated citizens who have nonetheless been forced to a status of employment of last resort, chronic underemployment, or public assistance.

America has thus become a country of chronic financial insecurity—a nation that is at once two—characterized by growing prosperity at its summit and widespread desperation at its bottom, a society of gaping economic shortfalls amid a dynamic field of financial plenty. To paraphrase the opening lines to Charles Dickens's *A Tale of Two Cities*, "These are best of times; these are the worst of times."

Global competition—the boon of some—has become the bane of others. Plants that once supported entire communities are now closed to achieve greater operating efficiency. Lives, families, and often entire regions have been disrupted and, at times, destroyed. Even many of the nation's best areas are frequently littered with triage of ghost towns that at one time sustained productive neighborhoods, jobs, and incomes.

Thus, a paradox of economic inequality continues to evolve. For while the aggregate national income has been growing at an 2.5 percent average annual rate for the past three decades, the typical hourly earnings of the bottom two-thirds of American workers have stagnated, and, in many cases, even deteriorated.

Indeed, the reality is that, in many sectors, the average weekly wage has fallen to less than three-quarters of those of the foremost U.S. trade competitors—among them Germany and Japan—and in relative terms now approaches those of some mid-level third world countries. Yes, in absolute terms, the average household income has increased at the margin in recent years—but again, this is testimony to the *failure* of economic policy, not to its success, as too often, it is because homemakers are being forced into the workforce just to make ends meet.

Indeed, today, upward of 50 percent of American families have been coerced into "two wage earner" status just to meet their budgets—often leaving children unattended in the most fragile and formative phases of their lives.

That inadequate family income can be partially offset by increased labor is economic fact, but it is not a tribute to successful economic policy. For the United States today remains a nation that is not chronically unemployed, but qualitatively underemployed when it comes to middle-class working men and women.

Some would counter that dramatic increases in consumption over the recent decades are themselves indications of mounting prosperity. Yet if consumption and well-being were synonymous, alcoholism would be a virtue. It is real income levels vis-à-vis long-term industrial trends that are statistically significant—and if people can indeed afford many more and better things today, it is only because advances in the market-driven technology base have made them increasingly more affordable.

It is concurrently ironic, yet no accident, that this paradox of economic inequality is paralleled by an emerging one of missed educational opportunity. For today, at a time when the skills of many Americans are inadequate to meet evolving twenty-first-century shop floor requirements, national policy makers are concomitantly constantly being required to raise immigration quotas for software developers, engineers, and other highly trained workers to meet national high-tech industrial production needs.

Such workplace realities converge in a compelling way to suggest that one requisite solution to America's growing critical-skills crisis must be a renewed, sustained commitment to training at all levels—that to reduce present income inequalities, education and lifelong top-to-bottom workforce training must be key.

REFORMING THE NATION'S K–12 EDUCATIONAL SYSTEM

Such reform must commence at education's bottom rung, with an effort to preserve America's economic base starting early within its schools. For the challenge of sound, balanced economic diversification is daunting—and also financially unattainable unless the present hemorrhaging of productive private capital away from job-generating entrepreneurial investments into public-engineering causes at the expense of education is now effectively stanched, as there are opportunity costs to social experimentation.

If increased productivity is indeed the proper path to the global competitiveness needed to expand the nation's job base, then enhanced human skills are the tools needed to make enhanced productivity a workplace reality. A study conducted at the University of California, San Diego has, in fact, suggested that each additional year of schooling increases an individual worker's productivity by an average 2.8 percent.[23]

More than two decades ago, in 1983, the Carnegie Foundation's famed report *A Nation at Risk* called the graduating products of America's K–12 schools a "rising tide of mediocrity." To wit: "Our recent unchallenged preeminence in commerce, industry, sciences, and technological innovation is being overtaken by competitors throughout the world. . . . What was unimaginable a generation ago has begun to occur—others are matching and even surpassing our educational attainments."[24]

Regrettably today, as the nation moves further into the twenty-first century, all evidence remains that this warning has not been heeded—that far too little progress has been made in the quest for educational excellence. Today, far too many U.S. school systems remain foundering islands of incompetence in a sea of public policy indifference.

Accordingly, even America's best and brightest—the approximately 2 million K–12 students whose testing ranks them in the top 5 percent in national achievement—often seriously trail their counterparts in other countries, and the best students in the critical areas of science and math, in particular, rank merely "at the bottom of the best" of other industrialized nations. U.S. twelfth-grade students, for example, recently performed well below the international average of twenty-one countries on a test of general knowledge of science and mathematics, whereas eleven nations outperformed them in a fifteen-nation assessment of advanced mathematics skills.

Even worse, the national high school dropout rate has actually deteriorated (i.e., worsened) since 1983. Of those pupils who reach the ninth-grade level, a full one-third disappear before high school graduation. Another third finish high school, but aren't in any way ready for college or the workplace. Only the upper third of students, then, leave high school actually prepared for productive citizenship.

Meanwhile, America's business competitors are continually advancing and surpassing it in primary education. Of the twenty foremost developed nations, the United States ranks sixteenth in high school graduation rates and fourteenth in college graduation rates. As a consequence, the nation now ranks forty-ninth in the world in overall literacy; twenty-eighth out of forty countries in mathematical literacy; and behind the European Union in public R&D expenditures, science and engineering graduates, and the production of scientific literature—and her frontline workers lack basic skills to the degree that American businesses must now spend over $30 billion annually on remedial education and training.

Small wonder that the bipartisan Hart-Rudman Commission on National Security found that after terrorism, the second greatest threat to national security is the failure of math and science education. Indeed, in a unanimous consensus, it found that this educational failure is a greater threat to America's future well-being than any conceivable conventional war within the next quarter century.[25]

The problem is not primarily one of money—the United States already outspends most other major industrial nations per capita on K–12 education, while their students consistently outperform those here. A Cato Institute study has found that whereas federal educational spending, in real terms, stood at about $25 billion in 1960, it now approaches $110 billion and continues to grow.[26] Indeed, since 1980 alone, funding for American public schools from all sources has more than doubled. To quote economist Walter Williams:

> If money were the answer, Washington public schools would be the best in the nation—if not the world. Per student expenditures are $10,500 a year, second highest in the world. With a "student-teacher ratio" of 15.8, they have smaller-than-average class size. What is the result? In only one of the city's 19 high schools are as many as 50 percent of students proficient in reading and at no school are 50 percent of them proficient in math.[27]

Hence, while typical federal solutions have consistently proposed more bricks and mortar, American children still can't read or calculate their math. Fiscal realities suggest, therefore, that the remedy for the nation's educational deficiencies lies not in increased expenditures of tax dollars, but rather in the more productive use of the training resources that are actually available.

Succinctly put—and as a definitive Hudson Institute study makes vividly clear—it is disastrously poor classroom productivity, not too little spending, that is the central cause of the expanding crisis now enveloping America's K–12 education system. To quote economist Thomas Sowell:

> Our education system is turning out increasing numbers of people who have no skills that anyone would pay for out of his own pocket. They thus have little choice but to become busybodies in government or in programs paid for with taxpayers' money or foundation grants designed to get taxpayer money later. This is called public service.[28]

Indeed, at a time when economic, demographic, and competitive forces have combined to create a workplace wherein one's basic learning tools are of paramount importance, the present elementary and secondary school systems operating in many regions of America are actually regressing in their abilities to impart the job skills needed by high school graduates entering the workforce.

The key public policy question thus becomes: Can such regression be reversed? While there may be no one solution, it is clear that better teachers must be supported by sounder education policies, lending promise to some combination of a significant number of prospective remedies—among them restoring the primacy of the hard disciplines in the K–12 curriculum, teacher competency testing, better productivity controls, and development of superior vocational training.[29]

Such reform cannot come soon enough—as upward of 90 percent of all future jobs will require at least a high school education. Thus, to prosper, America cannot continue to allow its educational focus to lag behind the pace of technological change. Already, declining literacy and numeracy are denying many young people access to even entry-level jobs. Yet no small part of the problem stems from the underutilization of existing educational resources, which, if used more productively, would enable the K–12 educational infrastructure to do more with less.

As today, America remains committed to the 180-day school year—a relic of the economic dictates of an agrarian age wherein children were required to spend their summer months working on family farms, an industrial phenomenon that is no longer a prime socioeconomic concern. By contrast, the more urban offspring of her principal trade competitors in Europe and Japan now spend 220 to 240 days in the K–12 classroom. Germany, for example, requires its high school students to study core hard-discipline academic subjects 3,528 hours per year, compared with just 1,460 hours for America's youth.[30]

In like manner, typical Japanese K–12 students receive an average of five hours per day of homework, compared with just one hour for their U.S. counterparts. This is doubtless a significant factor why Japanese students consistently score median 70 percent achievement levels on standardized mathematics scores, compared with 40 percent for American students, and 67 percent on science scores, contrasted with 55 percent for U.S. teenagers.[31]

The notion that America can somehow achieve educational parity with its principal trade competitors with a dramatically lower level of intellectual commitment thus constitutes an academic arrogance that cannot continue if the nation is to remain an economic superpower.

Yet, systemic overhaul of the attendance dimension to the K–12 training process is not the total solution. In tandem with consideration given for extending the school year quantitatively, a concerted focus also must be lent to improving it qualitatively—making better use of the time that is available.

As presently, much of a typical American school day is spent—indeed often wasted—on nonacademic activities. No more than 40 percent of U.S. high school students' productive classroom time, for instance, is now spent on the combination of math, science, history, civics, geography, and foreign languages—less than one-half that of their German, French, and Japanese counterparts.

If America's schools are going to effectively compete intellectually, then, they must begin by *getting back to basics*—commencing with immediate reinstatement of a primary focus on communications skills, mathematics, and the scientific disciplines within the nation's K–12 system. Greater opportunity for the acquisition of fast-track skills as well as increased incentives for individual students to excel likewise are required if the nation's secondary school graduates are gain a secure foothold on the path to successfully competing in the highly sophisticated twenty-first-century job market.

In her founding years, America's citizens were generally among the most literate on earth. The education of its youth has always been its path to progress. The nation now stands at a crucial crossroads confronting its critical public policy choices: Will it, by policy choice, rescue the educational opportunities of its coming generations or forever consign them to menial labor and their nation to the ranks of second-rate economic powers?

MEETING EDUCATION'S PROMISE
THROUGH VOCATIONAL TRAINING

Understanding these policy imperatives leads to the realization that there presently are serious systemic inadequacies in imparting knowledge in an information-based economy that must be expeditiously addressed. They are challenges that invoke the need to draw upon education's technology-generating strengths. For if creating a state-of-the-art twenty-first-century national workforce is the linchpin to "new economy" development success, then workforce training must be made a paramount priority.

Indeed, creating a capability-rich labor force must build upon the educational infrastructure reforms embedded in the pioneering No Child Left Behind program to include such initiatives as

- an agenda that includes developing reading capabilities at an early age;
- K–12 enrichment in the hard disciplines: mathematics, science, and communication skills;
- ongoing, state-of-the-art workforce training; and
- ample funding for college and university training and research.[32]

With the ever-evolving changes in the information-driven technologies cited in the preceding analysis, it is estimated that most real-time workplace skills are becoming obsolete every two years. This shop floor reality, in turn, mandates pressing needs for vastly improved vocational skill development as well as entrepreneurial training for those seeking to invest their time and financial resources in fostering new business start-ups.

Such targeted workforce training, moreover, must be not only technology driven, but also structured in ways that ensure continuing access to realistic, real-time educational upgrades, carried out in conjunction with mentor and apprentice partnerships with the private sector within the workplace to ensure that workforce training efforts reflect true marketplace demands and not the mere best guesses of public bureaucrats.

With employment in the service sector now exceeding 83 percent of the U.S. workforce and growing, the need for more education-driven professional services training also must be emphasized. Here again, the key public policy question becomes one of how manpower development strategies may best be formulated to serve national development goals.

Hence both public policy prudence and private individual commitment are required. For foundation education and training are essential keys to ensuring equal access at the economic starting gate—and as noted, they are public services whose equal access the Constitution explicitly mandates government to provide.

They are, in fact, especially critical as the twenty-first-century Information Age continues to unfold, with the types of jobs now being created invariably coming in the high-skilled, knowledge-driven sectors. Within the emerging high-tech global marketplace, what you learn is what you earn!

Several factors underlie this profound transformation. Within the ever-evolving "new economy" paradigms of production, previous ways of working, based on manual assembly, are constantly being replaced by more sophisticated computer-driven ones engaging work-specific specialties as the knowledge-based economy applies human logic as well as mechanical tools to the technical operations of production. As a consequence, yesterday's rote outputs churned out by production assembly lines are now constantly giving way to robotics, machine vision, and CAD/CAM operations.

These shop floor realities need not mean that fewer workers be employed, of course, only that different skill sets are required that must be upgraded constantly. They also explain why traditional economic development strategies, because they impact upon the wrong determinants, no longer effectively work—as well as why sound human resource investment must be made paramount in any comprehensive national economic development strategy.

A leading-edge, holistic training formula, therefore, is invoked—and it is here that President Kennedy's educational initiatives in the early 1960s offer a development example that is at once instructive and inspiring. Then, a mounting external threat—Russian satellites and missiles—led to a massive program to upgrade the nation's human skills.

The imminent danger of the loss of U.S. military supremacy thus goaded policy makers into action. Articulated in the challenge of putting the first astronaut on the moon, America enacted the National Defense Education Act, which for more than a decade led to significant enhancements in scientific education, language skills, and national literacy.

Yet curiously, after the race to the moon was won, the nation's focus on educational quality was once again almost totally abandoned. It is no accident, then, that uniform high school test scores have concurrently fallen by more than 5 percent since the 1960s.

The inherent folly of such a policy course obviously cannot continue—as today, it is U.S. economic supremacy at stake, mandating that workforce training priorities rank among the foremost within the panorama of future national development strategies.

Just getting by is no longer good enough. A greater educational vision is needed so that all citizens can again dare to dream. No free nation can guarantee full equality of outcome. But through greater vision and planning, it can ensure equal opportunity in imparting workplace skills.

TECHNOLOGICALLY RESTORING THE AMERICAN DREAM THROUGH EDUCATION

In the 1960s, as shown, President Kennedy's National Defense Education Act forged a decade and more of top-to-bottom national educational reform. Today, with the lessons learned again increasingly ignored, a similar commitment is required to restore full and equal educational opportunity.

America today must wake up to the unavoidable reality that prosperity is not a given. Rather, it is an aspiration realizable through more rational development planning—with the challenges that it poses requiring dynamic solutions forged by forward-looking leadership.

In this, America must not fail! For no nation can fulfill its economic promise until all citizens share equitably in its proceeds. In the requisite quest for new technology-based development, then, policy makers must not lose sight of this one long-standing pillar of U.S. economic strength—that all jobs, top to bottom, are important and contribute to a common prosperity.

A rising tide *does* lift all boats—as Kennedy made clear—and there is no denying that many are better off today because of technological advance. But equity dictates that the nation not be satisfied with the status quo, with a society that continues to be markedly divided between "winners" and "losers" within its economic marketplace. Ignoring mounting inequality is not what democratic capitalism is supposed to be about. Life, like poker, may not invariably be fair, but steadfast public policy can ensure that the house rules themselves are honest.

Today, the GI Bill of the 1950s and the National Defense Education Act of the 1960s are gone. U.S. K–12 elementary and secondary systems are no longer world-class. In standardized tests, in fact, the bottom 25 percent of students in countries such as Japan and South Korea often score well above the median levels of their American counterparts. Small wonder, then, that the nation is turning out just half as many Ph.D.s in the science and engineering fields as it did three decades ago.[33]

The academic performance problem is compounded by the reality that many who now run the nation's K–12 schools don't value the importance of basic skills to the same degree as the employers who manage the enterprises wherein their graduates will work. Consequently, too much time in America's undergraduate college education today must be devoted to what its principal trade competitors do in high school.

There is a valid role for government in both education and technology development. Indeed, they are inexorably linked—as in an age of CAD-CAM manufacturing and other advanced information-driven production systems, economic development is, first and foremost, education.

For today, in the Information Age, there are few physical empires worth conquering, no strategic natural resources that need seizing to secure comparative advantage. For those who succeed in the future will forge their empires from man-made brainpower—building from where today there stands but empty intellectual space.[34]

Accordingly, to preserve its status as global economic hegemon, America must do better in education—and it can, given a firm commitment to both lifetime learning and a top-to-bottom workforce training approach that optimizes its global competitiveness within the ever-evolving "new economy." As a nation, America has historically led economically because it has been strong educationally—and today, the world has entered into an education-driven entrepreneurial age.

NOTES

1. M. Friedman (1962), pp. 3–4.

2. Will and Ariel Durant in *The Lessons of History*, cited at www.uga.edu/ihe/perspectives/perspect0102.

3. H. G. Wells in *The Outline of History*, cited at www.classicreader.com/author.php/aut.

4. Franklin Roosevelt, the "Four Freedoms," cited at www.americanrhetoric.com/speeches/fdrthefourfreedoms.htm; home.att.net/~jrhsc/fdr.html.

5. Henry David Thoreau quoted in L. Peter. 1977; cited at www.quotationspage.com/quotes/Henry_David_Thoreau.

6. M. Cary and T .J. Haarhof (1940), pp. 193–194.

7. Ibid.

8. Ibid., p. 195.

9. Ibid., pp. 212 ff.; H. Couch and R. Geer (1940), pp. 391 ff.

10. See P. Drucker (1969), p. 131.

11. L. Thurow (1996), p. 287.

12. On this federal research spending decline, which continues, see R. Inman and D. Burton (Spring 1990), p. 132.

13. On the effectiveness of this R&D, see J. Pearson (1988), passim; R. Johnson and C. Edwards (1987), pp. 39 ff.; D. Lampe (1986), passim.

14. See sources cited in n. 13.

15. R. Reich (1991), p. 228.

16. M. Woolfe (1992), p. 56; K. Phillips (1990), p. 137; P. Drucker (1989), pp. 149–50; R. Reich (1987), pp. 86–88; L. Thurow (1985), p. 136.

17. T. Stewart (October 19, 1992), pp. 54–57.

18. Quoted in J. M. Keynes (1980).

19. On this, see R. Reich (1991), pp. 264–65.

20. L. Thurow (1992), pp. 45 ff.; R. Kuttner (1991), pp. 217 ff. The Pentagon has identified twenty-two separate evolving technologies that it believes to be critical to future national security.

21. L. Thurow (1992), pp. 51–52; D. Calleo (1991), p. 166.

22. R. Reich (1991), pp. 264–65; Alan Greenspan, cited in D. Coyle (2001), p. 209.

23. T. Stewart (October 19, 1992), pp. 54–57.

24. On this, see L. Dobbs (September 15, 2003), p. 40; U.S. Department of Education (1983), p. 1.

25. U.S. Department of Education (1983).

26. Hart-Rudman Commission on National Security (2001).

27. W. Williams (December 26, 2002), p. 1; C. Thomas (July 14, 2004), p. 10.

28. See T. Sowell (May 11, 1994), p. 21; L. Perelman (May 1990), passim; T. Geier (August 1, 1994), p. 17; B. Kantrowitz and T. Winger (1992), p. 92.

29. On this, also see T. Sowell (July 17, 2002), p. 21.

30. "State Exhibit: Window to Future Jobs" (April 10, 1989), passim.

31. Ibid.

32. Ibid.

33. L. Thurow (1996), p. 286.

34. Ibid., pp. 307–8.

Part III

"RESPONSIBLE REMEDIES"

An American Agenda

From those flames, no light, but rather darkness, visible.

—John Milton, *Paradise Lost*, Book 1, Lines 62–63

The State, the last complex instrument to be mastered by capitalism, must not itself act. Let it prepare the ground by guaranteeing *security*; let it predispose the minds of men through *education*; and let it establish *freedom*, so that the economic machine, as transformed, and as to be transformed further still, by the individual, may function so as to achieve the maximum of economic rationalization that will mark the triumph of capitalism.

—Amintore Fanfani, Italian economist and politician

The bourgeoisie, by the rapid improvement of all of the instruments of production, by its immensely facilitated means of communication, draws everyone, even the most barbarous nations, into civilization. The cheap prices of its commodities are the heavy artillery whereby it batters down Chinese walls, wherewith it forces the barbarians' intensely obstinate hatred of all foreigners to capitulate. It compels all nations, on pain of extinction, to adopt the bourgeois mode of production; it thereby compels them to introduce what it calls civilization into their midst; that is, to become bourgeois themselves. In a word, it creates a world after its own image.

—The grudging assessment of "capitalism" of Karl Marx and Friedrich Engels in *The Communist Manifesto*, 1848

Chapter Nine

What Doesn't Work: The Economic Problem with the Liberal Pabulum

Democracy will cease to exist when you take away from those willing to work and give to those who will not!

—Thomas Jefferson

As a consequence of the findings documented by this inquiry, America faces crucial political choices. In an economy every day more global, the nation cannot continue to prosper employing the failed economic policies of the past, constituting public-sector palliatives that do no more than meddle in the operations of the competitive private market while charging exorbitantly for the so-called "service" in the process.

On the contrary, to thrive economically the free market must be unleashed— not bled—if the national policy goal is to sustain full employment by providing the meaningful, well-paying jobs that only a strong private sector can provide.

The goal of a private-sector-led economic renaissance, of course, stands in direct contrast to those who would stimulate a faltering economy through the failed doctrines of a hodgepodge of public cures—be they minimum wages, public-sector jobs, income transfer payments, mandated equalities of outcome, or preferential development incentives.

Indeed, the economic threats that such policy courses pose are notoriously counterproductive, making it imperative to critically evaluate that litany of liberal public-sector socioeconomic programs—so often proposed, so seldom successful—that offer no real remedy, yet needlessly encumber taxpayer dollars. The fundamental reasons for the reality of their failures merit further exploration.

159

WHY MINIMUM-WAGE LAWS DON'T WORK

A minimum-wage law is perhaps as perfect an example as there is of a liberal public policy whose ultimate effects are precisely the opposite of those intended. Because it prohibits those whose contributions' market values fall below its statutory minimum from gaining productive employment—in direct contravention of the law of supply and demand—it unabashedly prices them out of the labor market.

In so doing, it concurrently diminishes both incipient marketplace demand and real output, as denominated in domestic product terms—and thereby contributes to even greater unemployment. By creating competition among the poor for scarce jobs, then, its net impact, paradoxically, is to create the very poverty that it is designed to stamp out.

While government can *legislate* minimum wages, it cannot dictate that private employers must hire at those rates—and any astute businessman intent on staying in business will generally not hire at wage levels not dictated by the realities of the competitive marketplace merely to humor the "social justice" whims of a monopolistic government. Moreover, profit-maximizing private firms will always award basic training opportunities to those cheapest to train. Accordingly, economist Walter Williams asks:

> Are low-skilled workers made better or worse off as a result of a minimum wage? It is almost a no-brainer that being hired at $5 an hour puts more food on the table than not being hired at $9 per hour. What's more, minimum wages reduce training opportunities. Most of us gain new skills through on-the-job training. Minimum wage laws deny that opportunity.[1]

Satirizing the crass political rhetoric of the minimum wage issue, a recent *Wall Street Journal* editorial similarly asserted:

> John Kerry says that he wants to raise the minimum wage to $7 an hour from $5.15, and his proposal has us thinking: "But why stop there? Why not make it $10 an hour, or $20, or for that matter, whatever a U.S. Senator makes?"
>
> Wage floors aren't manna from Heaven. Here on Earth, they tend to price certain kinds of jobs out of the job market. Businesses hire and pay workers what they think their skills are worth relative to other ways that they can spend their capital. Force the price of labor too high, and suddenly businesses hire fewer workers, especially those at the lower rungs of the skills ladder. . . .
>
> Bill Clinton's Small Business Administration followed a select group of workers after the last increase in the minimum wage in 1997 and found that it slowed hiring at small businesses and more than doubled the likelihood that low-wage workers at the largest firms would become unemployed.[2]

The economic bottom line and the consummate irony, then, is that those who would today benevolently engage in a "living wage" crusade on behalf of low-wage earners do a grave disservice to the very people they are trying to help. For people in minimum-wage jobs usually don't stay there permanently. Generally, both their pay and their status increase as they accumulate experience and develop skills.

Indeed, most studies show that low-income people evolve into average-income people and then higher-income people as they progress in life. But a wage minimum can slam the door of the American Dream in their faces at the starting gate by denying them even a chance to set out on such a productive employment path.[3]

WHY THE PUBLIC-SECTOR JOBS SOLUTION DOESN'T WORK

In tandem with minimum wages, for decades the big government solution to the rising unemployment caused by unwarranted governmental intervention into the free marketplace has been to focus upon tax-funded public-sector WPA/CETA—and job corps—types of programs. Yet a wealth of empirical economic evidence makes clear that such make-work efforts, however well intended, simply do not work either.

Why? The reasons are rudimentary. Because they are public entitlement programs, they are bureaucratically rigid and enjoy no strategic focus, training people for functions for which there is no market demand.

The jobs created, moreover, are not those that destined to build a modicum of future prosperity—productive, permanent jobs that ensure full-time employment and rising incomes in real terms. For without question, the technologies of the future—particularly those high-performance manufacturing and other information-driven industries—will require premier-quality job performers who will, in turn, demand high-quality jobs.

But what constitutes a "quality job"? By classic definition, it is one that will provide wages and fringe benefits, decent working conditions, job security, employment stability, and rising incomes in real terms. Those features defined as necessary to meet the test for high-quality jobs, therefore, are generally not characteristic of artificially created public-sector jobs.[4]

What's worse, such public-sector job creation programs are invariably a drain on the productive economy—robbing resources from private-sector workers whose jobs contribute to national economic strength. For almost by definition, the public jobs established are ones for which no private demand exists; if there were, they already would. But when government creates make-work jobs for which there is no real market demand, it actually increases unemployment in a variety of ways.

Why? The cause is simple. The money used to pay for such public-sector jobs comes from private-sector producers. Thus, because taxes fund these programs, private businesses have less money to employ people in their own industries.

Therefore, unemployment is not reduced—a private-sector job has merely been replaced with a public-sector one. Perhaps this sounds like a zero-sum exchange—but in reality it is not. For the job that is lost in the private sector is in a business that creates a product or service that is in demand. The governmentally owned job, on the other hand, provides a service that customers do not want—because if they did, the workings of the free market process would have already provided it.

In addition, because bureaucratic inefficiency is common to all governments, it generally takes more tax dollars to get a public worker to do an amount of work equivalent to that of an employee of a private business that must rely upon profits to survive.

Finally, because the taxpayers—who now no longer have the money that was used to create the public-sector job that they didn't want—also now find themselves with less money to buy those goods and services that they genuinely *do* want. Economic production thus is slowed and unemployment actually *increases* throughout the economy.

Most tragically, in this convoluted process, however, is that an even greater disservice is done to the so-called beneficiary of the artificially created job. For in reality, public-sector job programs are little more than a twenty-first-century form of medieval indentured servitude. When a worker is trained and employed in a job that the free market process does not demand, he or she is denied the opportunity to find, and prosper in, a job that the market truly does require.

In this instance, then, job security hinges upon the benevolence of the American taxpayer—and while the employees may initially be able to eke out livings by raking the municipal leaves, they will never develop the type of employment record and work-related experience that will enable them to provide for their families in the manner that Americans both deserve and have come to expect from the free market. In fact, such programs generally do little more than to discourage many would-be productive workers and teach them bad work habits.

WHY THE "POLITICS OF DEPENDENCY" SOLUTION DOESN'T WORK

Accordingly, though the failed public-sector "training and employment of last resort" approach has remained a foremost recourse within the liberal political medicine bag for some, its remedy remains basic—that is, to abandon traditional public remedies and negotiate a new social contract between industry, labor, academia, and government to develop critical new private-sector job skills. Such a remedy produces not *bureaucracy-driven* but *market-driven* technology-based vocational and entrepreneurial training opportunities that prepare program graduates for the complex workplaces of the future.

This is a critical policy imperative. For the bureaucratic alternative to productive private jobs is public-sector transfer payments—modern big government's vernacular for the public dole. As in the present pork barrel paradigm, the welfare state corollary to public-sector jobs is the mushrooming monolith of entitlements—the notion that, as the name implies, society somehow owes everybody something and that it is the duty of bureaucracy to ensure that it is delivered.

In pursuit of this grand ideal, the Great Society was for decades in the second half of the twentieth century given carte blanche in the formulation and dispensation of entitlements—yet bought little. For the only poor who succeeded throughout its mandate generally did so not through public-sector largesse but rather, most often, the old-fashioned way: through diligence and hard work.

Some have not succeeded, and poverty remains rampant within many of America's inner cities in particular. In remedy, some have advocated, in fact, a somewhat callous, though pragmatic, cure for the public dole phenomenon in what is euphemistically called a "quick as hell theory of full employment." Eliminate transfer payments, welfare, and all other liberal excuses for not finding a job in America, they argue—and the country will create full employment "quick as hell"!

Arguably, this is not the inhumane course that most liberals make it out to be. Many of America's underclass today, particularly in urban areas, suffer not so much from material impoverishment as from behavioral underdevelopment—the absence of a functional work ethic. Indeed, in many cases, given attractive income transfer alternatives, in a sheer capitalistic sense, it is often more financially profitable not to work. From a personal economic standpoint, in fact, the welfare option for many can be a sound, market-based decision.

Yet from the standpoint of formulating constructive, cost-effective public policy, the reality that people are impoverished merely because they reject the effort or the discipline required to perform productive work makes it not only appropriate but imperative that they confront the consequences of their choice.

Historically, Americans have prided themselves as a work ethic society and have disavowed the welfare ethic. But championing the former as the alternative to the latter concurrently imposes upon societal governance an obligation to promote full employment opportunity by preserving the economic health of private job producers. To do less, in the apt words of economist

Lester Thurow, would be tantamount to "locking the Church doors and then claiming that people lack virtue for failing to attend the service."[5]

The process of formulating cogent policy is today too often confounded by contemporary political confusion between the term "entitlements" and the notion of "rights" as secured by constitutional guarantee. Yet the operational dichotomy is here clear and fundamental: An entitlement is a gratuity provided at the expense of others; a right paves the way for self-reliance.

More pragmatically put, rights allow the enterprising and the ambitious to work their way up the economic ladder. Entitlements presume that a society owes something to individuals whether they have earned it or not, and keep them mired in indolence at the bottom of the ladder. Rights, then, help a society to grow, whereas entitlements merely slow its growth and sap its character.

Notwithstanding the cogency of this dichotomy, the notion of the desirability of the public-sector handout has continued to escalate—often even demanded as a public obligation—as a dramatic transformation has transpired within the nation's ethical and social values.

In the not too distant past, citizens were too proud to accept welfare. Diligence and hard work were deemed redemptive, and "public compassion" was defined as ensuring popular well-being not in terms of the number of people put on welfare but instead upon the number of people for whom welfare was no longer a necessity.

Today, however, the nation's liberal political class has serendipitously redefined traditional public-sector handouts as "entitlements"—in so doing, spawning an entire new generation who reject John D. Rockefeller's faith in "the dignity of work . . . the opportunity for every man to make an honest living."[6] Whereas people in the past sought recourse to benevolent public assistance only as a last resort, today they line up demanding it as a mainline right—as something they are owed.

In tandem, the flawed notion continues to be perpetuated that through some miraculous federal sleight of hand, and with still more tax dollars, people can mystically be politically transformed from welfare status into productive frontline workers. Yet this is a rationale bred of economic ignorance, not of workplace reason. For the notion that government can somehow create economic security is illusory at best. Indeed, government's great specialty has been to undermine, not underwrite, economic security through the tax dollars required to sustain it.

What happened to the axiomatic recognition that for government to guarantee a right to entitlements for some, it must deny others the right to their own earnings? Whither the concept of compensating civic service? Today, for liberal policy makers and their dependent political constituencies, benefits-linked work requirements are deemed demeaning, and hence too great a price to pay. They fervently believe that while the proper role of government is to disburse entitlements, there are no corresponding obligations accruing to the "entitlee."

Unworthy successors to John Kennedy, they have thus come to parody his name—completing the full circle from Captain John Smith's 1607 puritan edict—"Those who do not work, shall not eat!"—to the current liberal social credo: "Ask not what your country can do for you . . . demand it!"

Notwithstanding, however economically debilitating, entitlements continue to expand both because they retain powerful, vociferous lobbyists—and because their proponents usually possess a stronger voice for *keeping them* than their opponents have in *taking them* away. And while the welfare reforms of the mid-1990s may have changed the legalistic dynamic within which the system operates, the underlying ethos that made the reforms necessary in the first place remains an all too tempting target for those would preach the "politics of dependency."

Consequently, because of a convoluted liberal golden rule stipulating: "That which is once given shall never be taken away," nearly two-thirds of all federal spending today is committed to funding "entitlements," consuming some 16 percent of GDP—draining the capital lifeblood from the private economy, destroying work and savings ethics, weakening family values, limiting individual freedoms, and in so doing, undermining the very fabric that has been the embodiment of U.S. society.

WHY THE EQUALITY OF
OUTCOMES SOLUTION DOESN'T WORK

Notwithstanding its primacy, this continuing social devolution is the very antithesis of those socioeconomic values that have historically been the cornerstone of American national existence. For the Founding Fathers bequeathed to U.S. citizens three fundamental rights: individual liberty, legal parity, and equal market access. They did not guarantee to anyone a risk-free economy or an inherent or automatic stipend from the earnings of others more productive.

A fundamental premise of the rights-based economic system that they resolutely put into place, in fact, is that one's financial reward from society must be commensurate with one's willingness to contribute in return. In ensuring personal well-being, absent physical or mental disability, then, the only "entitlement" one has, or should expect to have, from government is the opportunity to participate diligently, and without prejudice, in the competitive free marketplace.

Statutory entitlements, therefore, are not at all what the Founding Fathers intended. Thomas Jefferson consistently contended that "dependence begets servitude," and the consensus of his contemporaries equally makes clear that the notion of a welfare state is an egregious perversion of their original intent. For the term "equality," as framed in the Declaration of Independence, meant *equality of opportunity*, not *equality of outcome*.

Indeed, the federal Constitution, one must again recall, guarantees only the pursuit of happiness, not happiness itself. Not everyone is destined to be economically prosperous or to enjoy an equal living standard, any more than all marathon runners are "guaranteed" the right to finish first in the race. They are merely afforded equal access to line up at the starting gate.

Built-in inequality has, in fact, long been an indispensable catalyst for any free society to advance. For it is the individual's desire to overcome and excel that is the key to all human industry and social progress—as well as the essence of democratic capitalism. If all are guaranteed equal outcome, what is the incentive to produce—and who will pay for the reward?

If casino poker players, beginning with equal stakes, were all guaranteed an equal outcome—with everyone ending up right where he began—who would bother to play the game? Life, like poker, may not invariably be fair, but both winners and losers are essential to the process of economic advance.[7]

Was it not the father of modern Western capitalism, Adam Smith, who taught that it is not from the goodwill of the merchant that goods are gotten, but from everyone pursuing his or her enlightened self-interest? To wit:

> It is not from the benevolence of the butcher, the brewer, or the baker that we may expect our dinner, but from their regard for their own self-interest. We address ourselves not to their humanity but to their self-love; and never talk to them of our own necessities but of their advantages. No one but a beggar chooses to depend upon the benevolence of his fellow citizens.[8]

Though this fundamental market-driven truth is the essential precondition for all economic progress, however, it is concurrently the singular dimension to the free market that those who found their careers upon the "politics of victimization" find so vexing. For in their view, the admixture of equal rights and unequal outcomes creates basic incompatibilities between the economic principles of capitalism and the political precepts of democracy.

The issue at stake then thus becomes: How can a political system promote unequal outcomes while concurrently proclaiming the equality of all citizens and universally distributed human rights? Capitalism, in their view, must somehow be evil or immoral.

Yet fair and free economic competition need not be a social or moral issue at all. The reality that a person is working in his self-interest does not mean that he is a bad person or even that he is not benefiting other people. Adam Smith's baker may well have been a selfish man, but his market-based success suggests that he probably made exceptionally good bread and sold it at reasonable prices. This is not antisocial behavior. It is merely a pragmatic categorical rejection of the demeaning doctrine of equality of outcome.

Accordingly, it comes as no surprise that the most vocal patron saints of the liberal shibboleth of the equality of outcomes doctrine are not risk takers at all, but rather liberal officeholders and bureaucrats—street front demagogues who find useful political theatrics in appealing to those among their constituencies who retain underdeveloped approaches to the precept of achieving earnings through diligent work.

Indeed, the dramatic mushrooming of taxpayer revolts within recent decades has come in direct reaction to the self-seeking aspirations of those who work to sustain their livelihoods through such political pandering.

Yet their concerns, if unrequited, are equally unfounded. For unfettered, America's system of free market capitalism continues to work well. It works precisely because it preserves individual freedoms while promoting individual opportunities and preserving individual options. Indeed, recurring allegations that it fosters inordinate inequalities are no more that a statist myth.

One would be hard pressed to find any American—even the least blessed—willing to trade his or her lot for everyday life in Moscow or Calcutta, let alone Zambia or Bangladesh. Unlike socialism, the capitalistic market continues to hold tangible, tantalizing economic opportunities for the disadvantaged to move up and become tomorrow's privileged class. The key question that arises, then, is: At a time when the socialistic remedy is failing so spectacularly elsewhere throughout the world, does it make sense to embrace it in America now?

WHY THE SOPHISTICATED STRATEGIES SOLUTION DOESN'T WORK

Beyond their obvious and inherent failures within the socioeconomic services arena, the dramatically different ultimate results produced by the sophisticated strategy versus fiscal responsibility public policy approaches is illustrated by two separate business climate surveys annually produced—the first is program-based, whereas the second is cost-based.

For years, the Washington-based Corporation for Enterprise Development (CFED) has graded each state according to the types of public-sector incentive programs offered to its local business community—with higher grades awarded commensurate with invasiveness of service level. Yet the job generation results in those states wherein the CFED's comprehensive strategy approach has been specifically applied have been uniformly devastating.

One study discovered, in fact, that while the employment bases of those ten states receiving a CFED grade of A for exemplary development policy had grown 7.52 percent in a select consecutive eight-year period, those states indicted for "failed economic policy" (receiving grades of D and F) increased their employment at a quite phenomenal 16.66 percent aggregate rate.[9]

While the job base of Michigan—whose policies are perennially cited by CFED as comprising the premier development program in the country—grew by just 2.09 percent in this period, the survey's very bottom five states, those receiving Fs for their approaches, grew three times as fast, at a collective 6.09 percent rate.[10]

While the policy-driven CFED rankings have been performing so abysmally, however, the state employment bases in the annual Grant Thornton Index—which measures the *costs* of those public policies—have functioned quite predictably. For in the eight-year period analyzed, the job bases of Grant Thornton's five *best-rated* manufacturing states collectively grew by 27.70 percent; whereas those of its five *worst-rated* states grew by just 7.06 percent.[11]

For the same tax reasons, it is likely no accident either that a handful of northern Indiana counties on Michigan's southern border in that same time period created more jobs with companies formed specifically to serve the Michigan side of that border than did the strategy cited by CFED as being the premier industrial development approach in the entire country. Why? Primarily because Michigan ranked fourth whereas Indiana ranked thirty-fourth among the states in aggregate property tax burden.[12]

The message from the data aggregates again is that if public policy costs are competitive, sophisticated development strategies might—just *might*—make some difference at the margin. But if they grow inordinately out of line, a jurisdiction is merely squandering finite revenue resources by funding countervailing business development incentives to create jobs that will soon migrate to other regions in search of better business climates.

WHY THE MANAGED MARKET SOLUTION DOESN'T WORK

A favored corollary to the sundry big government approaches cited is the ongoing quest to publicly intervene to pick winners and losers in the competitive free marketplace, also known as the "managed market approach"— a favored, albeit fatally flawed, job creation tool particularly preferred by U.S. state and local jurisdictions whereat, unlike federal-level efforts in most countries, the most active economic development activities in America take place.

At the state level, for example, various packages of costly preferential financial and tax incentives have traditionally comprised a prime thrust of business development efforts—frequently becoming the main weapons of choice in intense internecine interjurisdictional bidding wars.

There is, in fact, no better policy laboratory for examining the economic impact of gratuitous public-sector intervention aimed at attracting businesses within the free market than in this theater of business operations. For the lessons learned are especially germane in seeking to ascertain the proper role of the public sector in the private industrial development process.

Business investment decisions, of course, fuel the economic engines that power private job and income growth. To influence such decision making, the states commonly offer superficially attractive market baskets of discretionary financial and tax incentives to would-be producers to stimulate investment. Such preferential incentives come in many forms—industrial zone concessions, property tax abatements, investment and/or job creation tax credits, production cost and business inventory deductions, sales tax exemptions, and the like.

Such inducements are frequently called "tax expenditures," since the revenues foregone are equivalent to budgetary outlays. Technically defined, they are revenue losses incurred due to tax law that allows special exemptions, exclusions, or deductions—or that provide preferential tax rates, targeted credits, or tax liability deferrals.

Financial incentives, in turn, are portfolios of public-sector capital benefits that may include interest subsidies in the forms of loan guarantees or revenue bonds, project grants, direct loans, equity or near equity capital financing, and similar forms of concessionary financing.

States often attempt to justify their use of preferential financial and tax incentives on the pretexts of:

- promoting investments to create jobs and achieve a growing economy;
- equalizing interstate tax differentials when competing for ambulatory firms;
- lowering the costs of capital to promote greater capital formation;
- offsetting the effects of other noncompetitive state mandated costs; and
- creating the illusion of a probusiness attitude fostered by government.

Whatever their initial utility, however, their use has now proliferated to the degree that the process of business location in America has evolved into a fierce cold war competition, with each state having more weapons within its arsenal than it needs, yet no state willing to disarm for fear of losing parity in the ongoing interstate battle for business migrants.

Indeed, from a business management standpoint, state and local governments now offer lucrative discretionary inducements to the extent that they have generally become viewed as a prerequisite to, rather than a determinant of, new investment.

Nonetheless, the principal arguments against the conventional incentives approach to development are overwhelming. Practically every analysis completed within the past two decades has concluded that most standard business incentives packages neither substantially encourage new investment nor boost output nor create jobs—yet the revenue losses to the implementing jurisdictions can be substantial.

To the contrary, evidence is strong that financial and tax incentives of the types now employed to attract investment themselves are not meaningful—typically accounting for less than one-tenth of the aggregate values in a weighted spectrum of prime locational determinants.

A mounting body of economic evidence suggests, in fact, that while such incentives can reinforce other determinants, and may be the deciding factor in marginal cases where all other costs are identical, such overarching considerations as composite tax levels, relative costs of regulatory compliance, a reasonably priced skilled labor force, and efficient transportation weigh far more heavily than preferential incentives in most business investment decisions.

The prime reason for such findings is that conventional development incentives do not operate in isolation but rather function in direct response to the growth dynamics of the economic and political systems of which they are a part. Hence such factors as the jurisdiction's overall tax levels, its indirect costs of working through regulatory and other bureaucratic processes, and its ability to ensure the sustained fiscal stability needed for sound development to take place usually have far greater influence than financial and tax incentives upon business location decisions.

As to be effective, incentives must make a sizable impact upon industrial production costs. Yet analysis after analysis has demonstrated that public-sector incentives in general, and tax inducements in particular, have such inconsequential effects upon production factor costs that they have virtually no influence upon ultimate location decisions. Because of the serious policy implications of such findings in discerning government's proper role in the competitive marketplace, therefore, a review of the principal arguments regarding the use of such inducements is instructive.

The overwhelming in-the-field evidence suggests that while the theory underlying business incentives may assume that a corporation can be induced to expand or relocate through the discretionary lowering of select financial and tax input costs, and that the result will then serve the public good, the reality is quite different than the assumption. Indeed, there appears to be little, if any, direct correlation between a jurisdiction's inventory of incentives and its ultimate success in generating net employment growth.

While the intent behind their use to promote sound development may be laudable, their implementation may actually hinder needed development in the long run. Examination of key factors related to the dynamics of the development process explains the reasons for this phenomenon, and in so doing, reveals that there are few winners and many losers in most traditional public-sector development approaches. A review of the evidence is compelling.

First, from a strict cost-benefit standpoint, conventional incentives make little macroeconomic sense. Indeed, they can be quite costly yet add little to national productive capacity. Not only is the combination of direct and indirect costs of conventional preferential inducements costly, it also fails to generate new wealth—another key litmus test of an effective development approach—contributing little to the national economy, but merely rearranging economic activity among the various states and municipalities.

Interstate competition for industry today is little more than a zero-sum game wherein the benefits to one state or party are always balanced, or often even exceeded, by costs to others. Indeed, there is no evidence that incentives increase the size of the investment pie. Rather, it is merely sliced in different ways.

Second, the participating governments, for a variety of reasons, are even greater victims than the national economy at large in the interstate business inducements sweepstakes. Chief among the reasons for this irony is that in the event of business failure, there is no effective mechanism for fiscal recapture of the revenues foregone.

If job creation is properly defined as a primary goal of economic development, in fact, then the overwhelming majority of all state locational investments probably are inappropriate from a public revenue standpoint. For most employment generation studies concur with a remarkable degree of unanimity that no more than 12 to 15 percent of all new businesses succeed in creating durable jobs.[13]

If these figures are indeed accurate, then, at least 85 percent of all potential public-sector investments in new ventures are a waste of public revenues. In fact, the proportion is probably much higher. For many of the fast-growth companies created are often not integral to the jurisdiction's durable economic base at all, but rather are part of its local services economy. Hence, were they to go out of business, they would merely be replaced by other firms that meet local needs, irrespective of the public subsidies.

Third, regardless of the success or failure rates of particular business ventures, state governments are always net losers to the federal government in offering tax incentives to businesses. The reason for this fiscal backfire is basic. Since corporate state and local taxes are generally deductible when computing federal tax liability, the U.S. government receives a substantial portion of the subsidy that the state intends for the corporate beneficiary when it offers an incentive. Since the average U.S. corporate marginal rate stands at 35 cents on the dollar, the financial impact of this anomaly is that the federal government gets more than one-third of the tax savings accruing to a business that receives a state tax incentive.

From a company-specific standpoint, therefore, though this federal deductibility has not materially altered the relative tax differentials among the states in the locational decision process, it does substantially diminish the actual cash value of a tax benefit received. From the state's standpoint, in turn, the net result is a curiously peculiar form of reverse revenue sharing with the federal government in the amount of thirty-five cents on the dollar.

Fourth, while states often offer financial and tax incentives as goodwill gestures to businesses indicative of a propitious business climate, they generally tend to have the opposite effect. For the prospective firms receiving preferential financial and tax incentives are, in actuality, receiving the same governmental services as the indigenous businesses, but at a much lower cost. This disparate phenomenon frequently causes existing in-state firms to perceive that they are victims of unfair competitive advantage.

If the jurisdiction can afford to offer the tax expenditures encumbered by the incentives, then in theory it could also afford, with the same monies, to lower taxes overall, or, alternately, to constructively increase the level of services provided for everyone. Therefore here, one of three adverse fiscal developments must inevitably occur:

1. Either increased taxes will be required upon indigenous firms to maintain the same levels of public services; or
2. Public services will have to be reduced to lower levels to subsidize the artificial lowering of operating costs of the incoming competing firms; or
3. The increased tax burden may be shifted onto residential taxpayers.

While this latter option may not be inherently economically significant from an actual tax impact standpoint—since, in the last analysis, it is customers, not corporations, who, directly or indirectly, always pay all taxes anyway—it is the direct impact of such levies upon residents that has occasioned most of the popular tax revolts of the past three decades.[14]

Fifth, they tend to target the wrong companies, impacting at the wrong stage of their product development cycles. Today, as noted, many states and nations continue to believe that the quintessential key to attracting "footloose firms"—which typically account for less than 2 percent of any jurisdiction's employment shifts—comes through costly preferential tax and financial incentives packages.

Upon closer scrutiny, however, it becomes readily apparent that such is not the case. Indeed, the historic critical paths of American industrial migration from the Midwest Rust Belt—first to the nation's South and Southwest, thence abroad to such newly industrialized nations as Korea, Taiwan, Mexico, and Brazil—seeking the more favorable production costs that characterized the second half of the twentieth century illustrates the futility of interjurisdictional incentives wars.

At the onset, such industrial out-migration is not, in itself, surprising. Indeed, it is a natural phenomenon that characterizes the product cycles of most manufacturing industries as they mature. In their infancies, they need to be proximate to the agglomerations of research and development expertise and financial services infrastructures that spawned them—and to the attendant skilled technicians capable of performing appropriate modifications in product design and production processes dictated by marketplace demand.[15]

But as the products, over time, become more conventional and standardized, their markets invariably become more competitive—and as the businesses become more cost sensitive, they tend to seek out the least expensive manufacturing locations. It is these firms, in fact, for whom the traditional financial and tax incentives programs hold the greatest capital appeal—and are concurrently precisely the ones that will again eventually move out when other incentives elsewhere become more appealing.

The key question for public policy makers thus becomes: To what degree should the jurisdiction preferentially subsidize such aging firms over younger, more vibrant enterprises whose longevity within it are more assured?

Finally, and most basically, conventional incentives are demonstrably largely irrelevant to the dynamics of the industrial development process—playing a very minor role in the location and expansion plans of financially healthy firms. David Birch of MIT, in his studies of job generation within America, for instance, has found that less than 0.1 percent of all job growth within a jurisdiction comes from relocation. Except for Alaska (+2.9 percent), in fact, he identifies no single state wherein any business in-migration or out-migration has accounted for more 1.5 percent of net employment shift.[16]

Roger Schmemner of Duke University likewise found that even in the southeastern United States, where relative production factor costs have historically been lower, and financial and tax incentives have been integral parts of local development processes, the in-migration of relocating firms typically has accounted for only about 3.8 percent of net new employment in the region.[17] Roger Vaughan, in *Wealth of States*, likewise argues that "there are very few foot-loose firms. . . . In growth areas, in-migration accounts for less than 2% of net job gain."[18] And Michael Kieschnick concludes: "Even if tax incentives are a good public investment, they will influence only a tiny proportion of new investment in any state. While the evidence is unclear about whether such targeted incentives are good public policy, it is unequivocal about whether they are a significant policy. They are not."[19]

The economic bottom line? Decades of empirical evidence make clear that the public-sector strategy approach to promoting economic development—artificially-mandated job creation and individual income growth—simply does not work.

For an overarching axiom previously stated deserves restatement here: that is, that levels of bureaucratic overhead—regulatory and tax costs levied upon job producing entrepreneurs—and not sophisticated public strategies, remain the single most important determinant of job and income growth within any taxing jurisdiction. It is to their mitigation that prudent public policy must turn.

TOWARD A MORE MARKET-DRIVEN
APPROACH TO NATIONAL DEVELOPMENT

It is therefore clear that government's traditional tools to promote the private-sector economy—public-sector job programs, the "politics of dependency," mandated equality of outcome, managed markets, and smokestack chasing—no longer yield results, if indeed they ever did.

Each day, as global industrial restructuring takes place, incontrovertible evidence mounts that the public-sector interventionist approach to job development simply does not work. Rather than spawn economic miracles, in fact, its application has failed wherever it has been attempted.

The reason for its failure is founded in its very nature, as public-sector strategies are reflective of symptoms, not real cures. As such, they are generally imposed to compensate for economic base erosion caused by previous glaring inadequacies in public sector cost containment—costs that have already suffocated private-sector economic activity—and are offered only as revenue-costly countervailing subsidy substitutes for those tough cost-cutting fiscal options that could truly turn an economy around.

What are those options? The answers to that question hold the key to successful twenty-first-century global market competitiveness. For classic theory holds, as noted, that the prime goal of economic development is to create wealth and that net wealth is created primarily through the production of exportable goods and services. Such production, in turn, results from a process of free market innovation—finding new ways to employ resources more effectively to produce things consumers need and want.

Only private business is equal to this challenge, since government doesn't create wealth but consumes it. Its proper role in forging public policy, therefore, must be to facilitate—or at least not hinder—the private sector in its challenge of combining financial, human, and natural resources to produce those goods and services that contribute to wealth creation. For a nation promotes the creation of net wealth not by implementing new programs per se, but by instead stimulating new private-sector development—and usually that goal is best approached by reducing, not increasing, the public-sector role in the competitive marketplace.

Indeed, in those genuine success stories wherein public-sector intervention has made a significant growth impact, favorable results have generally come largely because local public policy makers have actively sought to create the political environments most favorable for private-sector innovation and entrepreneurship to take place.

It is not surprising, therefore, that more relaxed tax and regulatory milieus have, in most cases, been the prime foci of such productive policy efforts. For sound economic development remains a free market process, not a legislated act. To the extent that it can be impacted by public-sector policy, then, such policy must be aimed at the ubiquitous challenges of both reshaping public attitudes toward private profits and removing public obstacles to private-sector growth.

These are the imposing challenges of economic development that, as a societal imperative, clearly must be met. For it is economic growth that defeats poverty. It is economic growth that raises living standards for rich and poor alike. It is economic growth that fuels technological innovation and scientific progress. While government cannot create such economic growth—and indeed, is often its enemy—it can nonetheless foster a milieu favorable for growth to take place, an environment that encourages people to take reasonable economic risks in quest of those equitable returns that empower civilizations to progress.

To these ends, if America is to sustain its economic preeminence, it must begin by optimizing the incentives for its prime producers to produce— reinvigorating the nation's industrial environment with public policies that promote, not penalize, increasinly private wages and profits and encourage job-producing entrepreneurs to expand their operations to meet future critical job and income needs.

For in the last analysis, in the quest to sustain economic prosperity, the market is a better determinant than the bureaucrat—and the regimented mentality of government is no substitute for a private form of management that must rely upon profits to survive. The critical first public policy steps to these ends are articulated in the recommendations presented in the appendix to this inquiry.

NOTES

1. W. Williams (November 19, 2003), p. 8; L. Thurow (1996), p. 287.

2. *Wall Street Journal*, June 24, 2004, p. 15.

3. W. Williams (November 12, 2003), p. 7.

4. On this, see M. and R. Friedman (1980), pp.128 ff.

5. L. Thurow (1980), pp. 203–204.

6. John D. Rockefeller, quote at <www.brainyquote.com/quotes/authors/john_d_ rockefeller>.

7. M. and R. Friedman (1980), pp.135–37.

8. A. Smith (1930), vol. 1, p. 16.

9. See G. Heck (1989), pp. 47–48.

10. Ibid.

11. Ibid.

12. See G. Heck (1988), p. 202.

13. cf. *The State of Small Business* (1983), pp. 67 ff.; C. Armington and M. Odle (1982a), passim; idem. (1982b), vol. 6, no. 3, pp. 3–5; D. Osbourne (1987b), pp. 61 ff.; D. Birch (1979), pp. 74–75.

14. See A. Lyons (December 1985), pp. 4–15; R. Vaughan (1979), p. 44.

15. R Ady (1983), pp. 8–10; W. Thompson (1982), pp. 222 ff., passim. The product development cycle was probably best described by economist Joseph Schumpeter (1939, chap. 3) early in the twentieth century within his analysis of technological development as a sequential, three step process of invention, innovation, and imitation.

16. D. Birch (1979), pp. 43 ff., 137 (quoted), appendix A.

17. R. Schmenner (January 1981), pp. 3, 7; idem (1982), pp. 50–53, 179.

18. R.Vaughan (1981), p. 261.

19. M. Kieschnick (1981), p. 87; R. Schmenner (January 1981), p. 7.

Epilogue

America: A Shining City on a Hill

In framing a government which is to be administered by men over men,
the great difficulty lies in this: you must first enable the government to
control the governed; and in the next place, oblige it to control itself.

—James Madison in "Federalist #51"

As America seeks to build twenty-first-century economic governance for the
twenty-first-century "new economy," it is challenged to do so within the context of *its* special calling. The late Ronald Reagan was fond of quoting Massachusetts governor John Winthrop's poignant 1630 sermon aspiring to establish America as a "shining city on a hill." It must remain its vision still.

Gleaning the lessons of economic history—and what the convictions articulated by Reagan and the Founding Fathers posit in that quest—this inquiry's
analysis has demonstrated the critical role of profit motive in creating that
economic surplus that affords any civilization the freedom to advance.

For only when the basic requirements of physical existence have been
met can human energy be devoted to productive intellectual endeavor. It is
such profit-generated economic surplus—and the attendant quest for civic
advance—that empowers civilizations to progress.

Today, in America, that economic surplus is being eroded by costly bureaucratic excess that is not good governance. It is instead its antithesis—the
moral equivalent of running up huge bills on one's children's credit while on
a drunken binge.

Yet when the public-sector cure becomes the problem—as, in this case, it
has—still more creative decision-making paradigms are invoked until they
ultimately reach the point where, piled one upon the other to great heights and
intermixed, they come to resemble the federal government itself: a massive

bureaucratic aggregate of nonresponsive remedies mistargeted at symptoms rather than at underlying causes.

As such, there are no magic cures—for such futile attempts, in themselves, create new problems faster than they solve old ones—as the problem creation itself comes to subordinate, and eventually suffocate, any lingering hope for problem solution that may be genuine.

But this too should come as no surprise. For while the self-presumed wisdom required to manage newly created public problems grows geometrically, the knowledge needed to administer requisite solutions grows merely arithmetically. The end result, therefore, is no more than contrived, top-down micromanaged bureaucratic fiscal panaceas.

Yet isn't there a certain logic to suggest that the economy, and society itself, would be better off if America were to shed her penchant for governmental placebos—to again unfetter the "invisible hand" to let those natural free market forces that have clearly stood the test of time work their economic wonders once again?

This is a question that has repeatedly arisen throughout this inquiry's exploration of America's two-centuries-long experiment in free market democratic capitalism—seeking remedy for the nation's economically debilitating and deepening immersion into Big Brother government.

There is no excuse for such statist experimentation. For generally, it may be said that the nation's initial free market experiment has been a spectacular success—as nowhere at any time throughout history have so many benefited so abundantly from the productive output of an economic system. Indeed, unfettered democratic capitalism has functioned magnificently—validating Thoreau's appraisal that "a nation is governed best when governed least."

Reflexively, advocates of reincarnate socialism counter that paternalistic governments provide services that can't be valued in terms of profit and loss—that they must instead be measured in warm bundles of "bureaucratic compassion." Thus, the ideological confrontation is political war, but more so, it is class warfare.

Proponents of unfettered capitalism contend, in turn, that governmental dictates in themselves create, de novo, unnecessary, untoward bureaucratic economic outcomes that are inherently unequal and inefficient, while in the process stifling the innovation needed to remedy the presumed inequality.

Critical times call for creative solutions, and at critical times, creates them. It is no accident that in 1776, the challenge of America's quest for political and economic freedoms invoked the genius of the Founding Fathers. It is equally no accident that its Declaration of Independence and Adam Smith's *Wealth of Nations* both appeared in that year.

It is likely no accident either that James Watt's perfected steam engine was likewise patented in that same year. For as this inquiry has shown, personal freedoms and economic prosperity through technological progress are inexorably linked. Great times invoke great ideas—and it is the Founding Fathers' great legacy that they established the intellectual and economic milieux propitious for great ideas, both philosophical and economic, to coalesce and emerge.[1]

Their contributions are reflective of their intent. In seeking to guarantee "life, liberty, and the pursuit of happiness"—that system of natural liberty held out as an ideal by no less than Adam Smith—they established a democratic administrative exemplar that has earned at once the awe and envy of the world.

America remains blessed that two priceless principles, democratic freedom and economic freedom, came together two centuries ago to form the cornerstone of its governance. Embodied in the Bill of Rights appended to the U.S. Constitution by the Founding Fathers, they remain an integral part of its national fabric. Its system of free market capitalism is their vital offspring, and one that has provided unprecedented economic blessings. In the words of Woodrow Wilson: "The American Revolution was a beginning, not a consummation."[2]

Undeniably, the American system of governance was among the most daring experiments in democratic socioeconomic administration ever attempted by rational human beings. Indeed, it was the crucible wherein the society was shaped that became the planet's foremost workplace for economic man.

Yet today, aspirations have dimmed as the suffocating bureaucratic system that has followed in its wake has, within the past half century, become at once the antithesis of democratic government and the nemesis of democratic capitalism—as well as the single greatest threat to the survival of the Founding Fathers' remarkable vision—as everywhere, bureaucratic automatons are given carte blanche to mess within the daily lives of citizens.

Consequently, while government's ability to expand continues to increase *exponentially*, its ability to administer has increased only *linearly*. Graphically put, this is a body growing faster than its head—making it not an exaggeration to conclude that if this bureaucratic elephantiasis is not soon arrested, the American free market system may not survive its domination.

Already the prophets of doom are with us, as evidenced in the litany of schizophrenic liberal obituaries—at once gleeful, albeit conveying ominous foreboding—eulogizing the demise of capitalism that commenced in the early 1990s: a self-serving emotional outpouring again not unlike that of one who kills his parents, then pleads for mercy on the grounds that he is an orphan.

Yet such doomsday jeremiads are not new within the span of Western history—nor are apocalyptic forebodings an entirely new phenomenon. On New Years Eve in 999, the pope and the Holy Roman emperor together knelt with assembled leaders in the citadel of Rome to prayerfully await the world's end.[3]

Feelings of impending doom likewise were not uncommon as the later Middle Ages drew toward their wretched close—and the final, closing acts of the second Christian millennium a half decade ago were accompanied by similarly dismal sentiments from some. But again, this was not new.

Indeed, more than a century and a half ago, Karl Marx, commencing with publication of his *Communist Manifesto* in 1848 and culminating with the publication of his three-volume *Das Kapital* in 1867, preached in chapter 32 of the latter, "The death knell of capitalist private property sounds. The expropriators are expropriated."

Seven decades later, in 1918, Oswald Spengler unveiled his famous doomsday tome, *The Decline of the West*, heralding "the moment when money is celebrating its last victories"—and eight years later, in 1926, a youthful John Maynard Keynes penned his initial analogous economic salvos in the form of a booklet whose pessimistic title, *The End of Laissez Faire*, clearly signaled its forecast and intent.[4]

IS THERE, THEN, REASONABLE REMEDY?

The answer can be an unqualified "yes" if the nation's political leadership is willing to heed the cogent economic messages emanating from the past. For history's lessons clearly teach that societies that actively seek out free-market-driven economic progress more often reap the dividends of an enlightened and progressive civilization than those that do not.

Indeed, the present analysis has demonstrated that the very essence of civilization—and its forward march—depends directly upon that production of capital surplus generated by the pursuit of profit motive. This capital surplus then fuels the technological and cultural advance that gives life its quality, its value, and its meaning.

America's current crisis of capitalism, therefore, is not just a crisis of an economic system, but also a crisis of culture and creativity—and of the lifestyle ambience and intellectual satisfaction that derive from it—a reality axiomatic to the degree if any nation, over time, ever loses its ability to promote dynamic technological advance, its cultural progress will concomitantly stagnate.

Unfettered, the free market has been America's prime engine for economic growth—indeed, capitalism without economic growth is systemically impossible. Unleashed, it can continue to lead the way in sustaining economic well-being. Unbridled, it can resume the production of high-quality jobs for all Americans.

Today there are those who would argue that so long as the free market remains the primary means for dividing the economic resource pie—in a static zero-sum world, a bigger piece for one means a smaller piece for someone else. Yet this is utter nonsense, for the miracle of capitalism lies in its unique ability to create more "economic pie" for everyone—not in the technicalities of how to slice a finite portion.

Indeed, as eminent economist Joseph Schumpeter concluded slightly less than a century ago, "enlightened entrepreneurship," more than any other force, promotes economic advance and precludes economic stagnation. For the hidden secret of economic growth is both forthright and fundamental: creative individuals with money—in a word, entrepreneurs.

It is such entrepreneurs, as engineers of economic change, who forge the incipient dynamism of the competitive marketplace—and in so doing, activate the forces that shape societal well-being. It is entrepreneurs who make it possible to have one's cake and eat it too through the simple exercise of baking still more cake. Through them, the wealth of nations is built. Without them, all civilization would be mired in a socioeconomic swamp.

This would be the inevitable result, in fact, were there not those capital risk takers willing to commit their private resources on the promise of a fair return—were there not those willing to pay wages to working men and women before they realize their first profits.

At the bottom line, therefore, the precept of democratic capitalism is neither an oxymoron nor a tautology—but instead a unique synergy of political and economic ideologies—freeing the creativity and imagination of individuals to explore the possibilities inherent in the human process.

In so doing, it stimulates enterprise and invention while delighting irreverently in progressive change. It thrives because it at once limits the power of the state and efficiently liberates the economic energies of individuals, empowering them to realize their ambitions and potentials.[5]

Capitalism, at full flower, thus works both equitably and efficiently. It is neither economically unjust nor religiously immoral. It is, instead, humankind's most promising path to a more prosperous socioeconomic future, as civilization and private profit have historically always progressed together hand in hand.

Succinctly put, capitalism works because work bred of profit motive works—and it works well! It is no accident that Americans today are better fed, clothed, and transported than citizens of any other nation, past or present;

that U.S. social class distinctions have dramatically narrowed; that the status of U.S. minorities has improved; and that U.S. technology, science, and culture continue to grow richer exponentially.

That progress did not flow from an all-encompassing security blanket of entitlements. Instead it is a product of the initiative and drive of responsible citizens competing, cooperating, and collaborating within the free and open marketplace.

Nor is it is mere happenstance! For capitalism is at once the sustenance of the rich and the best economic hope for the aspiring, working poor. Contrast the striking parallels between capitalism and socialism within the past half century—the United States and the erstwhile Soviet Union, the two Koreas, the two Germanys, Hong Kong and Communist mainland China.

Indeed, there is no instance on the entire planet wherein socialism has outperformed capitalism—or even where it has actually succeeded and prevailed. There is a clear, defining economic difference. Capitalism requires economic expansion as a factor of its success. Socialism requires economic contraction as a factor of fostering dependency—and its survival.

This is the administrative system that liberal statists now forward for national economic salvation. Yet their would-be cure ignores one fundamental economic truth: *to get more from government, one must first give more to government*. As President Gerald Ford asserted in the opening presidential campaign debate of September 23, 1976, "the government powerful enough to give you everything you want is also powerful enough to take everything you've got."

CAN THE U.S. BRAND OF
DEMOCRATIC CAPITALISM SURVIVE?

What is the remedy? Is there indeed a cure? If so, its ultimate quest must commence by concentrating upon the Achilles' heel of the professional political process—constantly reminding would-be policy makers up for reelection that the facts of life remain largely economic and that our citizenry will accept no less than foresight and prudent stewardship in our economic leadership.

Yet if this goal is to be realized, America needs reaffirmation of that precept that has historically been the prime source of its economic greatness: that government prospers best when people prosper most—when they are permitted to keep more of their personal incomes within their wallets.

To this end, the nation needs a government dedicated to the precept of working for its people, rather than coercing its people to work for it. This means a government committed to a stewardship of doing more with less, and administered with sufficient foresight to get itself and its workings economically out of the way so that people can better help themselves. For in the last analysis, it must not be forgotten that laissez-faire means no more than "leave us alone!"

Accordingly, the federal government generally makes its greatest contributions to solving the nation's most pressing economic problems by reducing its own economic role, on both the tax and spending sides of the budgetary equation, and by cutting back on that regulatory excess whose oversight renders inordinate private compliance and public administrative expenditures necessary.

But voluntarily, of course, that will never happen, given the bureaucratic incentives for governmental expansion and the disincentives for contraction detailed throughout this inquiry. If government is to be effectively put back in its cage, therefore, the necessary coercion must perforce come from a compelling exogenous force.

To this end, to succeed, those seeking to reduce the size of government will need both the political power of moral suasion and ready recourse to the persuasive power of popular coercion, as well as a strategic vision—an action agenda to make it happen, thereby empowering the private sector's ability to prosper.

But how does one get from here to there? Ronald Reagan was fond of saying that economists are people who see things working in practice and then spend their whole careers experimenting to see if they would work in theory.

America's new free market plan must be more precisely focused. For every policy target, there must be a policy tool, as without a blueprint, government can be compelled neither to be more efficient nor to balance its accounts. If it is to do better in fiscal practice, therefore, it must first do better in financial theory.

For just as success in private-sector competitive survival requires a strategic course of action, so American government needs a new business plan that details in explicit terms a more professional approach to economic policy—in its proceeding, cognizant of the cogent words of Theodore Roosevelt that "[i]t is not what we have that will make us a great nation, it is the way in which we use it."[6]

THE CONTINUING NEED FOR THE
"ECONOMIC VISION THING"

Such a quest, though challenging, can again productively commence by searching for answers within the faith-endowed socioeconomic legacy left by Ronald Reagan. His vision was one of optimism imbued with confidence. In restoring respectability to economic governance, he built upon an abiding belief not only in the divine but in his vision for the American people—and in so doing, created a decade of prosperity for the nation.

Throughout its history, America's leaders have entertained great visions. In 1961, moved by his perception of a mounting U.S. technological gap vis-à-vis the Soviet Union, President John F. Kennedy mounted a massive—and ultimately successful—educational campaign designed to restore the nation's traditional industrial strengths.

His goal culminated in his vision to place a man on the moon within the 1960s—a dream posthumously fulfilled on July 20, 1969. His initiative precipitated the greatest peacetime mobilization of resources ever undertaken— as the Apollo Project took ten years to implement and ultimately wound up costing the nation more than $25 billion! But for an entire generation, America's technological preeminence and economic prosperity were restored.[7]

Yet well over a century and a half before, in January 1803, President Thomas Jefferson entertained a similar vision—asking Congress for the then considerable sum of $2,500 for an expedition west of the Mississippi River "for the purpose of extending the foreign commerce of the United States." Like Kennedy's dreams of space conquest, Jefferson's ends were equally noble and futuristic, culminating in the successful westward expedition of Meriwether Lewis and William Clark in 1805.[8]

Magnificent achievements both—but could either of these, America's two boldest expeditions of discovery, have ever occurred without the committed, dedicated, determined leadership and the transcendent vision of a Thomas Jefferson or a John Kennedy?

They dared to dream, knowing full well that while those who dare to dare may sometimes fail, those who don't—or won't—invariably do. Success favors those who dream and dare. Christopher Columbus did not succeed because he was lucky; he did so because he had a vision—because he elected to go in a direction where no one had ever sailed before. To paraphrase that famed line from *South Pacific*, "If you don't have a dream, how can you make that dream come true?"

To this end, America's leaders must themselves be more economically prospective—focusing upon the future because that is where everyone will be. Few deny that the nation's job-generating private sector is in trouble today, dragged down by the mushrooming fiscal deadweight of its public-sector counterpart. Yet to date, there has been no master plan to redress this imbalance—a circumstance reminiscent of the stoic philosopher Seneca's assessment of his imperial Rome at the time of Christ: "Our plans miscarry because they have no aim. When a man knows not what harbor he is heading for, no wind is the right wind."

Throughout history, the Alexanders, Caesars, Napoleons, Jeffersons, Roosevelts, and Kennedys all led from conviction. They were willing to lead because the cause was just, even if the timing wasn't propitious. Indeed, John Kennedy's *Profiles in Courage*, written in the 1950s, was penned as a compendium standing in documentary tribute to the consummate success of such courage of conviction in the face of overwhelming odds.

Today, the political stage has dramatically shifted—with the defining difference that too many national leaders have abdicated their positions of leadership to their partisan managers and nightly tracking polls. They have gotten too smart by half in their quest to manipulate the masses—in substituting form for substance.

They are no longer driven by conviction or ideology, but instead by media marketability. This helps to explain why, while they may be flourishing politically, the nation is weakening economically. For the bottom line is that enlightened leadership, tied to strong economic principles and moral values, invokes a vibrant economy—yet the converse is true as well.

Today, the American spirit is dimming—waning in the face of an evolving crisis in economic stewardship. Where is the Ronald Reagan of the 1980s, whose defining vision of "Morning in America"—a "shining city on a hill"—singularly pulled the nation up from the deepening morass of late-1970s stagflation?

Where is the John Kennedy of the 1960s, whose vision of a new frontier led to the Apollo Project—a lofty cause that, not coincidentally, culminated two decades later in Ronald Reagan's Strategic Defense Initiative, which hastened the demise of the Soviet Union—and rallied the nation behind a technological crusade that fortified the foundations for building the American Century? Unfortunately, today the Apollo Project would probably never happen: Kennedy's advisers would tell him that there was too much political downside risk.[9]

Where are the Jeffersons and Madisons and Churchills of the new millennium? Where are those leaders willing to first identify, and then take on, tough economic challenges? Let it not be forgotten that Winston Churchill's famed Battle of Dunkirk speech—"We shall defend our island whatever the cost may be. We shall fight on the beaches; we shall fight on the landing ground; we shall fight in the fields and on the streets; we shall fight in the hills; we shall never surrender"—was prefaced with the somber appraisal: "The news from France is very bad."

America finds itself today where Great Britain was at the onset of the twentieth century. After a hundred years of nearly unchallenged economic superiority, it confronts a world of mounting economic competition. The question therefore becomes: Will the United States be equal to the challenge in the *twenty-first* century, or will it follow Britain into industrial decline?

Will future historians record that U.S. policy makers were, at the onset of the twenty-first century, wise enough to identify, and then remedy, emerging economic policy shortcomings, or will they record that the turn of the third millennium also signaled the eclipse of the American Century?

A RETURN TO AMERICA'S HISTORIC ECONOMIC VALUES

"There is a tide in the affairs of men," Shakespeare's Brutus said, "that taken at the flood, leads on to fortune." The United States today stands at that tectonic watershed—facing the defining choice, through tax and regulation reduction, to restore its political and economic freedoms, or to continue on its present slippery slide down the steep slope to statist subjugation. The outcome will determine whether the twenty-first century will again be the American Century—a seismic turning point—the defining difference between a belle epoque and a fin de siècle.

If America truly seeks a new world order that reflects its traditional values and principles, then the place to begin is within the markets and the workplaces of its own economy. "Fix America first" may be a dangerous and shopworn slogan, but in the light of today's evolving economic realities, it is not altogether wrong. For as in post–World War II, it, as a nation, is summoned once again to global economic leadership—and it owes equally to its citizens, to the world, and to posterity to be equal to the challenge.

But while time remains, it is finite—and the nation must act now. There is a Prussian parable that holds:

For want of a nail, a shoe was lost;
For want of a shoe, a horse was lost;
For want of a horse, a rider was lost;
For want of a rider, a battle was lost;
For want of a battle, a kingdom was lost;
And all for the want of a horseshoe nail.[10]

Hence, America's shining beacon to the world, the American Dream, must now more than ever be aggressively pursued and preserved. In this quest, the nation's opportunities remain as vast as its vision will allow. It is limited only by the daring of its dreams, the reality of its resolve, and the power of its purpose. It is, after all, the fulfillment of Ronald Reagan's noble vision: It is the United States of America.

Fully mindful, therefore, of the twentieth-century multinational moral philosopher George Santayana's admonition that those who fail to remember history are condemned to repeat it—the nation must proceed decisively, heed-ing equally the cogent lessons of economic history. Thus, for those who seek "the ability to change that which can be changed; the patience to accept that which cannot; and the ability to discern between the two"—there is the countervailing counsel attributed to the eighteenth-century British parliamentarian-philosopher Edmund Burke that "all that is necessary for the triumph of evil is for good men to do nothing"!

NOTES

1. Indeed, his was a fulfillment in an unbroken string of successes in the progression of technology. Leonardo da Vinci, cited in chapter 2, had many wonderful conceptual inventions, but none could be built without a source of propellant power that was beyond his imagination. The steam engine was his "missing link"—and today the industrial captains of capitalism continue to produce the power-generating technologies that issue from James Watts's invention of the steam engine in 1776. (On this, see L. Thurow [1996], pp. 10, 279.)

2. W. Wilson, cited in L. Peter (1977), p. 49; W. Simon (1978), pp. 19 ff.

3. B. Goudzwaard (1979), p. xiv.

4. K. Marx (1929), vol. 1, chap. 2; O. Spengler (1926), p. 507; M. Novak (1996), p. 80.

5. M. Novak (1982), pp. 14, 72, 79.

6. B. Rogge (1979), p. 287; P. Peterson (1993), p. 29.

7. W. Cook (July 11, 1994), p. 54.

8. D. Boorstin (July 11, 1994), p. 61.

9. J. Wanniski (1989), p. 13.

10. Cited in L. Thurow (1996), pp. 292–93.

Appendix

The American Competitiveness Agenda: Preparing for the Post–Information Age

> We cannot have symphonies unless we first build factories. We cannot support poets unless we first have machine tool operators. And for every teacher within our schools, there must be dozens of laborers, farmers, and managers working to create that economic surplus that first makes it possible to construct and maintain our schools.
>
> —Fletcher Byrom in *Corporate Policy Applied to a Finite World*

This inquiry has explored two millennia of economic history in its quest to discern the impacts of bureaucratic excess—in the forms of direct taxation and indirect taxation, or regulation—on the rise and fall of nation states. Based upon governing convictions articulated by the Founding Fathers and Ronald Reagan and the economic remedy prescribed in textbox A.1, twenty principal recommendations—divided equally between administrative and institutional reforms—are advanced below.

A.1. A Free Market Formula for Building Prosperity

PRODUCTION	−	TAXATION & REGULATION	+	EDUCATION & RESEARCH	=	PRODUCTIVITY, COMPETITIVENESS, & GLOBAL MARKET PROSPERITY

FINANCIAL AND REGULATORY REFORMS

Reduce Bureaucratic Inefficiencies through Budget Balancing[1]

Bureaucratic costs can, of course, be significantly reduced through judicious admixtures of more effective management with more relevant public-sector work incentives. But even in the best-case scenario produced by such an approach, the results achieved would be spread unevenly across the span of public agencies.

The goal could be reached equally effectively, on the other hand, by simply forcing government to live within its means, and then letting the bureaucrats themselves blend the proper mixture of management controls and bureaucratic incentives needed to survive and function efficiently.

Foremost among such options could include a constitutionally mandated federal balanced budget, with exceptions allowed only in time of war or other carefully circumscribed dire public emergency. In this process, increases in discretionary spending could be limited to inflation's annual rate of growth, and entitlement spending to the annual rate of population growth.

The case for such a drastic measure directly targeting governmental right-sizing has been made and needs no lengthy repeat discourse. America's present fiscal problems are caused not because it taxes too little but because it spends too much—because governmental spending continues to grow faster than the national income required to sustain it.

Yet the resulting deficits, unfortunately, merely pay for today's profligate spending by mandating tomorrow's tax increases—in the process, handcuffing government's ability to meet the needs of *future* generations because of the long-term fiscal overburden caused by *present* public spending.[2]

As a result of an absence of effective constraints within this spiraling appropriations process, then, governmental spending in recent decades has now cascaded into a raging torrent fed by a multitude of revenue tributaries funded by private sector tax levies. Indeed, the recent evolution of the term "tax expenditure" in American fiscal vernacular in itself suggests a governmental presumption that it owns all of the nation's money and that any portion that may remain with the taxpayer does so only at its sufferance.

Yet even that residual portion is gradually diminishing. For once incorporated into governmental budgets, public-sector spending programs seldom, if ever, end. Most often, as the failure of governmental fiscal reform efforts demonstrates time and again, they continue to be a financial drain upon the tax base regardless of whether their original objective is ultimately achieved.

Hence, in good times and in bad, in periods of recovery and recession, government expenditure goes only in one direction—up! Yet this spending spiral invariably invokes even higher taxes, and higher taxes mean less take-home pay for citizens. The process is self-generating. Because government spends more, taxpayers come to have less of their own revenues for personal priorities—and in a tragic cycle, still more people become still more dependent upon government, triggering the need for even more public-sector spending.

By compelling the federal government to live within its means, on the other hand, citizens are merely requiring it to do what every single American family must do to survive. They are asking elected officials who would call themselves responsible public servants to direct their focus to the ultimate bottom line: the national balance sheet.

This is no radically new approach. Indeed, it is no more than an endorsement of the populist precept that working men and women should not be asked to do more for government until government learns to do more with what it already has. For a budget-balancing amendment is no less than a social contract between a nation's leaders and its people—a pledge by the governors to the governed that as servants of the people, they will be as committed to the goal of financial responsibility as the laws that they pass require their constituents to be.

There are limits to growth. The country is today constrained by finite fiscal resources. At the same time, if the public goal is to produce innovation, productivity, better outcomes at lower costs, and more entrepreneurial bureaucratic management, balanced budgets effectively build the requisite compelling pressures. To these ends, then, the budgetary process must now be inverted, as bottom-up budgeting no longer works.

As the preceding analysis makes clear, the nation's emerging fiscal crisis has produced a situation where it can no longer afford to say, "This is the problem," address it—and then worry later about how it will get the money to pay for it. Clear limits must be set at the top of the fiscal pyramid while forcing its underlying layers to live within the resulting resource base.

Restrict Federal Spending to a Constant 20 Percent Share of GDP

Spending limitation is a natural complement to budget balancing, providing safeguards that preserve the goal of federal fiscal responsibility. This too is a critical imperative. For in addressing the question, Which is preferable—a $2 trillion budget with a $500 billon deficit or a $2.5 trillion dollar balanced budget with 25 percent higher taxes?—the answer is "neither" if economic prosperity through fiscal sanity is to prevail.[3]

The concept's critics invariably contend that both spending limitation and a balanced budget requirement frustrate the process of representative government—and raise the cogent question: Isn't this what we elect our legislators to do? But the reality lies in the corresponding question: Are they doing it today? That answer is clearly "no."

Conversely, when it is argued that mandatory limits to the ability to spend are required, such a representation is not a denial of the workings of democratic process but merely a call for a judicious separation of the power to tax from the power to spend for which there is strong historic precedent. Britain's thirteenth-century Magna Carta—generally hailed as a foundation of democratic enlightenment—did precisely that. The executive branch, the king, could spend but could not tax. The legislative branch, Parliament, as representatives of the people, could tax but could not spend.[4]

This separation of official functions thereafter became the cornerstone for successful economic governance and remains a valid prototype to the present day. For within this delimited process, legislators still retain their basic rights to conceptualize and legislate. But they are now compelled to do it more judiciously, being mindful of resource constraints. To this extent, then, mandated fiscal restraint is no less than a reaffirmation of the time-tested precept of responsible representative government: There is your budget; now manage it in the most effective way![5]

This thus becomes a monumentally progressive step to the extent that if government is ultimately to be compelled to live within its means, its ability to grow must be constrained to its capability to grow its underlying sustaining economy. Indeed, historically, precise de facto ratios have evolved to divide resources between those in public service and those whom they purport to serve. Within the United States, for instance, federal spending predicated upon government's capital take from the economy for most of the past half century has hovered around the 20 percent of GDP level.

In recent decades, it has at times crept well above this 20 percent Plimsoll mark to in excess of 23 percent. Yet history's lessons make clear that such upward drift must end if prosperity is to issue from the private sector. Firm spending ceilings must be established to explicitly fix the relationship of public consumption to private production before the rapacious appetite of government ingests still more intolerable levels of productive private enterprise.

The case for such a revolutionary policy course is at once both compelling and simple. Relative shares of GDP are firmly fixed so that both the public and private sectors are guaranteed proportional allocations of national productive output. By thus linking public spending to private production, the close connection between industrial economic growth and government's capacity to distribute benefits is concurrently underscored.

Directly tying public spending to GDP growth could, in fact, compel elected leaders to at last concede that there is no real relationship between the *quantity* of tax dollars spent and the *quality* of public services received. This is a recognition—as the escalation of the federal budget in recent decades and the corresponding attenuation of real economic growth that has attended it make clear—that the long prevailing faith in unlimited public funds must be brought to a definitive end.

Create a Federal "Rainy Day" Trust

A budget-balancing constitutional amendment fixing federal outlays as a share of GDP could concurrently stipulate that all revenues received in excess of the threshold ceiling be consigned to a federal economic stabilization trust.

Such a fund could initially be structured to serve as a fiscal restoration fund—with its proceeds dedicated to reducing the federal debt—and, once eliminated, retooled as a "rainy day" fund forcing government to save in economic upturns for less buoyant economic times. If such an approach sounds not radical but rather rational, that is because it is really no more than what modern heads of household who aspire to be financially prudent now do in their private lives.

The preceding analysis has made clear that economic growth through fiscal responsibility is a national challenge invoking federal solutions. Thus there is no better place to start than within the U.S. government itself. To this end, creation of a federal "rainy day" fund would allow for countercyclical budgeting in times of economic downturn without raising taxes— using financial surpluses built up in good times to offset deficits incurred in bad times.

At the same time, this approach decisively rejects the conventional wisdom oft held by those in government that the solution to recession is to remove capital from the productive private sector, in the form of tax increases, to underwrite the costs of pasting of remedial legislative Band-Aids over perceived critical economic wounds. On the contrary, it moderates the rate of taxation while preserving essential services—thereby restoring revenue-producing income growth to private industry.

Provide Sunset Clauses for All New Programs

General Hugh Johnson once observed, "the nearest thing to immortality in this world is a governmental bureau!" Yet were the promulgation of new bureaucratic programs to be accompanied by the devolution of old ones—if that vital "creative destruction," breaking down the old to make way for the new, that takes place in the free market also worked within the halls of government—its present problems of inefficiency and obsolescence would not now be so self-compounding. Today, such is not the case, as bureaucratic dinosaurs remain very much alive and well, openly roaming streets and alleys within Washington's Beltway, foraging upon economically sustaining private productivity and profits.

Incorporating sunset provisions into every newly created program that requires substantial recurring commitments of federal funds—thereby mandatorily subjecting their performance to periodic review—would effectively attack this Jurassic anomaly. For under this approach, public programs that do not produce demonstrably cost-effective reviews would be scrutinized on an ongoing basis to ascertain their continuing merit.[6]

There is a compelling argument to be made, in fact, that only through incorporating sunset clauses in the enabling legislation of all future major revenue-consuming programs can the nation be assured of the comprehensive public oversight required to ensure they remain cost-effective. Today, the nation's leadership unfortunately only sunsets economically regenerating productive federal tax cuts. Why not more providently sunset federal spending instead?

Require Privatization Impact Statements for New Federal Programs

Together with oversight reforms for existing bureaucratic programs, prudent public policy oversight simultaneously mandates that major recurring executive program or policy initiatives under legislative consideration for implementation or renewal be accompanied by privatization impact statements. These statements should require that their proponent public agencies justify why they can perform what they propose in more cost-effective ways than can the private sector, while employing the same types of stringent cost-benefit analyses that all private firms must undertake to compete and survive.

Such statements could be generated by the proponent agency advocating the new program or policy and be made publicly available on a widespread basis prior to their consideration by the primary committee evaluating it in the congressional house of origin, thereby enabling private firms and citizens alike to readily ascertain their capability to bid out the proposed public-sector initiative into the private sector.

Ascertain the True Costs of Governmental Functions

Accurately determining the public-sector costs of services delivery is critical to any decision to proceed with privatization. This goal can best be accomplished by a shift in federal accounting procedures from fund accounting to financial accounting practices. The distinction is not semantic but instead is operationally critical. For fund accounting identifies only the direct costs of governmental services delivery. It does not quantify such indirect inputs as capital costs, administrative overhead, and employee fringe benefits—factors that can make actual operational costs as much as 30 percent greater than budgeted costs.[7]

Financial accounting differs from fund accounting in quantifying these hidden liabilities in that, in addition to line item budgetary expenditures, it also calculates a program's indirect costs, opportunity costs, and privatization conversion costs. A shift to this more comprehensive "total cost" accounting system—using standardized accounting practices—would thus provide the requisite data needed to enable federal privatization to proceed more intelligently. For in employing it, public policy makers and private-sector vendors alike would be able to optimally gauge the cost tradeoffs of privatization initiatives as they are proposed, deliberated, and bid.

Establish Public Competition as a Market-Driven Process

In establishing market-driven federal privatization, the Governmental Restructuring Implementation Committee approach introduced by the provincial government of British Columbia also merits careful contemplation. Pursuant to it, the committee formally entertains private-sector bids to perform select public-sector functions in a six-step process of bid submission and evaluation.

Should a similar system be contemplated in America, once the full costs of public programs have been established through the reformed governmental accounting practices recommended above, a Joint Congressional Committee on Governmental Restructuring could be created parallel to, and in tandem with, the respective congressional budget committees. This new committee would exist not to create more federal bureaucracy, but rather to reduce it by engaging in extensive, ongoing budgetary review to identify appropriate program candidates for privatization.

Its overarching fiscal mission, however, would be to solicit, receive, and evaluate proposals from private firms to directly bid out specific functions of the federal budget now being performed by public agencies. Were a private firm convinced that it could better administer the country's parks than the National Park Service, for instance, it would be permitted, and indeed encouraged, to submit a bid.

If, in turn, the bid were to be favorably evaluated, the function's parent governmental agency would be given a prescribed limited period to justify why it should continue as a public function. Should it fail to do so to the committee's satisfaction, the latter could recommend to its parallel congressional budget committees that the activity be privatized.

Implementation of this approach would thus constitute a revolutionary budgetary advance. For in effect, government would be reinvented by retooling Congress, allowing for the workings of competitive market processes in the provision of public services. In the process, the same market efficiencies that now endow America with the highest living standards in the world would be made universally available to its citizens in the provision of public services.

Use ESOPs to Promote Public Competition

To further expand venues and opportunities for privatization, financial and tax incentives to promote the formation of privatized employee stock ownership programs (ESOPs) would likewise play a constructive role in encouraging public employees to bid out their current missions as private-sector activities.

This approach recognizes that the nation's economic interests are not best served if the cost savings from privatization are consumed by corresponding increased public assistance payments required to sustain erstwhile public-sector employees displaced by the privatization transfer—as there is no positive public policy goal achieved in a zero-sum exchange whereby unemployment is merely displaced from the private sector to the public sector.

ESOP incentives targeted to rational privatization initiatives can readily resolve this problem. For by altering the nature of the incentives offered to public employees, the present bureaucratic impediments to greater productivity cited in chapter 3 are broken through profit motivation induced by free market means.

At the same time, public employee unions should be afforded full opportunity as well to bid in quantitative and qualitative improvements to their members' on-the-job performances if they wish to maintain them as public-sector functions and thereby forestall their privatization. Through such competitive means, therefore, privatization can be institutionalized as a more vibrant, across-the-board, no-holds-barred, open-market competitive bidding process.

Reform the Federal Regulations Promulgation Process

Institutionalize Regulatory Budgeting in the Policy Formulation Process

To lend concentrated focus to the cost of public regulation, mandatory promulgation of an annual Federal Regulatory Budget should be made a policy priority. Pursuant to it, to empower more effective congressional oversight, the executive branch would each year be required to develop in significant detail accurate estimates of the private regulatory costs imposed by the full operational spectrum of agencies and programs over which it presides.

Each year, in turn, Congress would be statutorily required to formally approve the Federal Regulatory Budget, making such adjustments as it prudently deems necessary. By making explicit the costs of the federal regulatory burden, then, this process would enable direct crosschecks between the administrative costs officially sanctioned by government and those actually run up by executive agencies in pursuit of their statutory mandates.

It would concurrently mandate legislative—as well as proponent agency—approval of compliance costs; in so doing, making possible a regulatory report card by specific agency and program that would constitute a critical first step toward fiscal remedy by forcing bureaucratic and political officials alike to directly confront the market costs of the regulations they impose.

Provide for Detailed Cost-Benefit Analyses for Each New Rule Proposed

In 1995 Congress directed the Office of Management and Budget to assess the economic impact of all federal regulations. A concurrent measure, Executive Order 12866, required federal agencies to analyze the effects of proposed rules economically significant to the degree that they impose private-sector costs exceeding $100 million.

But such initiatives, however laudatory, have subsequently proven to be subjective in their focus and clearly do not go far enough. To quote economist Richard Rahn, "Too few governmental regulations are today subjected to rigorous cost-benefit tests. Many governmental agencies do not take the requirement seriously, act in good faith, or even present accurate data. For regulators have a strong incentive to underestimate the true costs of their regulations."[8]

The reality that each year's new traunch of federal regulations costs the economy another $50 billion or more to the federal budget clearly mandates a new oversight assessment approach—one requiring that all regulations subject to congressional oversight be accompanied by objective cost-benefit analyses standardized across federal agencies in formats that provide both direct and contextual information, and in so doing, monetize the values of *effects*, as well assess the costs, of each promulgation proposed, thereby forecasting net benefits over time.

Such analyses should then become the basis for congressional determination of whether any given federal rule or regulation has produced sufficient public benefit as to justify its continuance over time. In making the agency cost-benefit review more discerning, the nation's regulatory report card can ensure that the unwarranted growth of the regulatory state is taken seriously by enabling better federal policy decision making based on superior information.

Make the Regulatory Approvals Process Elective Rather than Rejective

Submitting administrative rules approval directly to congressional jurisdiction and explicit approval would likewise make a material contribution to restoring proper oversight in rules promulgation. Pursuant to such a hands-on oversight approach, each congressional committee could be made explicitly responsible for those rules promulgated by the federal agencies subject to its jurisdiction and required to endorse each rule by record roll call vote ninety days prior to its proposed effective date.

In effect, then, this approach would compel Congress to approve those follow-on policy mechanisms implemented to enforce the laws that they pass, in addition to the laws themselves. By mandating that all new regulations be explicitly endorsed, rather than merely tacitly accepted, by congressional committees, this promulgation reform would effectively regulate the regulators by requiring greater managerial oversight on the part of America's elected officials.

In short, holding Congress accountable for the consequences of regulation to the same extent that it now is for creating and appropriating for programs that it implements can head off spending excess, as requiring express approval of proposed regulations would ensure that lawmakers bear direct responsibility to voters for each operating component of the bills that they pass as well as for their newly-levied regulatory costs.

Provide Sunset Clauses for All New Regulations

Just as for recurring federal programs, in addition to promulgations reform, sunset clauses prescribing fixed date terminations for each new federal rule enacted can also ensure focused periodic, circumspect consideration of regulatory policies. For only through systematic chronogically-mandated review can prudent stewardship provide that rules continue to serve the public good for which they were originally intended.

Recourse to this sunset clause approach introduces two highly salutary effects into the public policy-making system. First, it requires elected officials to periodically validate whether past regulations remain valid. Second, it creates a deliberate natural policy inertia—for by requiring bureaucracies to rectify past follies, it reduces their time available to create new ones.

Create In-House Government Efficiency Task Forces

Producing tax savings through governmental efficiency is a systemic process that must be both compelled from without and impelled from within. An optimal internal approach could come in the form of an executive order establishing permanent oversight task forces within each federal agency to annually examine each operational function of the department's activities to ascertain which regulatory processes or bureaucratic practices can be modified to establish more economically responsible and fiscally sound government oversight.

To ensure that such review activities are a constant, ongoing process, these task forces could be also mandated to annually report their findings to the president, Congress, and the Government Accountability Office. Their reports could simultaneously be statutorily made public to any citizen seeking to ascertain how wisely tax dollars are being spent on a program-by-program basis. Incentives to do better would thus be systemically induced by the focus of the public spotlight.

Reform the Federal Regulations Administration Process

Promote, Not Penalize, Collaboration in Regulatory Compliance

As modern industrial society becomes more complex, the futility and deleterious impact of antitrust legislation upon trade competitiveness becomes concomitantly apparent. There are several reasons for this reality. First, with the rise of a global economy, local market share is no longer a principal determinant of whether a monopolistic practice poses a potential hazard to the domestic economy—or indeed whether a firm has acquired a monopolistic position within the broader world environment.

Second, in like manner, in this global economy, if a domestic conglomerate is broken up, a foreign conglomerate can readily move in to fill resulting market voids. In such an instance, then, what is actually accomplished by breaking up carefully constructed vertically integrated operating efficiencies of America's large oil, auto, aircraft, or telecommunications industries?

Indeed, experience reveals that such enforcement actions merely compel enterprising firms within such industries to diversify as *horizontal* conglomerates, pursuing lines of business they may initially know very little about— a factor that unfortunately inadvertently contributes to a vitiation of U.S. workplace productivity. In such a situation, then, the real victims are domestic workers in Connecticut and California, while *keiretsu* in Japan marvel at, and move in to profit from, this monumental tribute to economically bereft sanctimonious self-righteousness.[9]

Finally, antitrust laws, as currently structured, are hopelessly myopic in that they protect only against price. Quantitative rather than qualitative in their focus, they ignore such aesthetic qualities as workmanship and lifestyle ambience. Who would want to cross the ocean on a commercial aircraft purchased on the basis of cost consideration alone? Indeed, the evolving global marketplace invokes the need for greater private-sector collaborative research and development, not less.[10]

In a number of instances, this phenomenon is already occurring. With the passage of the Cooperative Research Act of 1984, for instance, many multi-lateral R&D ventures have been launched. Another encouraging example of much needed public-private collaboration is the waiving of antitrust provisions to allow Big Three automakers to join with the Department of Commerce, the Department of Energy, and other federal agencies in the development of pollution-free, technologically advanced, futuristic automobiles.[11]

These are positive developments. For in a competitive marketplace, it is sufficient that antitrust laws safeguard against sheer predatory pricing and price-fixing cartels. All other forms of collaborative industrial endeavor in the quest for better-quality, lower-cost products can only serve the common good within the operational contexts of the free market process.[12]

Establish Market-Driven Ends, Not Bureaucracy-Driven Means

The selective use of general market incentives, rather than punitive disincentives, also can ensure more uniform compliance with specific, predetermined regulatory standards. Indeed, it is becoming increasingly evident that the best way to regulate economic activity is to impose financial charges for noncompliance rather than impose rigid rules for operation across a broad range of industrial sectors.

Among them, protection of precious natural resources is one of the most expensive, yet vital, responsibilities of federal regulation—as today, enforcing environmental rules costs America's economy more than $1 trillion annually. Here, an expanded use of incentives rather than disincentives could ensure more uniform compliance.

Increasing numbers of market microeconomists and production experts, in fact, are reaching the conclusion that the best way to regulate business operational activity is to establish goals and impose financial charges for remediation, rather than merely enforcing intractable rules for prevention whose oversight incurs high transaction costs.

Accordingly, this goals-driven regulatory approach could, for example, offer rational capitalistic incentives to diminish engagement in polluting activities—with sufficient revenues provided for environmental remediation, if necessary—and with costs of cleanup levied directly upon, and proportionate to, the most prodigious uses of ecologically damaging materials.

Use of this compensatory regulatory technique—creating fixed opportunity costs to pollute—therefore, would be wholly market based, offering positive feedback for voluntary compliance without spending public-private resources on expensive environmental verification processes.

In compelling producers to face up to the costs of pollution, it simultaneously allows them decide how best to respond. At the same time, it offers distinct rewards for pollution reduction. For here, the parties involved are forced to confront the economic consequences of their actions—a needed safeguard deeply embedded within both the opportunity cost approach to environmental regulation and the lessons of economic history.

Creating such regulatory opportunity costs rather than detailed oversight and enforcement procedures is, of course, not a new technique. Indeed, in an extreme, albeit undeniably effective, early application, famed eighteenth-century BC Babylonian lawgiver Hammurabi promulgated a simple, albeit attention-getting, building code for contractors: "Should a building that you erected collapse, killing people, you will be executed—and should the owner's son be killed, your son will be executed!"

This is a superb example of how a rule should read—set goals and offer compliance incentives, but don't micromanage the compliance process!

INSTITUTIONAL AND EDUCATIONAL REFORMS

Developing a Long-Term National Savings and Investment Agenda

As the preceding analysis suggests, inadequate private investment can be, and usually is, a major long-term factor in forging any nation's structural productivity, and ultimately its economic challenges. Indeed, more than any other major industrial country, America has a special reason to be concerned about its national savings rate. A century ago, it was the highest in the developed world—and was an abiding source of economic strength. A half century ago, it was about in the middle—but today, it endures the lowest savings rate.[13]

This is a factor that can readily be addressed by restructuring the levies now imposed upon capital investment. The argument is frequently made that if America is to invest more, Americans are first going to have to save more. Yet such a generic assessment is only partially correct—primarily representing a failure to properly distinguish between middle-class savers and institutional and high-net-worth investors.

The nation's present much lamented savings enigma is less a genuine savings crisis than it is a significant capital disequilibrium in that America's middle-class individual savings are currently not predominantly structured as individual accounts but rather as collective savings—Social Security accounts and private pensions—that actually discourage other forms of private savings. Indeed, some estimates are that they now suppress the national savings rate by as much as 40 percent, reducing the GDP growth by about 5 percent, or $500 billion, each year.[14]

Given the reality that global technology-based competitive advantage issues directly from productivity-enhancing capital investments, the key public policy issue thus becomes: How can their substantial collective portfolios best be channeled into job-creating equities that optimally serve the national economic good? For if greater investment—made possible by mobilizing and repackaging the capital surplus assets of the affluent and institutions—is to now take place, the financial incentives structures that govern current savings and investments processes must be substantially reworked.

Why? Because the U.S. tax code today penalizes equity investments more severely than that of any other principal American international trade competitor. Other major countries structure their tax codes to favor increased savings and investment, but the United States's code discourages savings and investments by taxing corporate profits twice. Other nations promote savings and investment by discouraging consumptive household borrowing. In America, household borrowing is encouraged through full tax deductibility while dividend income, at the same time, is double-taxed! This is a prime reason why America is a "borrow and buy" nation, while its principal trade competitors, particularly those in East Asia, are "save and produce" ones.

Other principal trade competitors also discourage short-term market manipulation; yet today, it is the quintessence of the huckster's American Dream. As a consequence, when deductibles and other levy offsets are factored into aggregate tax burden, studies continue to find the United States having historically endured among both the highest capital gains tax rates and the lowest investment and savings rates among the world's major industrial nations.[15]

In short, the U.S. tax structure is today upside down, for in its arcane approach of punishing equity while favoring debt, it trades short-term consumptive advantage for long-term economic stasis.[16]

The lessons of the 1991 Bush-Democratic tax increase and the 1981 Reagan tax cut remain reciprocally clear. Whenever taxes are raised, the economic surpluses of prudent investors are generally not increased but merely rearranged—either recommitted abroad, or alternately diverted to tax shelters or similarly less taxable noneconomic uses.

Whenever such taxes are decreased, on the other hand, the examples of economic history demonstrate that investment capital literally comes out of the woodwork to be put to work in the kinds of productive equity that build a national economy, making the quest to favorably enhance the overall public tax climate a foremost policy priority.

What can be done to "right-side" the existing U.S. tax structure—to bring economic surplus back into more productive use? Perhaps the most powerful tools for raising the rate of sustained industrial investment are incentives that afford more favorable capital gains treatment to those willing to make long-term investment commitments of perhaps five to ten years in duration, thereby rewarding patient investors.

Under this restructured approach, capital gains taxes could be made inversely more regressive as a function of time—impacting substantially higher on short-term stockholdings—while progressively diminishing to the extent that the holdings are held longer term.[17]

New investment tax incentives could also be created, perhaps in the form of partial tax credits, for capital gains realized through the long-term purchases of corporate stock equity. Such credits could be offered to pension funds and other institutional investors as well as to new individual investors who have no immediate compelling reasons to engage in rapid retrading.

Simultaneously, continuing to reduce marginal capital gains tax rates could offer an even more powerful inducement to invest—and at no real cost to the public treasury. For there is compelling evidence that suggests that throughout history, whenever the maximum statutory rate is reduced—as it was from 35 percent to 28 percent in 1978 and then to just 20 percent in 1981 and 15 percent in 2003—the lowest marginal rate since the 1930s Great Depression—the aggregate yields of capital gains taxes paid have actually increased without fail.[18]

The reason: capital gains taxation is an institutional drag upon any economy. Recent studies show, moreover, that it regressively impacts most heavily upon workers and consumers. To the extent that its effect is minimized, therefore, the principal objective of long-term capital investment—and hence the nation's revenue-producing economic vitality—are enhanced.

The economic impact of the remedy proposed would be monumental—as today, America has moved from being an employee society to being an ownership society. More than 70 percent of all citizens now own stock and more than a quarter of all U.S. federal income tax returns—more than 35 million—annually report dividend income. Yet of this number, more than 60 percent have combined wage and salary earnings of less than $50,000 annually. Thus, were the dividend taxation approaches recommended now implemented, a new form of populist capitalism would more rapidly evolve and spread throughout America.[19]

Ensuring Ample Capital Access for Modernizing Businesses

Inadequate access to fixed plant investment capital today too often continues to inhibit the twenty-first-century refurbishing of many U.S. businesses, thereby limiting their abilities to provide jobs and innovation to the economy.

For America's private sector confronts significant obstacles and constraints in acquiring capital, many of which result from governmental tax and regulatory policies.

At the federal level, for instance, shifting taxation policies have frequently seriously diminished the availabilities of both venture and expansion capital. Current Securities and Exchange Commission (SEC) regulations, by increasing transaction costs, have likewise made capital markets inaccessible to many firms requiring sums of less than $10 million.

Hence, while such policies and regulations may serve valid public purposes, they can concurrently create market imperfections that severely limit the access of growth-oriented firms to private-sector capital. To this extent, then, the nation endures, at a minimum, a serious capital allocation problem— a capital supply shortfall brought on by imprudent public policy.

Yet America's industrial future is linked to the intrinsic strengths of its financing. To globally compete, the private sector must commit to a more effective advanced technology growth strategy. But that goal is attainable only through the maintenance of a strong, nurturing financial services infrastructure. For just as the smokestack industries actively sought out supportive physical facilities three decades ago, so now advanced technology industries move in the direction of comprehensive capital infrastructure support.

Indeed, the economic span of civilizations previously considered makes clear that nations that invest in state-of-the-art production facilities progress, whereas those that tax and consume their corporate incomes in nonproductive quests are destined to fall further into stasis.

This realization is critical to the quest to sustain economic prosperity through high-tech industrial advance. For as preceding chapters demonstrate, many of America's current economic woes stem from a severe excess of governmental tax consumption and an attendant, resultant shortfall in private-sector investment.

Hence, to ensure sustained advanced technology growth, a comprehensive variety of new funding sources must be found to underwrite the costs of capital-intensive industries built through innovation. Ongoing competition today for investment capital is as critical in promoting commercial competitiveness as that among products for finite market share upon which conventional trade policy traditionally has been based. The requirement for broader, deeper, more effective financial services infrastructures has thus become acute.

One potentially effective approach could be to amend the U.S. Tax Code to allow for deductibility of capital contributions to private-sector pooled risk loan guarantee funds. Here, the rationale is straightforward. Capital leveraging can play a critical role in business development financing. Loan guarantees, because they promote significant capital leveraging, can result in more loans funded, and hence, in more new business start-ups realized and more high-quality jobs created.

The rationale lies in the economics. Banks today typically are capitalized at around a 20:1 ratio. In other words, each dollar of equity supports twenty dollars of liability in borrowing. Loan guarantee funds, on the other hand, generally enjoy far higher capital leverage rates. Some operate successfully at ratios as high as 40:1 or even 50:1. If the ready availability of loan guarantees succeeds in increasing the creditworthiness of business transactions, the costs of borrowing can be significantly reduced—thereby promoting savings to the borrowers while simultaneously reducing the financial institutions' ultimate loan risk.

How could such business development loan guarantee programs best be structured at the national level? A long legacy of free market philosophy suggests that they be privately run—possibly as subsidiaries of consortia of publicly chartered financial institutions such as banks and savings-and-loan institutions, or, alternately, chambers of commerce—or some combination thereof—thereby assuring strong linkages to local lenders.

Several economic realities argue for this privately administered loan guarantee approach. Foremost among them, governmentally designed programs are usually characterized by an in-built bureaucratic rigidity that can inhibit their abilities to respond to private-sector business transactional needs on a real-time basis.

Conversely, there are numerous examples of privately administered loan guarantee funds that have succeeded measurably in preempting the traditional public-sector loan guarantee role through their greater efficiencies and flexibilities. The Massachusetts Capital Resources Corporation (MCRC), for instance, was originally created by a consortium of in-state life insurance companies that provided its initial capitalization in exchange for the elimination of a state tax surcharge that applied exclusively to them.

From modest beginnings, it has today succeeded in supporting the financing of local companies with strong growth potentials but which, because of that rapid growth, are already so highly leveraged that they are effectively unable to access further capital through conventional market sources. Accordingly, the ultimate achievement of the MCRC has been to channel private resources, administered by efficient private management, to the greater public good of high-tech job creation.

Another potentially effective capital leveraging approach could be to use U.S. Treasury cash reserves as interest-subsidized linked deposit monetary incentives to promote new business start-up, expansion, and modernization initiatives. Indeed, public-private interest subsidy programs today have already become common capital access leveraging mechanisms.

Operationally, under the interest subsidy approach, governmental units deposit their surplus funds in non-interest-bearing accounts at public financial institutions. The interest that would normally accrue to the depositing agency is then used instead to reduce interest rates for participation in targeted programs that serve the public interest.

While these programs have traditionally been employed to support such social causes as minority business enterprise and housing rehabilitation subsidies, there is no reason why their focus could not be redirected to such equally lofty goals as high-tech industrial development and its attendant venture and mezzanine capital financing requirements.

At the state level, Illinois, Missouri, and Ohio have for years, in fact, used linked deposit systems that employ the ready lure of state bankable cash reserves to entice private bank participation in programs deemed economically desirable from a public goods standpoint, including the promotion of small business lending.

At the national level, in turn, the U.S. Treasury, using the linked deposit mechanism, could similarly promote advanced technology industrial development by diverting a portion of the interest earned on current cash reserves deposited in private financial institutions to more productive use in incentivizing subsidized high-tech business start-up, expansion, and modernization lending.

Such an innovative approach would thus enjoy the dual laudatory economic effects of mobilizing productivity-enhancing investment capital while concurrently making such capital available on terms significantly below current market rates.

Arguments for employing such an approach are compelling. Federal deposits are public assets that should be employed to serve the public good. Not only could an economically-focused federal technology development linked deposit program serve to facilitate creation of higher-quality twenty-first-century domestic jobs, it would likewise serve to fortify the national economic interest globally by enhancing private-sector international trade competitiveness.

Targeting Tax Credits to New Process Technologies R&D

As demonstrated in the preceding analysis, technological advance has historically been a foremost force in the march of civilization. Because it dramatically accelerates civilized progress, it provides society with significant unexpected benefits—indeed, a societal equivalent of an economic "free lunch." Thus, creating business operating milieus amenable to technological advance contributes to cultural well-being as well.

Private firms are the prime creators of technology. Much technological innovation now comes, in fact, directly out of private industrial workshops and laboratories as investments in research improve the effectiveness of people and machines, thereby adding significantly to economic growth by developing new products exportable to the international marketplace.

Accordingly, because ultimate success within the "new economy" will be driven by the strength of its technological underpinnings, to ensure optimum competitiveness in the twenty-first-century global marketplace, governments at all levels must together work closely with private industry and academic consortia to foster both the creation of new industrial technologies and the development of new applications within them.

In this quest, the private sector, academia, and government face separate and distinct, yet equally imposing, challenges. In the first instance, within the now greatly downsized productive "new economy," manufacturers everywhere often lack sufficient funds to invest in the twenty-first century R&D and facilities modernization needed to enhance their trade competitiveness.

Their private capital challenges are numerous, as more creative ways of financing future investment must be developed—including leveraging public-sector R&D programs, seeking new and better ways to acquire research capital, and taking short-term earnings losses for R&D investments in exchange for future productivity-created profits.

New business-operating philosophies likewise must evolve. Within them, development of futuristic products and processes must be put ahead of short-term finance. Enterprises must focus equally upon advanced technological innovation, optimizing more effective use of cutting-edge technologies, and the design of next-generation high-performance manufacturing models.

For if America's economic future indeed lies in high-value production enterprise vital to today's industry, decision makers must be brought to a realization that the vast majority of the best future jobs and profits will derive not from scale and volume but from finding superior manufacturing solutions for emerging high-tech needs—as all future industrial progress will emanate from those market-driven production tools that successful frontline manufacturers are effectively able to develop and deploy.

Such innovation, as noted, must extend as much to processes as to products, as process-related technological investment is crucial for industrial productivity, making investments in fundamental production-related scientific and engineering research critical for sustaining long-term economic growth. Yet such innovation, of course, costs money.

But because R&D dollars typically yield productivity gains at rates at least ten times greater than those invested in fixed-plant facilities, they contribute materially to commercial competitiveness—and since technology lies at the source of man-made competitive advantage, new R&D initiatives targeted to more effective process technologies development become vital. This reality is the more critical because high performance manufacturing in the Information Age is more about systemic process than it is about rote production.

Hence, such development should be made a foremost focus of any new federal R&D tax incentives modification contemplated. For if there is, in fact, one definite Japanese trade secret—one embedded source of its competitive advantage to be emulated—it is largely technological production and not economic system in its nature, and centers upon that nation's unique focus upon manufacturing process technologies.

For Japan today spends about two-thirds of its private R&D capital on new process development and one-third on new product development. In the United States, that ratio is reversed. Most major Japanese manufacturing companies, for instance, now employ about five times more industrial robots than do their American counterparts. This reality is the reason why Toyota produces about half of the number of vehicles as General Motors with only about 5 percent of the number of workers.

Lack of focused manufacturing *process research* is a particularly serious R&D shortfall, for process research invariably creates larger economic payoffs than does product research. Again, the reason? While individual products are but minuscule components of the economy at large, and can take decades to have significant market impact, a new process for making existing products can impact immediately, since the markets for such products already are developed.

Process research likewise is a significant factor in sustaining global trade competitiveness—and one that has contributed significantly to the export initiatives of the various newly developed Far Eastern countries. For while low-wage states and nations can readily steal the manufacture of a new product from its inventor, it is more difficult to steal a process.

By way of example, though transistors, semiconductors, TVs, radios, stereo equipment, fax machines, videocassette recorders, CD players, and other such electronic consumer items were all American inventions, they are now almost exclusively manufactured in the Pacific Rim. In like manner, while Japan did not invent the microprocessor, for example, it directly copied the American semiconductor industry, learned how to produce superior-quality random access memory chips, and from them gained a dominant market share.[20]

Indeed, while until 1970 the United States dominated nearly the entire spectrum of the consumer electronics market, today it controls less than 5 percent, and its share continues to dwindle. The real development lesson to be learned here, then, is that it does little good to promote the invention of a new product if someone else can manufacture it more cheaply.

A key to effective development success in the twenty-first-century global economy, therefore, must be a sectoral focus on advanced process technologies—computer aided-design and computer-aided manufacturing, agile production, machine vision, advanced robotics, and other sophisticated machine tools—manufacturing systems that do not readily lend themselves to emulation.

Accordingly, if America is to sustain its industrial preeminence, a new approach is invoked to encourage private firms to develop those process innovations that will enable them to more effectively compete in the global marketplace. This course will not be easy. For innovation is expensive, and for many years exists only as a cost before it ultimately yields a profit. In other words, it must be an investment before it can become a return.[21]

Many of our principal trade competitors are already focused on such initiatives. In Japan, for instance, the marginal tax credit for R&D is 30 percent for general research and 50 percent for research on new industrial materials, allowing for expenditures in excess of a firm's rolling average expenditures over the previous three years, not to exceed 20 percent of taxes owed.

Within the United States, since the Reagan tax cut of 1981, American firms likewise have been able to expense R&D costs, and claim credits for R&D expenses that exceed average R&D expenditures for the preceding three years. Specifically, the federal tax system presently allows firms to

- deduct qualified research expenses in the year incurred; and simultaneously
- receive a 25 percent credit in increases in qualifying research expenses above the previous three-year running average.

Recent Bush-II tax reforms have likewise *temporarily* prudently doubled this productive tax credit to 50 percent of qualified research expenses. Because of the integral nature of process R&D, and because of the consummately successful results produced by the existing federal R&D tax credit while encumbering only limited public revenue resources, rational logic dictates that this doubling should now be made permanent—thereby putting the nation and its industry into a long-term fifty-fifty partnership in creating twenty-first-century quality jobs. Such provisions explain why America today remains industrially prosperous, why its federal tax policies of the 1980s have inspired two decades and more of investment.

Concurrently, investments in new technologies and machinery should be made wholly deductible within their first year—thereby eliminating arcane tax code provisions that depreciate acquired equipment over a protracted period, a practice that makes no sense in an era of rapid technological change. To quote business economist Peter Drucker, "What is needed within an entrepreneurial society is a tax system that encourages moving capital from yesterday into tomorrow, rather than one that prevents and penalizes it."[22]

Focusing Federal Lab Research on
Developing "Intelligent Machines"

Given the criticalities of technological R&D described, and to further the cause of trade competitiveness empowered through the enhancement of process technologies in particular, special federal focus should be concentrated on fostering private development of "intelligent industrial machines," particularly those with remote sensing and nanotechnology applications.

This is a crucial industrial necessity. For advanced cerebral information systems, together with their "arms and legs," robotics, are twenty-first-century advanced manufacturing imperatives that cry out for rapid, focused development nationwide. Accordingly, the establishment of an integrated nationwide network of federal laboratories focused upon the innovation and potential of "intelligent machines" in production processes should be made a foremost development priority.

The National Center for Manufacturing Sciences, based in Ann Arbor, Michigan, serves as a prototypical model for the R&D centers proposed, wherein for each new dollar in invested research, beneficiary companies derive an estimated five dollars in leveraged research in return—a return that now in aggregate exceeds $3 billion. Operationally, the modus operandi of the New York State Center for Advanced Technology in Automation and Robotics also serves as an optimal methodology in formulating new federal laboratory concept planning.

Present modern workplace demand for such new process technologies development facilities is monumental as field applications are myriad:

- Advanced technology production sectors across-the-board need a greater variety of intelligent machine systems that assure the continued manufacturability of new products and automatically reprogram themselves when new designs are introduced.
- The auto industry needs more sophisticated robotic systems with humanlike dexterity for vehicle assembly and materials handling.
- Precision tool manufacturers require automation systems that are readily adaptable for a wide variety of next generation applications.
- Future electronic manufacturers will likewise require more intelligent production systems that rapidly and easily accommodate new product lines.

- The medical sector will require more advanced robotic systems to collect hazardous waste at hospitals and from emergency care vehicles, thereby protecting doctors and other health care providers from infection.
- Surgeons also will require "intelligent operating systems" to assist them in delicate microsurgeries, thus allowing them to perform minute operations that would otherwise be too dangerous or even impossible.
- Food processors are similarly seeking advanced robotic and intelligent machines that can perform a variety of repetitive tasks adaptively.
- Agricultural and construction industries continue in their quest for more mobile, driverless machines with sensor-based controls for field work in assisting workers both in dangerous operating environments and in automating repetitive tasks.

To these ends, establishing new National Centers for Intelligent Machines would:

- benefit all companies within the advanced technology production and other state-of-the art industrial sectors, particularly those now most heavily dependent upon advanced information technologies;
- enable all companies to better structure their production and service facilities in the continuing quest for greater operating efficiencies, thereby building more competitive enterprises;
- through the employment of battlefield artificial intelligence and robotics, strengthen national security and provide better protection for U.S. military personnel; and
- strengthen industrial academic research at major national universities and laboratories.

Creating New Technologies Through Public-Private R&D

In tandem with the aforesaid R&D of private-sector firms, collaborative public-private research, conducted in conjunction with academic research institutions, likewise measurably strengthens the national technology base as yet another crucial by-product of technology-based development. Because it dramatically accelerates productive growth, it thereby contributes to enhancing private trade competitiveness in global markets.

Today, together with greater public-sector technological research focus, the nation confronts a concomitant need to strengthen those developmental pillars of its higher educational system that historically have constituted its academic technological infrastructure. Indeed, it enjoys a long, sound tradition of public-sector involvement in ensuring that its academic science and technology-based facilities remain dynamic.

Creative governmental programs contribute to academia-driven technology development in innumerable ways—in educating research scientists and engineers, in providing new research facilities and equipment, and in promoting that theoretical research needed by industry to develop derivative commercialized technologies. Sustaining investment in such activities thus is unequivocally critical to securing America's market future, as success within the global economy focuses increasingly as much upon great ideas as it does upon the superior products that issue from them.

Indeed, once started by seed capital research and development investment, the invention process becomes self-generating—as innovation becomes an engine of growth that stimulates additional innovation. Propeller airplanes, for instance, led to jet aircraft, and the discovery of electricity to advanced electrical appliances. Television threw the entire movie industry into serious economic decline until it was rescued by the subsequent invention of the VCR. Indeed, the process of invention invariably leads the way in which R&D itself is carried out, providing still further stimulus to innovation.[23]

A prime prerequisite for implementing a more cost-effective innovation-based economic strategy, therefore, must be the creation of more effective university-based public-private technology development systems. Indeed, in engaging them, academia becomes a frontline weapon in the combined public-private-sector quest to compete within the global economy as it is academia that possesses:

- the research laboratories capable of developing the products and new materials development required to meet ever-evolving global market demands;
- the in-house economists and econometricians needed to identify and define industrial trends and commercial opportunities as they emerge;
- the foreign trade experts trained in business development, exporting, and reverse investment processes;
- the regional specialists capable of evaluating commercial and political risk as well as the marketing specialists expert in formulating effective external sales campaigns; and
- the linguists required to effectively translate the marketing products supporting those campaigns into the host languages of the target markets.

In sum, America's major colleges and universities are themselves veritable "techno-centers"—active crucibles for that technology-based innovation needed to spawn revolutionary new processes and products—thereby minimizing production inefficiencies while reducing production costs so that the national economic base continues to expand.

Accordingly, with innovation holding the key to all future economic growth, cutting-edge R&D contributions of academia are quintessential for generating futuristic technologies that will keep the nation's job creation process dynamic.

Restoring a K–12 Focus on the Hard-Skills Educational Disciplines

If any nation is to retain economic preeminence, all citizens must be afforded equal access to compete in its productive economy. This is a reality recognized by Adam Smith when he called for a system of universal public education to "facilitate . . . encourage . . . and even impose upon almost the whole body of the people the necessity of acquiring those essential parts of education."[24]

Time is of the essence—with the need critical. For the findings of both economics and education today converge in a compelling way to concur that relative to the rest of the world, America is lagging behind in scientific literacy, with too few U.S. technology specialists being produced, as the nation now graduates less than half the Ph.D. scientists and engineers that it did two decades ago.

The nation suffers this ever-widening dearth of advanced scientific and engineering expertise at its peril. For because advanced technology development is the quintessential key to trade competitiveness, such expertise must be placed in the vanguard of its global trade offensive.

A substantial share of this failure to groom high technology talent as future "industrial quarterbacks" may be blamed upon inadequate scientific and mathematics training at the primary and high school levels, precluding prospective graduates from pursuing follow-on technology-based study within the nation's colleges and universities.[25]

For far too often in America's schools, the imparting of basic technical skills is today being subordinated to more politically correct social agendas, to the degree that the nation's secondary schools are often failing dramatically in their efforts to prepare their graduates for either science-based college majors or for the increasingly sophisticated demands of the competitive job marketplace.

Indeed, far too often also, those who actually do graduate find that the lower-skilled jobs for which they have been haphazardly trained no longer even exist, having migrated to lower-cost third world factories. As a consequence, nearly

two-thirds of all employers throughout the nation make the claim that a majority of current high school graduates are simply unemployable—coming to the
workplace unprepared to cope with the daunting challenges of modern advanced technology. Yet to either pursue a scientific/engineering degree or just
survive in the modern workplace, fundamental skills, particularly in secondary-
level mathematics and sciences, are essential and must be made nonnegotiable.

Aesthetics education, in itself, is admirable. But as analysis reveals, ongoing competitive testing results leave no doubt that U.S. high school students
must be immersed in *America's* hard disciplines first—not only because of
the human enrichment that they afford, but also because they must compete
in the U.S. job market—and because U.S. taxpayers will be required to pay
their maintenance should they fail to master basic employment skills.

The challenge is immense. For although the K–12 schools may, in some
sectors, adequately challenge the upper quartile, it often merely babysits the
rest. Yet the test of a great educational system is not only the abundance of
opportunities it affords to its A students, but also those it offers to its C students—as well as those who cannot effectively compete at all within conventional academic curricula.

Indeed, throughout the nation's history, some of its most accomplished citizens did not bring to their achievements the most distinguished of academic
transcripts. Accordingly, it has become an imperative to adopt a new federal
education agenda that effectively reverses current K–12 shortfalls:

1. beyond the accountability requirements of No Child Left Behind, further
   linking future education funding to demonstrably improved local educational performance; and, to this end,
2. implementing within every school district a more challenging standardized core curriculum of math, science, economics, and communications
   skills training—an agenda that explicitly mandates demonstrated core
   competencies in English, mathematics, science, and economics as a con-
   dition of graduation; and
3. beyond testing currently mandated by No Child Left Behind—which requires that states create and execute statewide reading and math exams by
   the school year 2005–2006 and similar science proficiency tests by school
   year 2006–2007—enforcing such curricula through sequential perform-
   ance-based threshold, SAT-type, norm-referenced achievement tests at
   each high school grade—with lengthier school years beyond the conventional 180 days, automatically prescribed, proportionate to the degree of
   shortcoming, for those schools failing to meet acceptable academic performance standards.

These, then, are ambitious goals, yet readily achievable without prescribing means—preserving local control while reflecting that future generations are now owed the opportunity to compete within the twenty-first-century job marketplace and concurrently recognizing that the right to equal access to education is as fundamental to the American system as is equality before the law.

They are the fundamental precepts that, at the same time, underlie this inquiry's contention that (1) every child can learn; (2) if the nation is to prosper economically, it can no longer tolerate schools that cannot teach and will not change; and (3) if public funding is to be provided for education, it must come with uniform accountability that makes unquestionably clear which schools are working and which are not and need fixing.

Fixing America's Broken Vocational Training System

Preceding analysis concurrently leaves little doubt that as economic dislocation produced by ongoing global restructuring continues to decimate large portions of the nation's industrial base, innovative sources of productive employment must be found to replace jobs that continue to be lost in many key manufacturing sectors.

Since in the future such jobs likely will not again be reproduced within identical manufacturing opportunities, new formal vocational schooling, apprenticeships, and other forms of on-the-job training will be required. For whereas in traditional twentieth-century paradigms of production no more than 40 percent of the jobs required education beyond high school, more than four-fifths of the jobs that today are replacing them require such skill levels.

Concurrent with restoring the basic core curricula focus of K–12 systems, the nation must simultaneously restructure its now broken vocational-training approach. For while current economic, demographic, and competitive forces have created a vastly different workplace wherein basic learning tools are of paramount importance, the U.S. technical training system, in many instances, remains woefully inadequate in its ability to impart job skills to prospective high school graduates.

Today, America remains the only major industrialized nation that lacks a coherent integral system of ongoing lifelong training and retraining for its adult workers—instead offering minimal, patchwork training programs on a sporadic basis. In the cogent counsel of economist Lester Thurow, "Adult reeducation is going to have to become a reality rather than a buzzword—much talked about but seldom ever seen. Education and training have to be the prime answers to rising inequality. To do anything else would be equivalent to applying cosmetics rather than antibiotics to a serious wound."[26]

America's principal trade competitors understand the need for top-to-bottom workforce training. Indeed, nations such as Germany, Britain, and France now commit up to three times as many financial resources per capita as the United States toward vocational training. Germany, in fact, employs a system of nearly universal apprenticeship training for high school graduates who do not go on to university. Such apprenticeships—subsidized through working partnerships of industry, labor, and government—are conducted partly in the classroom and partly in real time on the factory floor.

By contrast, U.S. production workers, the foot soldiers of American capitalism, for lack of opportunity, are effectively denied those critical midlevel skills that come through quality apprenticeship. As a consequence, they are being seriously shortchanged in their efforts to receive the training needed to effectively compete in the job marketplace, as the lack of adequate linkages between classroom offerings and workplace needs remains a particularly weak feature of the American educational system.[27]

In both Germany and Japan, for instance, on-the-job-training gives workers general as well as special skills. In the U.S. system, formal education aspires to teach basic skills, whereas only on-the-job-training specifically addresses workplace needs. Thus, while it may educate some people well, the formal approach remains woefully weak in its subsequent application to pragmatic economic needs.

Consequently, too many Americans today remain underinvested in their training, as the nation has become the world's best half-educated country. It is this training shortfall, combined with cross-border competition, that has produced declining real-term wages for the nation's working middle class.

Succinctly put, while America's present education system does a somewhat better job, albeit often marginally, of preparing the college-bound than it does of training the industry-bound for productive technical careers, this present errant course cannot continue. For the current widening gap in the U.S. technical training infrastructure is a serious shortcoming that also contributes to higher incidences of high school dropouts, often disenfranchising talented, mechanically minded students who may rightfully feel that their career needs are not adequately being met by conventional academic curricula.

To continue to succeed in the increasingly competitive global marketplace, therefore, the nation can't afford to continue to educationally shortchange either its productive economy or its future generations. It can't afford to initially pay for elementary and secondary education and then pay once again to retrain students so that they can get jobs. If it is to succeed economically, it must first fast-track high school participants in learning skills and then empower them through effective vocational training to industrially compete.

It must, moreover, create new training programs that focus on developing multiple industry-specific skills, rather than training students to do just one job. This core classroom curriculum, in turn, must be augmented by real-time factory visits and diversified by on-the-job vocational-training opportunities, thereby preparing graduates firsthand for the complex workplace of the factories of the future.

To meet the mounting needs of those destined for hands-on production careers, therefore, a dual-track high school curriculum is required—a two-plus-two agenda wherein students whose interests are in industrial endeavors pursue initial two year conventional high-school basic skills curricula, followed by shop floor technology training programs offered by proximate community colleges.

Such programs, when fully integrated into a follow-on two-year associate's degree at the community college level, would thus keep the mechanically gifted students moving toward increased technical proficiency, while simultaneously contributing to meeting today's ever-mounting demands for advanced workplace skills to fill tomorrow's jobs.

At the bottom line, employers, employees, and their unions alike must collaborate in preparing their constituencies to compete in the ever-evolving global economy rather than engaging in costly, ultimately futile, efforts to outlaw competition. Failing that, all participants, as well as American citizens at large, become the ultimate losers.

Building a state-of-the-art national labor force appropriate for twenty-first-century workplace requirements is undeniably a daunting challenge, but it must be undertaken. Indeed, many Far Eastern countries have already demonstrated that a superior national skills development system can be built within a decade or even less. Real-time imperatives of the emerging global market dictate that America now develop the will, resources, and policy focus to do it more quickly still.

Building Entrepreneurial Ethic through Free Market Economics

The preceding analysis has made clear that education is one of the vital keys to foreign trade competitiveness as well as a foremost deterrent to global outsourcing. For more than two centuries, American society has been distinguished by a powerful desire to succeed through creative private enterprise.

Today that tradition of entrepreneurial spirit is waning. Too often, public income maintenance has come to be perceived as an acceptable alternative to productive jobs, and efforts to link work requirements to welfare, though marginally successful since the mid-1990s, have nonetheless consistently been met with liberal resistance.

But again, the remedy is basic. For history's lessons show that a defining difference between dynamic free enterprise economies and those imbued with a long-standing welfare ethic has been education—better K–12 learning building the foundation for a strong entrepreneurial ethic imbued at an early age. Yet regrettably, today, far too many graduate from high school not even understanding the basic economic system in which they will compete for jobs.

As a result, America's business leaders continue to complain that a lack of economic literacy is a foremost socioeconomic problem. Repeated studies of the economic knowledge of U.S. high school students bear out their contentions—showing most graduates to be ill equipped to handle even the most basic business questions. Often less than one-third of most student bodies, for instance, understand investment's role in stimulating growth or the significance of competition in free market operations.[28]

A report issued by the National Joint Commission on Education headed by former Federal Reserve Board Chairman Paul Volker has documented alarming levels of economic illiteracy among U.S. high school students. Its comprehensive testing nationwide found that typical high school students could answer less than 40 percent of even the most rudimentary economic questions. In many cases, in fact, the students performed *just marginally above blind chance* in their multiple-choice responses to standardized economic tests. Economist Thomas Sowell explains the unfortunate end results of such disparities: "Economics as a profession bears some responsibility for this widespread lack of understanding. Very sophisticated analysis can be found in courses on campuses wherein a majority of the students have no real understanding of something as elementary as supply and demand."[29]

Obviously, such levels of economic illiteracy are unacceptable among high school graduates. For no sector of an economy can progress if its operatives are ignorant of its basic market rules. Economic understanding is even more critical if a nation is to seek to ensure full employment through entrepreneurial means. For as new small business start-ups become an ever more prodigious source of jobs, the need for an innate knowledge of basic business operations concomitantly increases.

Indeed, in the increasingly complex global marketplace, economics education has become a mainstream job requirement—a fundamental survival skill, and not just an elective for the college-bound—for individuals cannot be expected to capitalize on emerging market opportunities if they don't know that they are there, let alone how to develop them.

Regrettably, many American high school students never attend college, and many of those who do never take an economics course. But in the high schools of America's principal trade competitors, such as Japan and Germany, intensive, comprehensive economics education is required for graduation.

From a public policy standpoint, then, the bottom line on education is that in an ever more complex job marketplace, the criticality of economic literacy dictates that no jurisdiction can approach its full employment goals without substantial commitment to basic job skills training combined with widespread popular understanding of, and involvement in, the precepts of the free market system wherein all private-sector jobs are created.

Mandatory entrepreneurial economics education throughout the nation's K–12 schools—with a companion civics component that teaches how government raises revenues, how they are budgeted, and where tax dollars actually go—would explicitly meet this challenge.

Promoting New Business Start-ups through Entrepreneurial Training

For those with commercial rather than vocational skills, starting a new business today can be an attractive career option. Small businesses are, in fact, the primary source of job creation within America today—with firms employing fewer than twenty workers making up 90 percent of all American businesses, and well over half of all business receipts are now generated by their operations.

For nearly half a century, in fact, the overwhelming majority of all new jobs in the United States have been generated by small businesses. Within that period, firms with twenty employees or less have been responsible for more than half of all new jobs created; and companies less than five years old have generated more than 80 percent of the total national increase in employment.

Within that period also, highly noteworthy examples of the use of small business development systems to promote new job creation have been implemented. Among them are the Boston Compact and San Francisco's Renaissance Entrepreneurship Center. The Boston Compact was framed more than five decades ago as a deal between that region's business community and its system of public education whereby the public high schools agreed to upgrade their curricula in exchange for a commitment by local businesses to expand their hiring of local high school graduates.

The Renaissance Entrepreneurship Center, in turn, focused upon creating new jobs and businesses by training new entrepreneurs at the regional level. Its program offered fourteen-week, twenty-eight-session business courses in accounting, finance, management, marketing, and business plan development. Its goals were to aid individuals in first developing realistic business concepts and then opening and operating new small businesses that issued from them upon graduation from the programs.

A principal factor in the success of such programs—and those of other regions that have most effectively promoted job development through entrepreneurial training—has been their ability to forge new training partnerships between their business communities and local educational institutions, thereby developing private-sector solutions to what traditionally have been perceived to be public-sector problems.[30]

Training that specifically targets import substitution industries that contribute to economic diversification can often be a particularly prolific source of new business start-ups. For although in any region, about two-thirds of all industries are typically engaged in supplying goods and services to proximate markets, up to a third of those industries are nonetheless concurrently locally undersupplied in goods and services production, and offer promising opportunities for new business start-ups or existing business expansions. It is just such market opportunities that can best be captured through aggressive targeting and training.

The results speak for themselves. The business consulting firm Dun & Bradstreet has long estimated that of all new business start-ups within the United States, more than half will fail within the first five years of their inceptions. Yet the new business survival rate of enterprises created through entrepreneurial training that have continued for five years or more often exceeds 95 percent.

The reason for such success is basic: Prospective entrepreneurs are being explicitly trained in management skills that enable them to capitalize on specific preidentified market opportunities within their home communities. Specific trainees to be targeted by an entrepreneurial training initiative could be varied, to include

- dislocated industrial workers who are victims of technological advance;
- white collar workers displaced by ongoing economic change;
- "new to job market" women and minorities; and
- the incipient poor in rural areas.

Because of this significant job creation potential and the documented record of success, therefore, a new federal entrepreneurial training initiative could be launched to be executed by neighborhood banks in conjunction with the erstwhile Aid to Families with Dependent Children (AFDC), now relabeled the Temporary Assistance for Needy Families (TANF) program.

Pursuant to it, for instance, a certified financial institution could be granted a tax credit against its federal corporate income tax liability—of up to 50 percent of a TANF recipient's legally prescribed annual stipend—for its sponsorship of, and capital contributions to, entrepreneurial-training programs that result in new jobs created for recipients that replace their continuing need to receive TANF benefits.

To ensure income maintenance durability, an eligibility requirement could be that a recipient must have survived for one year in a business start-up produced by a small business development program under the financial institution's sponsorship.

In support of this initiative, in turn—following British and French models—in an age wherein the dynamic process of production change compels workers to constantly readjust to multiple career trajectories within an ever-evolving, intensely competitive global economy, the focus and financing of unemployment compensation could be shifted from that of subsidizing the process of waiting for the restoration of jobs that likely will never reemerge to programs of this nature that prepare them for the dynamic new jobs evolving in their futures.

In this approach, there is no downside, as the benefitting stakeholders in a dramatic reformation of the now shopworn twentieth-century unemployment compensation approach are universal. Employers are afforded an opportunity to custom-tailor skills of current employees to future job requirements.

Employees, in turn, will no longer be passively waiting as they transition from employer-subsidized public support to taxpayer-subsidized public assistance, but instead are offered venues to a more productive, prosperous future—and the American economy will inevitably be a stronger and more competitive one in which every unemployed citizen is on a learning path to working.

The merits of such a job creation tax credit approach are readily evident. It would, from the onset, empower the federal government to form effective new alliances in addressing the socioeconomic problems that the Community Reinvestment Act of 1977 ineffectively sought to remedy through regulation, while concurrently contributing to the nation's full employment goals. All parties to the program thus would benefit:

- *The sponsoring financial institution would benefit in three ways*:
  1. It will have qualitatively upgraded its potential borrower pool through the vastly improved business management skills that the entrepreneurial training program provides, thereby enabling it to comply with Community Reinvestment Act requirements in a more financially prudent way.
  2. It will have enhanced its prospects for making more secure and profitable loans to new small businesses within its local lending area.
  3. It likewise will stand to make a tax credit "net profit" for each new job created for a present TANF recipient.
- *Society would similarly benefit in three ways*:
  1. Taxpayers will receive a 50 percent savings in welfare expenditures for each new job created. The one-year survivability clause will ensure that each job created is durable, thereby guaranteeing that there will be no loss of public-sector revenues.

2. By turning present tax consumers into future net tax producers, the public revenue base will be expanded by the new business start-ups and attendant new jobs created.

3. By promoting revenue savings that would otherwise be committed to public assistance, government will have served a significant public good by contributing to a fuller level of employment without risking tax dollars.

But most importantly, the recipients themselves will benefit—not only through having earned a job but by having gained an economic future. They will be proof positive that the flawed notion that public income maintenance is the optimal alternative to productive private employment is not only a false dichotomy, it is also bad policy.

Establishing Competitive Scholarships to Pursue Scientific Disciplines

Providing a skilled workforce is a genuine responsibility of government—and a shortfall that the workings of free market process often have not filled. For beyond the shortcomings of America's K–12 system, another major reason for its ongoing failure to produce more scientifically trained professionals is a lack of financial access to educational opportunity.

Yet for any society to progress, its most talented members, those demonstrating keen aptitudes for superior intellectual achievement, must be afforded every opportunity to develop and create. Accordingly, if the nation is to preserve its preeminence in technology-based development, it must more effectively capture the talents of its best and brightest and put them productively to work to secure its economic future.

To promote a greater pursuit of the scientific disciplines and to ensure that the most talented are afforded genuine opportunities to realize the full extent of their intellectual potentials, therefore, full-ride college scholarships could be offered to top high school graduates based upon the results of comprehensive nationwide exams taken in their junior year. Initially established as a $500 billion federal pilot program in the manner of Fulbright scholarships, it could target students intent upon succeeding as demonstrated by their election of demanding core curricula courses while in high school.[31]

Administered in a manner similar to Britain's A- and O-level exams, these exams would represent a renewed commitment to the nation's economic future via higher education, providing that its foremost academic achievers be granted four-year scholarships of $20,000 per year to undertake science-based training at their college or university of choice. As the training cycle progresses, the continuing pursuit of scientific, mathematics, engineering, or information technologies majors would remain prerequisite for the receipt of continuing scholarship benefits.

In like manner, investments in education and professional development to create new human capital should be made 100 percent tax deductible in their first year so long as they are job- or profession-related—and should be made available to either individuals or employers depending upon the source of the investment.

In sum, with prudent planning and committed public stewardship, the American Dream can be restored in fulfillment of the vision of the Founding Fathers and Ronald Reagan. But to achieve that lofty goal will require that the federal government get out of the business of special interest social engineering, for which it has no constitutional mandate, and back into that of providing basic public services, for which it does. The constraint of finite resources dictates that priorities must be set. The twenty recommendations contained in the national competitiveness agenda presented represent a critical first step to this end.

NOTES

1. On the case for constitutional *tax* limitation, see J. Perry (2004), passim.

2. H. Figgie (1992), pp. 179, 185.

3. See M. Friedman (1978), p. 16. Such constitutionally mandated spending limits are preferable to taxation limits in that they concurrently restrict the ability to engage in public borrowing to accommodate deficit spending.

4. On this see C. Adams (1993), pp. 458 ff.

5. See A. Wildavsky and C. Webber (1986), pp. 11 ff.

6. C. Edwards (February 2, 2004), p. 2.

7. On this see D. Osbourne and T. Gaebler (1993), pp. 215 ff.

8. R. Rahn (July 11, 2004), p. 1.

9. On this, see R. Kuttner (1991), p. 272.

10. See L. Thurow (1980), pp. 146 ff.

11. See P. Behr and W. Brown (April 17–18, 1993), pp. 1, 11.

12. See L. Thurow (1980), pp. 150 ff.

13. P. Peterson (2004), p. 44.

14. Indeed, from a strictly theoretical standpoint, a compelling argument can be made that these twin retirement institutions stand as explicit *disincentives* to greater individual savings by obviating the need for personal savings to ensure future security. (See R. Kuttner [1984], p. 60; P. Drucker [1989], pp.179–80; M. Jacobs [1991], pp. 271 ff.; N. Gingrich [2005], p. 38)

15. Cf. American Council for Capital Formation (March 1997), passim. In contrast, privatized personal retirement accounts would provide a large new tax-free shelter for savings and investments—the equivalent of a capital gains tax cut to stimulate the economy.

16. R. Kuttner (1991), p. 271; R. Reich (1991), p. 190; N. Kaldor (1992), p. 229. Yet this is no modern public policy epiphany. As early as the mid-nineteenth century, British philosopher–economist John Stuart Mill, in *Principles of Political Economy*, also wrote: "Unless savings are exempted from income tax, the contributors are taxed twice on what they save and only once on what they spend."

17. M. Porter (1990), p. 88.

18. See R. Chetty and E. Saez (June 2004), passim; American Council for Capital Formation (March 1997), passim.

19. Tax Foundation (January 2003), pp. 1–2; G. Norquist (June 23–29, 2003), p. 26.

20. L.Thurow (1996), p. 286.

21. On this, see L. Smith (October 19, 1992), pp. 74–76; L. Thurow (1992), pp. 157–59; idem (1985), pp. 272–73; P. Peterson (1993), chart 3.6.

22. P. Drucker (1986), p. 261.

23. W. Baumol (2002), pp. 11–12, 31; L. Thurow (1999), p. 83.

24. A. Smith (1980a), vol.1, f. 54, p. 785.

25. On this, see L. Thurow (1985), p. 193; P. Peterson (1993), charts 5.4 and 5.5; K. Newman (1993), p. 216.

26. L. Thurow (2003), p. 256.

27. L. Thurow (1996), pp. 287–88.

28. On this, see W. Walstead (1998), pp. 2–3; W. Walstead and J. Soper (1988), passim and pp. 10 ff. in particular.

29. Michigan Economic Education Council (n.d.), p. 3; T. Sowell (December 25, 2003), p. 27.

30. Regrettably, many of these innovative and productive programs have now died due to federal funding cutbacks in the late 1980s and early 1990s.

31. On this, see M. Smith (1992), pp. 430 ff. This is an initiative whose need is intuitively obvious. For today, as noted previously, it is ironic that as America seeks greater economic opportunity for all of its citizens, it is concurrently compelled to open its borders through increased H-1B visas for engineers and other highly skilled foreign workers.

Bibliography

Adams, C. *For Good and Evil: The Impact of Taxes Upon the Course of Civilization.* London, 1993.

———. *Those Dirty Rotten Taxes: The Tax Revolts that Built America.* New York, 1998.

Adams, J. R. *Secrets of the Tax Revolt.* New York, 1984.

Ady, R. "High Technology Plants: Different Criteria for the Best Location." *Commentary.* Council for Urban Economic Development, Washington, 1983.

Al-Hassan, A. A. *Kitab al-Hiyal* (The Book of Ingenious Devices). Baghdad, 1980.

American Council for Capital Formation. "The Impact of Capital Gains Tax Reductions on the American Economy." Washington, March 1997.

———. "Capital Gains Taxes and U.S. Economic Growth." Washington, July 1997.

American Petroleum Institute. "Oil and Natural Gas Industry Earnings." Washington, November 18, 2005.

Amoroso, B. *On Globalization: Capitalism in the 21st Century.* New York, 1998.

Armington, C., and Odle M. *Small Business: How Many Jobs?* Brookings Institution, Washington, 1982a.

———. "Sources of Job Growth: A New Look at the Small Business Role." *Commentary.* Council for Urban Economic Development, Washington, 1982b.

Atkins, C., and Hodge, S. "U.S. Corporate Income Tax System: Once a World Leader, Now a Millstone Around the Neck of American Business." *Tax Foundation Special Report #136.* Washington, November 2005.

Baecheler, J. *The Origins of Capitalism.* Oxford, 1975.

Bagby, M. *Rational Exuberance.* New York, 1998.

Balzac, Honoré de. Quoted at <www.quotationsbook.com> (July 7, 2006).

Barkley, R. *The Seven Fat Years.* New York, 1992.

Bartlett, B. "The Debate Over Outsourcing Needs Some Facts." National Center for Policy Analysis, Washington, October 12, 2004.

Bartlett, D., and Steele, J. *America: Who Stole the Dream?* Kansas City, 1996.

Barnes, H. E. A*n Economic History of the Western World.* New York, 1937.

Bartnik, T. "Business Location Decisions in the United States: Estimates of the Effects of Unionization, Taxes, and Other Characteristics of the States." *Journal of Business and Economic Statistics* 3, no. 1 (1985).

Baumol, W. *The Free Market Innovation Machine*. Princeton, 2002.

Bautier, R. *The Economic Development of Medieval Europe*. London, 1971.

Bearden, M. "A Bold Plan, Inked n Red," *U.S. News and World Report*, February 13, 2003.

Beaud, M. *History of Capitalism: 1500–1980*. London, 1984.

———. *A History of Capitalism: 1500–2000*. New York, 2000.

Beck, J. *The Effects of State Tax Burden on Economic Growth*. Cleveland, 1987.

Becker, G. "Memo to Clinton: Japan Inc. Didn't Make Japan Strong." *Business Week*, November 1, 1993.

Behr, P., and Brown, W. "An Industrial Departure: U.S. Forms Alliance with Detroit," *International Herald Tribune*, April 17–18, 1993.

Bell, J. F. *A History of Economic Thought*. New York, 1985.

Bennett, S. *Apathy in America*. Dobbs Ferry, 1986.

Berger, P., ed. *Modern Capitalism: Capitalism and Equality in America*. Lanham, 1987.

Best, T., et al. *The Imperative of Tax Reform*. Heartland Institute, Chicago, 1987.

Bieler, A. *La Pensée Éonomique et Sociale de Calvin*. Geneva, 1959.

Birch, D. *The Job Generation Process*. Cambridge, 1979.

Boissonnade, P. *Life and Work in Medieval Europe*. New York, 1927, 1959, 1987.

Boorstin, D. "Expeditions of the Human Spirit." *U.S. News & World Report*, July 11, 1994.

Braudel, F. *Civilization and Capitalism*. New York, 1981.

Bray, T. "Rising Competition Stalks U.S. Capitalism." *Detroit News*, May 9, 2004.

———. "Bush Proves Stronger on Domestic Issues." *Detroit News*, October 17, 2004.

Break, G. F. "A General Framework." In D. Skadden, ed., *A New Tax Structure for the United States*. Indianapolis, 1978.

Brockway, G. *The End of Economic Man*. New York, 1993.

Brookes.W. *The Economy in Mind*. New York, 1982.

Brookhiser, R. *The Way of the Wasp*. New York, 1991.

Budget of the United States, FY 2005. "Historical Tables: Introduction." Washington, 2004.

Budget of the United States, FY 2006. "Historical Tables: Introduction." Washington, 2005.

Buchanan, P. "Politicians' Betrayal of Working America." *Conservative Chronicle*, January 7, 2004.

———. "An Index of American Decline." *Conservative Chronicle*, March 3, 2004.

Burke: Selected Works, ed. E. J. Payne. Oxford, 1881.

Business Week. *Reinventing America*. New York, 1992.

Calleo, D. *The Bankrupting of America*. New York, 1991.

Calvin, J. *Institutes of the Christian Religion*. Philadelphia/New York, 1960/1986.

Cantor, N. F. *Medieval History: The Life and Death of a Civilization*. New York, 1967.

Carnegie Foundation. *A Nation at Risk: A Special Report.* U.S. Department of Education. Washington, 1983.

Cary, M., and Haarhof, T. J. *Life and Thought in the Greek and Roman World.* London, 1940.

Chamberlain, J. *The Roots of Capitalism.* Indianapolis, 1976.

Chapman, S. "Trade, Outsourcing, and the Truth about Jobs," *Conservative Chronicle,* March 24, 2004.

Chetty, R., and Saez, E. *Do Dividend Payments Respond to Taxes? Preliminary Evidence from the 2003 Dividend Tax Cut.* National Bureau of Economic Research (NBER) Working Paper No. W10572, Washington, June 2004.

Chow, R. *The Protestant Ethnic and the Spirit of Capitalism.* New York, 2002.

Cicero. *Orations.* In "Thoughts on the Business of Life." *Forbes,* July 18, 1994.

Cipolla, C. M. *Money, Prices, and Civilization in the Mediterranean World.* New York, 1967.

———. *Before the Industrial Revolution: European Society and Economy, 1000–1700.* London, 1976.

Claster, J. N. *The Medieval Experience: 300–1400.* New York/London, 1982.

Clifton, D., and Karas, E. *Cost of Government Day Report: Calendar Year 2005.* Washington, 2005.

Clough, S. B. *The Rise and Fall of Civilization.* Westport, 1951.

———. *European Economic History: Economic Development of Western Civilization.* New York/London, 1959/1968.

Clough, S. B., and Cole, C. *Economic History of Europe.* Boston, 1952.

Cohen, J. *Protestantism and Capitalism: The Mechanisms of Influence.* New York, 2002.

Coleman, S. "Outsourcing and Trade Are No Threat to Jobs." *Conservative Chronicle,* March 3, 2004.

Cook, W. "Signatures of Our Century." *U.S. News & World Report,* July 11, 1994.

Copeland, M. *Our Free Enterprise Society.* London, 1965.

Couch, H. and Geer, R. *Classical Civilization: Rome.* Edgewood Cliffs, 1940.

Cox, O. *The Foundations of Capitalism.* New York, 1959.

———. *Capitalism and American Leadership.* New York, 1962.

Coyle, D. *Paradoxes of Prosperity.* New York/London, 2001.

Crain, W. and Hopkins, T. "The Impact of Regulatory Costs on Small Firms." Small Business Administration, Washington, 2003.

Crews, C. *Ten Thousand Commandments: An Annual Snapshot of the Federal Regulatory State.* Cato Institute, Washington, 2004.

Croce, B. *Uomini e Cose della Vecchia Italia.* Bari, 1927.

Crouch, C., and Streeck, W., eds. *The Political Economy of Modern Capitalism.* London, 1997.

Crotty, R. *When Histories Collide: the Development and Impact of Individualistic Capitalism.* Walnut Creek, 2001.

Crutsinger, M. "Greenspan Warns of Painful Choices Unless Baby Boomer Benefits Are Trimmed." *Detroit Free Press,* August 28, 2004.

Davis, R. H. C. *A History of Medieval Europe.* Oxford, 1970.

Davis, S., and Hendrekson, M. *Tax Effects on Work Activity, Industry Mix, and Shadow Economy Size*. NBER Working Paper No. 10509, Cambridge, May 2004.

Deaver, M. K. *A Different Drummer: My Thirty Years with Ronald Reagan*. New York: 2003.

de Roover, R. "Partnership Accounts in Twelfth-Century Genoa," *Bulletin of the Business Historical Society*, no. 15, part 6, 1941.

———. *L'Evolution de la Lettre de Change, XIV–XVIII*. Paris, 1953.

———. "The Concept of 'Just Price': Theory and Economic Policy." *Journal of Economic History* 18 (1958).

———. "The Organization of Trade," *Cambridge Economic History of Europe*. Vol. 3. Cambridge, 1965.

———. "The 'Cambium Maritimum' Contract According to the Genoese Notarial Records of the Twelfth and Thirteenth Centuries." In *Economy, Society, and Government in Medieval Italy*, edited by D. Herlihy. Kent, 1969.

———. "Partnership Accounts in Twelfth Century Genoa." In *The History of Accounting*, edited by A. C. Littleton and B. Yamey. New York, 1978.

Desai, M. *Marx's Revenge: The Resurgence of Capitalism and the Death of Statist Socialism*. London/New York, 2002.

DeSoto, H. *The Mystery of Capital: Why Capitalism Triumphs in the West and Fails Everywhere Else*. New York, 2000.

de Toqueville, A. *On Democracy, Revolution, and Society*. Chicago, 1982.

Diodorus Siculus. *Bibliotheca Historica*. Ed. C. H. Oldfather. London, 1933–1967.

Dobbs, L. "Still Failing the Grade." *U.S. News & World Report*, September 15, 2003.

———. "Show Some Steel, Mr. Bush." *U.S. News & World Report*, November 24, 2003.

———. *Exporting Jobs: Why Corporate Greed Is Shipping American Jobs Overseas*. New York, 2004.

———. "The Myth of Outsourcing." *U.S. News & World Report*, May 2, 2004.

Donahue, J., and Nye, J. *Market-Based Governance*. Washington, 2002.

Dopsch, A. *The Economic and Social Foundations of Europe*. London, 1937, 1953.

Dougherty, P. *Who's Afraid of Adam Smith*. Hoboken, 2002.

Dowd, D. *Capitalism and Its Economics*. London, 2000.

———. *Understanding Capitalism: Critical Analysis: From Karl Marx to Amartya Sen*. London, 2002.

Drucker, P. *The New Society*. New York, 1949.

———. *The Future of Industrial Man*. London, 1965.

———. *The Age of Discontinuity*. London, 1969.

———. *Innovation and Entrepreneurship*. New York, 1986.

———. *The New Realities*. New York, 1989.

———. *Managing for the Future*. New York, 1992.

———. *Post-Capitalist Society*. New York, 1993.

Duby, G. *The Early Growth of the European Economy*. New York, 1974.

Dudley, S. "A Regulated Day in the Life." *Regulation*, Summer 2004.

Duffy, M., and Goodgame, D. *Marching in Place: The Status Quo Presidency of George Bush*. New York, 1992.

Dworak, R. *Taxpayers, Taxes, and Governmental Spending*. New York, 1980.

Edwards, C. "Farm Subsidies at Record Levels." Cato Institute, Washington, February 2, 2004a.

———. "The Era of Big Government." Cato Institute, Washington, February 2, 2004b.

———. "Downsizing the Federal Government." Cato Institute, Washington, June 2, 2004.

———. "Corporate Tax Reform: Kerry, Bush, Congress Fall Short." *Tax and Budget* 21, Cato Institute, Washington, September 2004.

Engler. A. *Apostles of Greed*. London, 1995.

Eurostat Press Office. *A Modest Decline in EU Overall Tax Burden Since 1999*. Luxembourg, June 13, 2003.

Fanfani, A. *Catholicism, Protestantism, and Capitalism*. Norfolk, 2003.

Farrell, C. "Is the Japanese Dynamo Losing Juice?" *Business Week*, June 27, 1994.

Figgie, H. *Bankruptcy 1995*. Boston, 1992.

Forbes, M. "Who Can Give Them Courage?" *Forbes*, March 14, 1994.

Ford, P., ed. *Works*. New York, 1904.

Friedman, B. *Day of Reckoning*. New York, 1989.

Friedman, K. *Myths of the Free Market*. New York, 2001.

Friedman, M. *Capitalism and Freedom*. Chicago, 1962.

———. *Tax Limitation, Inflation, and the Role of Government*. Dallas, 1978.

Friedman, R and Friedman, M. *Free to Choose*. New York, 1980.

Frum, D. *Dead Right*. New York, 1994.

Galbraith, J. K. *American Capitalism*. Boston, 1952.

Garrett, M. *The Enduring Revolution: How the Contract with America Continues to Shape the Nation*. New York, 2005.

Geier, T. "World Math Champs: U.S. Teens." *U.S. News & World Report*, August 1, 1994.

Genetski, R., and Ludlow, L. *The Impact of State and Local Taxes Upon Economic Growth*. The Harris Bank, Chicago, 1982.

Genetski, R., and Chin, Y. *The Impacts of State and Local Taxes Upon Economic Growth*. The Harris Bank, Chicago, 1978.

Gentry, W., and Hubbard, R. G. "Taxes and Wage Growth." National Bureau of Economic Research, Washington, November 2003.

———. "Success Taxes, Entrepreneurial Entry, and Innovation." National Bureau of Economic Research, Washington, April 13, 2004.

———. "Tax Policy and Entry into Entrepreneurship." National Bureau of Economic Research, Washington, June 2004.

Gibbon, E. A. *The Decline and Fall of the Roman Empire*. London, 1969.

Gilder, G. *Wealth and Poverty*. New York, 1981.

———. *Reconquering the Spirit of Enterprise*. San Francisco, 1990.

———. "Ronald Reagan and the Spirit of Free Enterprise." *Imprimis*, Hillsdale College, Summer 2004.

Gilbert, M. *Winston S. Churchill*. Boston, 1983.

Giles, D., and Tedds, L. *Taxes and the Canadian Underground Economy*. Toronto, 2002.

Gilpin, R. *The Challenge of Global Capitalism in the 21st Century*. Princeton, 2000.

———. *Global Political Economy*. Princeton, 2001.

Gingrich, N. *Winning the Future*. Washington, 2005.

Goudzwaard, B. *Capitalism and Progress*. Toronto, 1979.

Gore, A. "From Red Tape to Results: Creating a Government That Works Better and Costs Less." *Report of the National Performance Review*, Washington, September 1993.

Grassby, R. *Idea of Capitalism Before the Industrial Revolution*. Oxford, 1999.

Gray, J. *False Dawn*. New York, 1998.

Green, J. *The Book of Political Quotations*. London, 1982.

Greenberg, S. *Middle Class Dreams*. New York, 1995.

Greenfield, L. *The Spirit of Capitalism*. Cambridge/London, 2001.

Grieder, W. *Who Will Tell the People: The Betrayal of American Democracy*. New York, 1992.

———. *One World, Ready or Not*. New York, 1997.

———. *The Soul of Capitalism*. London/New York, 2003.

Grierson, R. "Theoretical Analysis and Empirical Measurement of the Effects of the Philadelphia Income Tax." *Journal of Urban Economics* 4 (April 1977).

Hahn, R., and Layburn, E. "Tracking the Value of Regulation." *Regulation*, Summer 2003.

Hall, P., and Soskice, D., eds. *Varieties of Capitalism*. Oxford, 2001.

Hanke, S. "The Theory of Privatization." In *The Privatization Option*, S. Butler, ed. Washington, 1985.

Harris, C. "The Magnitude of Job Loss from Plant Closings and the Generation of Replacement Jobs." *Annals of the American Academy of Political and Social Science*, September 1984.

Harrison, B., and Kantner, S. "The Political Economy of the States' Job Creation Business Incentives." *Journal of the American Institute of Planners*, October 1978.

Hart-Rudman Commission on National Security for the 21st Century. U.S. Government Printing Office. Washington, 2001.

Heaton, H. *Economic History of Europe*. London, 1948.

Heck, Gene. *Michigan in Perspective: A Critical Reexamination of the State's Economic Performance in the Recent Business Cycle*. Lansing, 1988.

———. *Building Entrepreneurial Michigan: A Strategy for the 1990s*. Lansing, 1989.

Heer, F. *The Medieval World*. London/New York, 1961.

Heilbroner, R. *Business Civilization in Decline*. London, 1976.

———. *21st Century Capitalism*. New York/London, 1993.

Heilbroner, R., and Bernstein, P. *The Debt and the Deficit*. New York, 1989.

Heilbroner, R., and Thurow, T. *Economics Explained*. New York, 1982.

Henderson, N., and Downey, K. "A Surge of Contractors Helps Explain the Jobless Recovery." *Washington Post National Weekly Edition*, February 9–15, 2004.

Herman. E. *Triumph of the Market*. Boston, 1995.

Hilke, J. *Cost Savings from Privatization*. Reason Foundation, Los Angeles, 1993.

Hilton, R. "Capitalism—What's in a Name?" In *The Transition from Feudalism to Capitalism*. London, 1976.

Hira, R. and Hira, A. *Outsourcing America*. New York, 2005.

Hitte, P. *History of the Arabs*. London, 1970.

Hodges, R. "Trade and Market Origins in the Ninth Century: An Archaeological Perspective of Anglo-Carolingian Relations." In *Charles the Bald: Court and Kingdom*. M. Gibson and J. Nelson, eds., New York, 1981.

———. *Dark Age Economics: The Origins of Towns and Trade, A.D. 600–1000*. New York, 1982.

Hodges, R., and Whitehouse, D. M. *Charlemagne, and the Origins of Europe*. London, 1983.

Hodges, S. "State Business Tax Climate Index." Tax Foundation, Washington, October 14, 2004.

Hodgett, G. *A Social and Economic History of Medieval Europe*. London, 1972.

Hollingsworth, J. R., ed. *Contemporary Capitalism: The Embeddedness of Institutions*. Cambridge, 1997.

Howes, D. "Are There More or Fewer Jobs? Surveys Don't Tell the Whole Story." *Detroit News*, August 29, 2004.

Hume, D. *Essays: Moral, Political, and Literary*. London, 1903.

Hunter, L. "Who's Afraid of the National Debt?" Institute for Policy Innovation, Washington, July 25, 2001.

Hutton, W., ed. *Global Capitalism*. New York, 2000.

Ibn Khaldūn. *Al-Muqaddimah: Kitāb al-'Ibar wa Diwān al-Mubtadā wa al-Khabar*. Beirut, 1978.

Ibn Taymīyah. *Al-Hisbah fī al-Islām*. Cairo, 1976.

Inman, R., and Burton, D. "Technology and Competitiveness: The New Policy Frontier." *Foreign Affairs*, Spring 1990.

Jackson, J. *Economic Development in Michigan: Choosing an Economic Future*. Institute for Social Research, University of Michigan, Ann Arbor, 1987.

Jacobs, M. *Short-Term America*. Boston, 1991.

Jacoby, J. "Giving Thanks for the Invisible Hand." *Conservative Chronicle*. December 10, 2003.

Jenkins, D. *Market Whys and Human Wherefores*. London/New York, 2000.

Jessop, B. *The Future of the Capitalistic State*. Cambridge, 2002.

Jett, W. *A General Theory of Acquisitivity*. San Jose, 2002.

Johnson, R., and Edwards, C. *Entrepreneurial Links between Corporations, Universities, and Government*. New York, 1987.

Joint Economic Committee of Congress. *Economic Benefits of Personal Income Tax Rate Reductions*. 107th Congress, Washington, April 2001.

Jones, B. "Black Gold." *Entrepreneur*, July 1994.

Kaldor, N. *The Economics and Politics of Capitalism as a Dynamic System*. Oxford, 1992.

Kane, T. "The Myth of a Jobless Recovery." Heritage Foundation, March 25, 2004.

———. "How Good Are the New Jobs?" Heritage Foundation, June 30, 2004.

———. "Trade and the Gods of Economic Statistics." Heritage Foundation, July 30, 2004.

——. "A Problem with Payrolls." Heritage Foundation, August 6, 2004.

Kantrowitz, B., and Winger, P. "Failing the Most Gifted Kids." *Newsweek*, November 1993.

Katz, C. "Thomas Jefferson's Liberal Anticapitalism." *American Journalism of Political Science* 47, no. 1, July 2002.

Kaus, M. *The End of Equality*. New York, 1992.

Kelly, K. *New Rules for the New Economy*. New York, 1998.

Kennedy, P. M. *The Rise and Fall of the Great Powers*. New York, 1987.

Kersey, P. "A Minimum Wage Hike Wouldn't Add Up." Heritage Foundation, Washington, July 22, 2004.

Keynes, J. M. *Economic Possibilities for Our Grandchildren: Essays in Persuasion*. New York, 1932.

——. *The General Theory of Employment, Interest, and Money*. New York, 1980.

Kieschnick, M. *Taxes and Growth: Business Incentives and Economic Development*. Washington, 1981.

Kiefer, D. *A Review of the Research on the 1964 Tax Cut, the 1968 Surtax, and the 1975 Tax Cut, Studies in Taxation, Public Finance, and Related Subjects*. Washington, n.d.

Knight, M. *The Economic History of Europe Until the End of the Middle Ages*. New York, 1926.

Kolb, C. *White House Daze*. New York, 1993.

KPMG. *Corporate Tax Rates Survey*. Washington, January 2004.

Krugman, P. *The Age of Diminished Expectations*. Cambridge, 1994a.

——. *Peddling Prosperity*. New York, 1994b.

Kuttner, R. *The Economic Illusion*. Philadelphia, 1984.

——. *The End of Laissez-Faire*. New York, 1991.

Lambro, D. "Public Is Skeptical of Governmental Health Care." *Conservative Chronicle*, April 21, 1994.

——. "New Jobs Doom Dems' Weapon." *Conservative Chronicle*, April 5, 2004.

——. "Dems Skew CBO's Taxing Report." *Conservative Chronicle*, September 1, 2004.

——. "Bush Must Employ Stronger Jobs Message in Ohio." *Conservative Chronicle*, September 8, 2004.

Lampe, D. *M. I. T. and the Commercialization of Biomedical Research*. Cambridge, 1986.

Lane, R. *The Loss of Happiness in Market Democracies*. New Haven/London, 2002.

Lash, S., and Urry, J. *The End of Organized Capitalism*. Madison, 1987.

LaTouche, R. *The Birth of Western Economy*. London, 1967.

Leonard, J. *How Structural Costs Imposed on U.S. Manufacturers Harm Workers and Threaten Competitiveness*. National Association of Manufacturers, Washington, 2004.

Leroy, M. *Histoire des Idées Sociales en France*. Paris, 1946.

Limbaugh, R. *See, I Told You So*. New York, 1993.

Lindbolm. C. *The Market System*. New Haven/London, 2001.

Lindsey, B. *Against the Dead Hand*. New York, 2002.

———. *Job Losses and Trade: A Reality Check*. Cato Institute, Washington, March 17, 2004.

Little, L. K. *Religious Poverty and the Profit Economy in Medieval Europe*. Ithaca, 1983.

Lopez, R. S. *The Birth of Europe*. New York, 1967.

"The Lost Factory Job." *Washington Post*, September 14, 2003.

Lot, F. *La Fin du Monde Antique et le Début du Moyen Âge*. Paris, 1927.

———. *The End of the Ancient World and the Beginnings of the Middle Ages*. London, 1931.

Lowry, R. "Bush's Economy by the Numbers." *Conservative Chronicle*. March 10, 2004.

Luskin, D. "Bush Fails to Get Deserved Credit for Tax Cut Benefits." *Detroit News*, August 27, 2004.

Luttwak, E. *Turbo Capitalism: Winners and Losers in the Global Economy*. New York, 1998.

Luzzatto, G. *Breve Storia Economica dell'Italia Medievale*. Picolla, 1958.

———. *An Economic History of Italy from the Fall of the Roman Empire to the Beginning of the Sixteenth Century*. Translated by P. Jones. London/New York, 1961.

Lyons, A., et al. *Michigan Business Tax Incentives*. Economic Policy Institute, Chicago, December 1985.

MacEwan, A. *Neo-Liberalism or Democracy*. London, 1999.

Machiavelli, N. *The Prince*. New York, 1952.

Makin, J., and Ornstein, N. *Debt and Taxes*. New York, 1994.

Malabre, A. *Lost Prophets: An Insider's History of Modern Economists*. Boston, 1993.

Malpas, D. "Record Jobs and GDP." Bear Stearns, New York, January 16, 2004.

Mandel, M. *The High Risk Society: Peril and Promise in the New Economy*. New York, 1996.

Al-Maqrīzī. *Kitāb al-Khitat Al-Maqrīzīyah*. Cairo, 1957.

Marx, K. *Das Kapital*. Tel Aviv, 1929.

McLaughlin, T. "The Teachings of the Canonists on Usury." *Medieval Studies*, part 1, 1939; part 2, 1940.

McMillan, C. "Manufacturing and Technology News." Annandale, April 2, 2004.

McMillan, J. *Reinventing the Bazaar: A Natural History of Markets*. New York/London, 2002.

McQueen, H. *The Essence of Capitalism*. Montreal, 2003.

Melman, S. *After Capitalism*. New York, 2001.

Merrill, P. Testimony before the House Budget Committee. Washington, July 22, 2004.

Meyer, R. *Structural Change and Job Dislocation*. Brookings Institution, Washington, 1984.

Michigan Economic Education Council, Eastern Michigan University. "Monograph." Ypsilanti, n.d.

Misiolek, W., and Ferguson, C. *A National Study of the Impacts of State and Local Taxes on Regional Economic Growth.* Center for Business Economic Research, University of Alabama, 1986.

——. *Preliminary Report: A National Study on Economic Growth, Tax Burden, and Governmental Expenditures.* Center for Business and Economic Research, University of Alabama, 1987.

Miskimin, H. *The Economy of Early Renaissance Europe.* New Jersey, 1969.

Mitchell, D. "The Historical Record of Lower Tax Rates." Heritage Foundation, Washington, August 13, 2003.

——. "Making American Companies More Competitive." Heritage Foundation, Washington, September 25, 2003.

Mitchell, W. *Essay on the Early History of the Law Merchant.* New York, 1969.

Mokyr, J. *The Lever of Riches: Technological Creativity and Economic Progress.* New York, 1990.

Moody, S. *The Cost of Tax Compliance.* Tax Foundation, Washington, February, 2002.

Moore, S. "Tax Cuts in 1998." Testimony before the Ways and Means Committee, U.S. House of Representatives, Washington, February 4, 1998.

——. "Putting Taxpayers First: A Federal Budget Plan to Benefit the Next Generation of American Taxpayers." Innovative Policy Institute, Washington, January 13, 2004.

Moore, S., and Kerpen, P. "Show Me the Money! Dividend Payouts after the Bush Tax Cut." Cato Institute, Washington, October 11, 2004.

Moss, H. St. L. B. *The Beginning of the Middle Ages.* New York, 1931.

——. "Economic Consequences of the Barbarian Invasions." *Economic History Review* 7 (1936–1937).

——. *The Birth of the Middle Ages: 395–814.* Oxford, 1965.

——. "Economic Consequences of the Barbarian Invasions." In *The Pirenne Thesis: Analysis, Criticism, and Revision.* A. F. Havighurst, ed., London, 1969.

Muller, J. *Adam Smith in His Time and Ours.* New York, 1993.

——. *Capitalism, Democracy, and Ralph's Pretty Good Grocery Store.* Princeton, 1999.

——. *The Mind and the Market: Capitalism in Western Thought.* New York, 2003.

Mulligan, C. *What Do Aggregate Consumption Euler Equations Say About the Capital Income Tax Burden?* NBER Working Paper No. 10262. Washington, February, 2004.

Mumford, L. *The Culture of Cities.* New York, 1938.

Munro, D., and Sellery, G. *Medieval Civilization.* New York, 1914, 1964.

National Priorities Project. *Where Do Your Tax Dollars Go?* Washington, 2004.

National Taxpayers Union. *The Silver Lining of Tax Day of 2004.* Washington, April 14, 2004.

——. *A Taxing Trend: The Rise in Complexity, Forms, and Paperwork.* NTU Policy Paper 113, Washington, April 15, 2004.

Nell, E., ed. *Free Market Conservatism.* Boston, 1984.

Nelson, R. "Old Bureaus Never Die." *Forbes*, October 11, 1993.

Newman, K. *Declining Fortunes.* New York, 1993.

Niskanen, W. *Reaganomics: An Insider's Account of the Policies and the People.* New York, 1988.

Nixon, R. *Seize the Moment.* New York, 1992.

Norberg, J. *In Defense of Global Capitalism.* Washington, 2003.

Norquist, G. "Step by Step Tax Reform." *Washington Post National Weekly Edition,* June 23–29, 2003.

Norton, R. "Taking on Public Enemy No. 1." *Fortune,* October 19, 1992.

———. "Our Screwed Up Tax Code." *Fortune,* September 6, 1993.

Novak, M. *The Spirit of Democratic Capitalism.* New York, 1982.

———. *The Catholic Ethic and the Spirit of Enterprise.* New York, 1993.

———. *Business as a Calling.* New York, 1996.

Olson, M. *The Rise and Decline of Nations.* New Haven/London, 1982.

Oman, C. *The Dark Ages: 476–918.* London, 1959.

O'Neill, J. *The Market: Ethics, Knowledge, and Politics.* London/New York, 1998.

Orenstein, M. *Out of the Red: Building Capitalism and Democracy in Post-Communist Europe.* Ann Arbor: 2004.

Osbourne, D. "The New Role Models." *INC.,* October 1987a.

———. *Economic Competitiveness: The States Take the Lead.* Economic Policy Institute, Washington, October 1987b.

Osbourne, D., and Gaebler, T. *Reinventing Government.* New York, 1993.

Osbourne, D., and Plastrik, P. *Banishing Bureaucracy.* New York, 1997.

Paine, T. *The Rights of Man.* New York, 1969.

Painter, S. *A History of the Middle Ages: 284–1500.* London, 1972.

Papke, L. "Sub-National Taxation and Capital Mobility." *National Tax Journal,* June 1987.

Parkinson, C. N. *Parkinson's Law and Other Studies in Administration.* New York: 1958.

Pearson, J. *Creating New Companies and Business Units Within Existing Companies via University Licensing Agreements* (monograph). Cambridge, 1988.

Penick, W. "Evolution of the Federal Tax System: 1954–1983," *Federal Tax Policy Memo,* National Tax Foundation ,Washington, July, 1983.

Perelman, L. *The "Acanemia" Deception.* Hudson Institute, Alexandria, May 1990.

Perrow, C. *Organizing America: Wealth, Power, and the Origins of Corporate Capitalism.* Princeton, 2002.

Perry, J. *The Case for Constitutional Tax Limitation.* Americans for Tax Reform, Washington, 2004.

Peter, L. *Peter's Quotations: Ideas for Our Time.* New York, 1977.

Peterson, P. *Facing Up.* New York, 1993.

———. *Running on Empty.* New York, 2004.

Peterson, W. *Controlled Capitalism: Capitalism or Socialism in 2004.* Bloomington, 2003.

Phillips, K. *The Politics of the Rich and Poor.* New York, 1990.

———. *Boiling Point.* New York, 1993.

Pirenne, H. "The Stages in the Social History of Capitalism." *American Historical Review* 19 (1914).

——. *Les Villes du Moyen Âge*. Brussels, 1927.

——. "Le Commerce du Papyrus dans la Gaule Mérovingienne," *Comptes Rendus des Séances de l'Académie des Inscriptions et Belles-Lettres*, 1928.

——. *A History of Europe*. New York, 1958.

——. *Economic and Social History of Medieval Europe*. London, 1972.

——. *Medieval Cities: Their Origins and the Revival of Trade*. Princeton, 1974a.

——. *Muhammad and Charlemagne*. London, 1974b.

Porter, M. *The Competitive Advantage of Nations*. New York, 1990.

Postan, M. M. "Credit in Medieval Trade." *Economic History Review* 1 (1927–1928).

——. "The Rise of a Monetary Economy." In *Essays in Medieval Agriculture and General Problems of the Medieval Economy*. Cambridge, 1973a.

——. *Medieval Trade and Finance*. Cambridge, 1973b.

Pounds, N. J. G. *An Economic History of Medieval Europe*. New York, 1974.

Pras, M. *The Politics of Free Markets*. Chicago, 2006.

Pryor, F. *The Future of U.S. Capitalism*. Cambridge, 2002.

Pryor, J. H. "The Origins of the Commenda Contract." *Speculum* 52 (1977).

——. "Commenda: The Operation of the Contract at Marseilles." *Journal of European Economic History* 13, no. 4 (1984).

Rahn, R. "Regulatory Therapy." *Washington Times*, July 11, 2004.

——. "Kerry Economically Scary?" *Washington Times*, August 26, 2004.

Reagan, R. *Reagan in His Own Hand*. Edited by K. Anderson. New York, 2001.

——. Speech, March 22, 1988, Washington, D.C. <www.reagan.utexas.edu.com> (July 7, 2006).

Reich, R. *Tales of a New America*. New York, 1987.

——. *The Work of Nations*. New York, 1991.

Reynolds, A. "Manufacturing Myths." *Washington Times*, August 31, 2003.

——. "The Unfairness of Fair Trade." *Washington Times*, November 16, 2003.

——. "Where the Jobs Went." Cato Institute, Washington, February 16, 2004.

——. "Trivial Outsourcing Pursuits." Cato Institute, Washington, March 14, 2004a.

——. "Jobs Melodrama Rerun." Cato Institute, Washington, March 14, 2004b.

——. "When More Is Less." Cato Institute, Washington, July 15, 2004.

Richman, L. "Bringing Reason to Regulation." *Fortune*, October 19, 1992.

Riedl, B. "How Washington Will Spend Your Taxes in 2005." Heritage Foundation, Washington, D.C., April 15, 2005.

Ringer, R. *Restoring the American Dream*. New York, 1979.

Roberts, P. C. "From Superpower to Third World Country." *Conservative Chronicle*, May 8, 2002.

——. "A War against the American People." *Conservative Chronicle*, July 31, 2002.

——. "Whither the Economy." *Conservative Chronicle*, October 10, 2002.

——. "Globalism Decimates U.S. Work Force." *Conservative Chronicle*, August 13, 2003.

——. "The Missing Case for Free Trade." *Conservative Chronicle*, March 17, 2004a.

——. "Outsourcing: A New Occupational Hazard." *Conservative Chronicle*, March 17, 2004b.

——. "America is Outsourcing Its Future." *Conservative Chronicle*, April 14, 2004.

——. "A Third World Country in the Making." *Conservative Chronicle*, May 19, 2004.

——. "Assessing the Assessments." *Conservative Chronicle*, June 30, 2004.

Roberts, R. *The Choice: A Fable of Free Trade and Protectionism*. Upper Saddle River, 2001.

Robbins, W. *Colony and Empire: the Capitalist Transformation of the American West*. Lawrence, 1994.

Robins, R. *Global Problems and the Culture of Capitalism*. Boston, 2002.

Robinson, W. *A Theory of Global Capitalism*. Baltimore/London, 2004.

Roepke, W. *The Moral Foundations of Civil Society*. New Brunswick/London, 2002.

Rogge, B. *Can Capitalism Survive?* Indianapolis, 1979.

"Ronald Wilson Reagan: The Final Chapter." *U.S. News & World Report*, June 21, 2004.

Rostovtzeff, M. *The Social and Economic History of the Roman Empire*. Oxford, 1926, reprinted 1966.

Rotwein, E., ed. *Writings on Economics*. Madison, 1955.

Rowling, M. *Everyday Life in Medieval Times*. New York, 1968.

Samuelson, R. "The Budget: Back to the Future." *Newsweek*, February 14, 1994.

——. "The Specter of Outsourcing." *Washington Post National Weekly Edition*, January 19–25, 2004.

Savage, T. "Let's Clear Up a Couple of Misconceptions on Tax Cuts." *Chicago Sun Times*, April 15, 2004.

Savas, E. "The Efficiency of the Private Sector." In *The Privatization Option: A Strategy to Shrink the Size of Government*. Washington, 1985.

Savoli, G. *Il Capitalismo Antico*. Bari, 1929.

Say, J. B. A *Treatise on Political Economy*. Philadelphia, 1819/1834.

Scarborough, J. *Rome Wasn't Burnt in a Day*. New York, 2004.

Schlesinger, A. *The Age of Jackson*. Boston, 1953.

Schmenner, R. "Locational Decisions of Large Firms: Implications for Public Policy," *Commentary*, Council for Urban Economic Development, Washington, January 1981.

——. *Making Business Location Decisions*. Englewood Cliffs, 1982.

Scheider, W. *Babylon Is Everywhere*. Westport, 1960.

Schlaes, A. *The Greedy Hand*. New York, 1999.

Schneider, F., and Enste, D. "Shadow Economies, Sizes, Causes, and Consequences." *Journal of Economic Literature* 38 (2000).

Schotter, A. *Free Market Economics: A Critical Appraisal*. New York, 1985.

Schreiber, J. *Le Défi Américain*. Paris, 1967.

Schumpeter, J. *The Theory of Economic Development*. Cambridge, 1934.

——. *Business Cycles*. New York, 1939.

——. *History of Economic Analysis*. New York, 1954.

——. *Capitalism, Socialism, and Democracy*. New York, 1950, 1962.

Scott, M. *Medieval Europe*. Oxford, 1964.

Scrycki, C. *The Regulators*. Lanham, 2003.

Shaviro, D. *Do Deficits Matter?* Chicago, 1997.

Sidey, H. "Back at Full Throttle." *Time*, August 23, 1993.

Silk, L. *Making Capitalism Work.* New York, 1996.

Simon, P. *We Can Do Better.* Bethesda, 1994.

Simon, W. *A Time for Truth.* New York, 1978.

Singer, D. *Whose Millennium? Theirs or Ours?* New York, 1999.

Sirici, R. "A Worthy Calling." *Forbes*, November 22, 1993.

Skadden, D., ed. *A New Tax Structure for the United States.* Indianapolis, 1978.

Skousen, M. *Economics on Trial.* New York, 1991.

Skowronek, S. *The Politics Presidents Make.* Cambridge, 1993.

Slemrod, J., and Bakija, J. *Taxing Ourselves.* Cambridge, 1996.

Smith, A. *An Inquiry into the Nature and Causes of the Wealth of Nations.* New York, 1909, 1937; London, 1980a.

———. *A Theory of Moral Sentiments.* London, 1980b.

———. *The Wealth of Nations.* London, 1930.

Smith, L. "What the U.S. Can Do About R&D." *Fortune*, October 19, 1992.

Smith, M. "A National Curriculum in the United States." In *Buying America Back*, J. Greenberg and W. Kistler, eds. Tulsa, 1992.

Smith, R. *Adam Smith and the Origins of American Enterprise.* New York, 2002.

Sobell, R. *The Pursuit of Wealth.* New York, 2000.

Sobran, J. "The Myth of 'Limited' Government." *Conservative Chronicle*, January 2, 2004.

———. "Reflections on Elections," <www.sobran.com> (November 5, 2002).

Sombart, W. *Der Moderne Kapitalismus.* Munich, 1916.

Sowell, T. "Random Thoughts on the Passing Scene." *Conservative Chronicle*, May 11, 1994.

———. "Teachers Are Why Johnny Can't Read." *Conservative Chronicle*, July 17, 2002.

———. "A Dose of Economic Reality." *Conservative Chronicle*, July 1, 2003.

———. "Profits without Honor: Part III." *Conservative Chronicle*, December 25, 2003.

———. "Manufacturing Confusion." *Conservative Chronicle*, January 21, 2004.

———. "Subsidies Are All Wet." *Conservative Chronicle*, March 31, 2004.

———. "Jobs and Snow Jobs." *Conservative Chronicle*, September 9, 2004.

Spengler, O. *The Decline of the West.* London, 1926.

Spufford, P. *Money and Its Uses in Medieval Europe.* Cambridge, 1988.

Spüler, B. "Trade in the Eastern Islamic Countries in the Early Centuries." In *Islam and the Trade in Asia.* Ed. D. S. Richards. Oxford, 1970.

"State Exhibit: Window to Future Jobs." *Detroit Business*, April 10, 1989.

Steinmo, S. *Taxation and Democracy.* New York/London, 1993.

Stevenson, B. "Delivering Municipal Services Efficiently." HUD, Washington, 1984.

Stewart, T. "U.S. Productivity: First, but Fading." *Fortune*, October 19, 1992.

Stigler, G. *The Economist as Preacher and Other Essays.* Chicago, 1982.

Strayer, J. *Western Europe in the Middle Ages: A Short History.* New York, 1955.

Strayer, J., and Munro, D. *The Middle Ages: 395–1500*. London, 1942; New York, 1959.

Swenson, P. *Capitalists against Markets*. Oxford, 2002.

Tawney, R. *Religion and the Rise of Capitalism*. New York, 1926; London, 1970.

Tax Foundation. "Evolution of the Federal Tax System: 1954–1983." *Federal Tax Policy Memo*, July 1983.

———. "Putting a Face on Dividend-Earning Taxpayers." *Foundation Fiscal Facts*, January, 2003.

———. *America Celebrates Tax Freedom Day*. Special Report No. 129, Washington, April, 2004.

———. "Retrospective on the 1981 Reagan Tax Cut," Washington, June 10, 2004.

———. "The Bush Tax Plan: How Big is the Tax Cut?" Washington, June 14, 2004.

———. "The Bush Tax Plan: How Big Is the Tax Cut?" *Tax Policy Update*, Washington: July 6, 2004.

———. *Wealthy Americans and Business Activity*. Special Report, Washington, August, 2004.

———. "Helped by Tax Cuts, Business Owners Producing Lion's Share of Income Tax Revenues," Washington, August 5, 2004.

———. "New CBO Study Confirms that Wealthiest Americans Bear Income Tax Burden," Washington, August 13, 2004.

———. "Bush Tax Cuts Erased Income Tax Burden for 7.8 Million Families." *Fiscal Facts*, August 17, 2004.

———. "Tax Freedom Day." *Tax Features*, April 7, 2004; April 17, 2005; April 12, 2006.

———. "Numbers of Americans Outside the Income Tax System Continues to Grow," Washington, June 9, 2005.

———. *The Rising Costs of Complying with the Federal Income Tax*. Special Report No. 138, Washington, January 10, 2006.

The State of Small Business: A Report of the President. Washington, 1983.

Thomas, C. "Both Parties Are Robbing the Taxpayers." *Conservative Chronicle*, June 4, 2003.

———. "Feds Should Drop Out of Education." *Conservative Chronicle*, July 14, 2004.

Thompson, J. W. "The Commerce of France in the Ninth Century." *Journal of Political Economy* 23 (1915).

———. *Economic and Social History of the Middle Ages*. New York, 1959.

Thompson, J. W., and Johnson, E. N. *An Introduction to Medieval Europe*. New York, 1937.

Thompson, W. "Industrial Location: Causes and Consequences." In *Michigan's Fiscal and Economic Structure*. H. Brazer, ed., Ann Arbor, 1982.

"Thoughts on the Business of Life." *Forbes*, July 18, 1994.

Tierney, B., and Painter, S. *Western Europe in the Middle Ages*. New York, 1970.

Thurow, L. *The Zero Sum Society*. New York, 1980.

———. *Dangerous Currents: the State of Economics*. New York, 1983.

———. *The Zero Sum Solution*. New York, 1985.

———. *Head-to-Head*. New York, 1992.

——. *The Future of Capitalism*. New York, 1996.

——. *Building Wealth: The New Rules for Individuals, Companies, and Nations in a Knowledge-Based Economy*. New York, 1999.

——. *Fortune Favors the Bold*. New York, 2003.

Trevor-Roper, H. *The Rise of Christian Europe*. New York, 1965.

Tyrell, R. E. "Economy Is Better than Critics Believe." *Conservative Chronicle*, March 14, 2004.

United Nations. *National Account Statistics: Main Aggregates and Detailed Tables, 2001*. New York: 2003.

Utt, R. "Have the Tax Cuts Saved America from Eurosclerosis?" Heritage Foundation, Washington, November 3, 2003.

U.S. Bureau of Economic Analysis. *Q&A's on Gross Domestic Product and Outsourcing*. Washington: August 3, 2004.

U.S. Bureau of Labor Statistics. *Effects of Job Changing on Payroll Employment Trends*. Washington, August 6, 2004.

U.S. Department of Education. *A Nation at Risk*. Washington, 1983.

Vaughan, R. *State Taxation and Economic Development*. Washington, 1979.

——. "State Tax Incentives: How Effective Are They?" In *Expanding the Opportunity to Produce: Revitalizing the American Economy through New Enterprise Development*. Corporation for Enterprise Development, Washington, 1981.

——. *The Wealth of States: Policies for a Dynamic Economy*. Washington, 1984.

Waley, D. *The Italian City Republics*. New York, 1969.

Wallace-Hadrill, J. *Early Medieval History*. Oxford, 1975.

Walsh, T. "CNN's Dobbs Changes His Tune." *Detroit Free Press*, August 25, 2004.

Walstead, W. *Economic Literacy in the Schools* (unpublished monograph). New York, 1988.

Walstead, W., and Soper, J. *A Report Card on the Economic Literacy of High School Students*. New York, 1988.

Wanniski, J. *The Way the World Works*. Morristown, 1989.

Webber, C. "Developments of Ideas about Balanced Budgets." In *How to Limit Government Spending*, A.Wildavsky, ed. London, 1986.

Weber, M. *The Sociology of Religion*. Boston, 1922, 1963.

——. *The Protestant Ethic and the Spirit of Capitalism*. New York, 1958.

Webster, A. *A General History of Commerce*. Boston, 1903.

Weisman, J. "Jobs Gone for Good." *Washington Post Weekly Edition*, September 15–21, 2003.

Wesbury, B. "The Blame Game." *American Spectator*, February 2004.

——. "The Earnings Mystery." Griffen, Kubik, Stephens, and Thompson, Inc., Chicago, July 2, 2004.

——. "Monday Morning Outlook." Griffen, Kubik, Stephens, and Thompson, Inc., Chicago, August 2, 2004.

——. "Monday Morning Outlook." Griffen, Kubik, Stephens, and Thompson, Inc., Chicago, August 9, 2004.

Wessel, D. "The Challenge of Jobs: As New Ones Rise, the Wage Gap Widens." *Wall Street Journal*, April 11, 2004.

White, M. *Property Taxes and Firm Location: Evidence from Proposition 13*. National Bureau of Economic Research, Washington, 1986.

Wildavsky, A., and Webber, C. *A History of Taxation and Expenditure in the Western World*. New York, 1986.

Williams, W. "Threats to the Rule of Law." *Conservative Chronicle*, June 12, 2002.

――. "Higher Taxes Lower Productivity." *Conservative Chronicle*, December 11, 2002.

――. "Fiddling While Rome Burns." *Conservative Chronicle*, December 26, 2002.

――. "The Morality of Markets." *Conservative Chronicle*, May 7, 2003.

――. "Dopey Ideas." *Conservative Chronicle*, May 21, 2003.

――. "Exporting Jobs." *Conservative Chronicle*, August 20, 2003.

――. "'Living Wage' Kills Jobs." *Conservative Chronicle*, November 12, 2003.

――. "A Politician's Public Service." *Conservative Chronicle*, November 19, 2003.

――. "Jobs Come and Jobs Go." *Conservative Chronicle*, December 3, 2003.

――. "Economics 101." *Conservative Chronicle*, August 11, 2004.

――. "Income Inequality." *Conservative Chronicle*, September 8, 2004.

Wills, G. "The End of Reaganism." *Time*, November 1992.

Wolman, W., and Colomosca, A. *The Judas Economy*. New York, 1997.

Woolfe, M. *Where We Stand*. New York, 1992.

Younkis, E. *Capitalism and Commerce*. New York/Oxford, 2002.

Zuboff, S., and Maxmin, J. *The Support Economy*. New York, 2002.

Zuckerman, M. "Where the Buck Stops." *U.S. News & World Report*, July 13, 1992.

――. "Three Cheers for Al Gore." *U.S. News & World Report*, September 12, 1993.

――. "What Scandal Cannot Dim." *U.S. News & World Report*, July 12, 2002.

――. "The Case of the Missing Jobs." *U.S. News & World Report*, February 9, 2004.

――. "The Old Protectionist Dodge." *U.S. News & World Report*, March 29, 2004.

――. "An Opportunity Lost." *U.S. News & World Report*, September 20, 2004.

Index

academia, 212
Adams, John, 46
administrative process, 199–201
AFDC. *See* Aid to Families with Dependent Children
affluence, 19
Aid to Families with Dependent Children (AFDC), 220
America: British taxation protested by, 88; crucial political choices of, 159; economic peril of, xiii, xv, 185–86; economic values of, 36–37; free market success in, 38; free market system threatened in, 179–80; future economic prosperity in, 135; government failing in, 47; immigration diversifying, 37–38; Industrial Revolution in, 30; industrial vitality preserved in, 19, 102; job creation in, 106–14; job growth in, 107–8; leaders crisis in, 17; liberal tax package of, 91; national savings rate in, 201; national wealth created in, 4–5; poverty increasing in, 51; producer incentives in, 175–76; prosperity in, 135; Protestants founding, 34–35; public policy choices critical to, xxiii; public policy objectives in, xxii;

R&D commitment declining in, 141; science/technology leading, 17; scientific literacy lagging in, 213; suburban growth in, 95; technology development eroding in, 141; trade competitiveness of, 105–6; training commitment required by, 148; training system in, 215; wealth in, 4–5
American Century, 16
American dream: education restoring, 154–55; Founding Fathers and, 223; free market ethic realizing, 37; punitive taxation influencing, 81; screening process in, 56
American economy: foreign trade needed for, 126; jobs created in, 107–8; something wrong with, 7; structural change in, 112–14
American industries: competitors surpassing, 149; leading-edge technologies invented by, 141; production costs reductions needed for, xv
American jobs: economy creating, 107–8; foreign labor markets taking, 107, 111; operating cost driving away, 134
American Revolution, 88–89

product commercialization, 141

product development: cycle of, 172–73; R&D investment in, 131

production, 103, 120; capital/technology factors of, 120–21; consumption v., 127; costs of, xv; in Rome, 100; sector, 133

productive growth, 84–86, 113

productive private industry, 89

productivity: direct investment required for, 125; factors of, 124; gains in, 207–8; global competition requiring, 148–49; global economy needing, 122–23; shop floor economic reality of, 113

professional development, 223

Profiles in Courage (Kennedy), 185

profit earned, 32, 33

profit motive: capitalism and, 181–82; civilization driven by, 34, 180; government actions impacting, xiii; as powerful economic force, xviii; Western cultures quest of, 22

profit system: in Christian doctrine, 33; functional efficiency in, 30

progrowth strategies, 6

prosperity: America's future, 135; in China, xix; exports creating, 127–28; free market formula for, xxiv, 189; government's role in, 70; middle class gaining, 95; no socialist state producing, xx; private investment causing, 18; surplus capital causing, 19; Western Europe realizing, 29; work producing, 35

Protestant ethic, 31

The Protestant Ethic and the Spirit of Capitalism (Weber), 32

Protestants, 34–35

public: administration, 57; carrier, 58–59; competition, 195–96; debt, 46; programs, 57

public policy: aging firms subsidized by, 173; America's choices in, xxiii; America's foremost objective in,

xxii; America's leaders crisis in, 17; capital supply shortfall from, 204; competitive spirit suffocated by, xviii; free market system and, 134–35; republicans role of, 13

public-sector: democrat cures from, 12; development approach, 171; economic development strategy of, 174; federal resources commandeered by, 47; handouts, 164; incentives, 170; job creation programs, 161–62; managers, 53; performance problem in, 56; private sector job replaced by, 162; productive growth not driving, 84; regulatory costs in, 61; spending programs, 190–91

public spending: earned income and, 91; taxes leading to, 81

quality of life, 123

Quayle, Dan, 7

Rahn, Richard, 197

Rather, Dan, 16

rational actions, 77

"rationalized government," 9–10

R&D (research & development): commitment, 141; investment, 131; Japanese assimilating, 143; new technologies through, 211–13; productivity gains from, 207–8

Reaganomics: tax cut from, 4–5; theoretical essence of, 92

Reagan, Ronald, 7, 83, 115, 186, 223; domestic policy of, 91; economic beliefs of, xxiii–xxiv; socioeconomic legacy of, 183–84; tax cuts of, xv, 4–5, 96, 114

real-term wages, 216

recession, 111

redistributive economics, 51–52

regulation(s): Adams, John, concerned with, 46; administration process reform of, 199–201; adverse impacts

About the Author

Gene W. Heck is a senior business development economist operating in Saudi Arabia and throughout the Mideast. Prior to joining the private sector, he was a member of the U.S. Diplomatic Corps, with postings to the U.S. embassies in Saudi Arabia and Jordan.

Dr. Heck has served as U.S. commercial attaché to Saudi Arabia, senior U.S. Treasury economic advisor to the Saudi Arabian Ministry of Finance and National Economy, as well as a governmental relations officer with Arabian American Oil Company (ARAMCO).

Dr. Heck holds a doctorate and three master's degrees from the University of Michigan, Ann Arbor; a master's degree (MPA) in public administration from Golden Gate University, San Francisco, California; and has completed the requisite course work for a master's degree in Arab economic history from the University of Jordan. He also serves as an adjunct professor of government and history with the University of Maryland.

About the Author